The American Homefront During WWII

The American Homefront
During WWII

The American Homefront During WWII

Blackouts, Ration Books and Rosie the Riveter

C. D. Peterson

First published in Great Britain in 2024 by
Pen & Sword History
An imprint of Pen & Sword Books Limited
Yorkshire – Philadelphia

Copyright © C. D. Peterson 2024

ISBN 978 1 39905 923 7

The right of C. D. Peterson to be identified as
Author of this Work has been asserted by him in accordance
with the Copyright, Designs and Patents Act 1988.

A CIP catalogue record for this book is
available from the British Library

All rights reserved. No part of this book may be reproduced or
transmitted in any form or by any means, electronic or mechanical
including photocopying, recording or by any information storage and
retrieval system, without permission from the Publisher in writing.

Typeset by Mac Style
Printed in the UK by CPI Group (UK) Ltd, Croydon, CR0 4YY.

Pen & Sword Books Limited incorporates the imprints of After
the Battle, Atlas, Archaeology, Aviation, Discovery, Family History,
Fiction, History, Maritime, Military, Military Classics, Politics,
Select, Transport, True Crime, Air World, Frontline Publishing, Leo
Cooper, Remember When, Seaforth Publishing, The Praetorian Press,
Wharncliffe Local History, Wharncliffe Transport, Wharncliffe True
Crime and White Owl.

For a complete list of Pen & Sword titles please contact

PEN & SWORD BOOKS LIMITED
47 Church Street, Barnsley, South Yorkshire, S70 2AS, England
E-mail: enquiries@pen-and-sword.co.uk
Website: www.pen-and-sword.co.uk
or
PEN AND SWORD BOOKS
1950 Lawrence Rd, Havertown, PA 19083, USA
E-mail: uspen-and-sword@casematepublishers.com
Website: www.penandswordbooks.com

The most often asked question of an author is "Why did you write this book?"

My answer is: "So some can remember, more will learn, and none may forget."

This book is dedicated to my family: Odessa, Gwen, Chris, Stephanie and Steve.

My sincere thanks go out to all the contributors listed in the book along with my special appreciation to Laura Hirst, Sarah Hodder, and Lucy May for their sound advice, for their everlasting patience and most of all for their enthusiasm for the project. Every writer should be as fortunate.

Contents

Chapter 1	America on Edge	1
Chapter 2	The War Production Colossus	19
Chapter 3	Civil Defense and Blackouts	53
Chapter 4	Rationing	73
Chapter 5	The War's Impact on Black People and Women	98
Chapter 6	The Impact on Children on the Home Front	121
Chapter 7	The Aliens Among Us	135
Chapter 8	Spies and Saboteurs	144
Chapter 9	Day to Day Life on the Home Front	149
Chapter 10	After the War	179
Four Essays – Reflections on the Home Front		187
Contributors		198
Notes		199
Index		205

Chapter One

America on Edge

Saturday December 6, 1941

America, at the beginning of the 1940s, had been grappling with efforts to climb out of the Depression. Pumping money into the economy in New Deal relief and social programs afforded uneven gains that had the middle class and well to do comfortable, visiting the World's Fair (held in New York in 1939–40), and dining out. In 1941 home construction exceeded all years dating back to 1929. Oil production was up. Steel production was up.

But that still left 10,000,000 unemployed.[1] The bank, business, and farm failures, along with the devastating dust bowl storms had driven millions into hunger and poverty but now some relief was on the horizon in the terrible form of the war in Europe. America had its eye on the war and, against its own will, recognized the need to prepare for war's eventuality. Through a succession of confusing agencies, the first programs of economic management and defense spending were initiated. But the biggest boost to US economic growth became Europe's need for arms.

While Americans felt the distant fire burning in Europe, it was not their fire. They were deeply divided in their views about the war in Europe, now more than three years old. Most Americans believed that the US would be drawn into the war including a substantial minority that wanted no part of a "war on foreign soil." WWI was still a sore memory just twenty years past. Americans had endured enough anguish from that conflict and from the suffering borne during the Depression. They felt they deserved the peace and prosperity they were enjoying, but they went about their lives under the gray cloud of war's inevitability.

With the outbreak of hostilities abroad, the United States worked to repatriate approximately 100,000 Americans who were caught up in Europe. The Special Division was created within the US State Department to handle matters involving the war and giving assistance to Americans who were abroad and being repatriated. Breckinridge Long was given responsibility of the Special Division. The US government chartered six ships from United States Lines to bring Americans home. By early November, 75,000 Americans had been repatriated from Europe.[2]

Isolationists held that the war in Europe was a dispute among foreign nations and that the United States should not become involved. One US Senator, Key Pittman of Nevada, went as far as to suggest that Britain should surrender at once. Isolationists advocated a two-part policy of building up the US defenses and pursuing neutrality. They believed that neutrality combined with the power of the US military plus the protection afforded by the Atlantic and Pacific Oceans would keep Americans safe. Congress passed a series of Neutrality Acts in the late 1930s. The acts banned American citizens from trading with nations at war, loaning them money, or traveling on their ships, all to prevent involvement in foreign wars.[3]

Organizations like the America First Committee worked to influence public opinion. Their efforts included mass rallies and propaganda campaigns through print and radio. The flyer Charles Lindbergh, an American hero, was a powerful spokesman. Speaking in 1941 of an "independent American destiny," Lindbergh asserted that the United States ought to fight any nation that attempted to meddle in the affairs of the Western Hemisphere but, he argued, American soldiers ought not to have to "fight everybody in the world who prefers some other system of life to ours."

Father Charles Coughlin, a Catholic priest based in Detroit, commanded a following of millions of Americans with his radio broadcasts, *The Hour of Power*. He used his broadcasts to inspire and publicize the creation of a political association called the Christian Front, a militia-like organization which promised to defend the country from communists and Jews. He founded a journal, *Social Justice*, to advocate his isolationist, ant-Semitic positions.

Five American women also earned prominence engaging in isolationist activities. In September 1939 Laura Ingalls (the famous aviator, not the author), shocked Americans and the Washington DC police as she flew over the White House dropping what appeared to be bombs. They were pro-Nazi, anti-war pamphlets. Ingalls, a regular America First Committee speaker, who was in the secret employ of the German government, was later arrested.

The leaflets she dropped were written by Catherine Curtis who was both an anti-communist and a strong anti-Semite. A former actress, Ms Curtis was a leader in a large, loosely affiliated organization called the Mothers' Movement (MOM). One Chicago branch of the organization, originated by Lyral Clark Van Hyning, stood out: *We, the Mothers Mobilize for America*. She claimed 150,000 members and edited a publication called *Women's Voice* with a circulation of 20,000. Her anti-Semitic histrionics were so extreme as to be almost laughable. (Harry S. Truman's middle initial stood for Solomon and he was a Jew.)

She said this about her followers:

My women are not intelligent. In fact, they are rather stupid. But they are a group of women who will work hard for me, and that's what's important. Later, perhaps, we will be able to attract a higher type of women.

Elizabeth Dilling organized anti-war mothers' sit ins and other demonstrations against intervention, Franklin D. Roosevelt (FDR) and his "Jew Deal"; her name for the New Deal. She especially attacked the efforts to provide Britain with ships and arms. Her third book, *The Octopus*, was so anti-Semitic she published it under a pseudonym. Ms Dilling's public views and her on again/off again divorce from her lawyer husband gained Americans' attention in the tabloids.

The most strident among the Mothers' Movements stood Agnes Waters who testified before Congress several times. Her hate-filled speech added Black people and the British to Jews, communists, and the Roosevelts to be pilloried. She was a failed presidential candidate in 1942.

Dilling and another woman were put on trial in 1944 for sedition. The trial went on for months, the stress from which probably led to the death of the judge. Many months later, the proceedings, like the war, burned away to nothing and these women faded from public view.[4] Their performances might have been thought of as just a side show had not their message been so hate-filled and contrary to America's best interest: to prepare the home front for war.

Those favoring intervention included The Committee to Defend America by Aiding the Allies (CDAAA), founded in May 1940 by William Allen White, a prominent Republican publisher in Kansas, and was directed by Clark Eichelberger, the head of the League of Nations Association. The CDAAA, with an estimated membership of 750,000, staged rallies and performances, took out full-page newspaper ads, and handed out flyers in an effort to gain support for aiding Great Britain. After Nazi Germany invaded the Soviet Union in June 1941, the committee dropped "by Aiding the Allies" from its name (becoming CDA) since many members opposed communism.[5]

Another interventionist organization, Fight for Freedom (FFF), was founded in April 1941 and headed by journalist Ulric Bell, who aggressively advocated entering World War II to defend both Great Britain and democratic values. Fight for Freedom claimed journalists, writers, movie stars, and politicians as supporters. Walt Disney Studios produced a program cover for a FFF rally featuring Mickey Mouse, Donald Duck, and Goofy.[6]

The two organizations often worked together and coordinated with President Franklin Roosevelt's aides or British propagandists to rally public support. The democracies of Western Europe, they argued, were a critical line of defense against Hitler's fast-growing strength. These organizations also informed Americans that Germany was murdering civilians in the countries it occupied. In November 1941, the CDA sponsored rallies throughout the country, protesting the Nazi regime's mass murder campaign.

The fray was joined by an extraordinary organization called the German American Bund formed, their leaders said, to represent Americans of German descent. They worked to align themselves with the America First groups against any intervention against Germany. In the late 1930s the truth became clear that they were, in fact, pressing the policies of Nazi Germany.

With a membership estimated to be 25,000, they rallied and paraded in paramilitary uniforms and opened youth-oriented camps in several states. Their most visible rally was held in Madison Square Garden in 1939. (Marshall Curry produced a chilling short documentary about the rally, "A Night at the Garden.") By the end of the decade, with several of its leaders arrested and American sentiment tilting against Germany, the Bund fell apart. Its leader, Fritz Julius Kuhn, was imprisoned and later deported to Germany.[7]

Americans were aware that western Europe was not the only part of the world engulfed in war. Japan had invaded Manchuria and was engaged in all out attacks on China and other southeast Asian neighbors in an order to establish a Greater East Asia Co-Prosperity Sphere. Italy, under fascist leader Benito Mussolini, had attacked Ethiopia, essentially with impunity.

Spain was embroiled in a vicious civil war brought by the fascist, Generalissimo Francisco Franco, against the Republican government. Franco's efforts benefitted from strong support from Germany under Adolf Hitler, while the Republicans were aided by the USSR under Josef Stalin.

America was (re)discovering Latin America. Stories were circulating that Hitler was making plans to sneak into the hemisphere via sending troops on freighters or by using commercial airlines to ferry civilian-dressed Gestapo. Axis partner Italy's Alitalia Airlines also had plenty of routes into Latin America.

Americans saw the Panama Canal as very vulnerable. Rumors had the canal bombed and ammunition for canal defenses blown up. Reports of a landslide at Culebra Cut brought fears that with the Pacific Fleet cut off from the Atlantic, the East Coast was vulnerable to attack. There was indeed a landslide at Culebra Cut but it was in 1913.

The interest in South America grew to the point that FDR appointed Nelson Rockefeller, whose family had long had dealings south of the border, to head cultural and commercial relations with the region.

Individual Americans also took greater notice of South America. Spanish lessons became popular. Radio networks beamed to and from Latin America. Nightlife took on a Latin flavor, with rumba and samba bands playing in such venues as the Copacabana and the Latin Quarter. Even Broadway joined in with Cole Porter's *Panama Hattie* starring Ethel Merman.[8] A genuine Latin star also arrived on the scene – Carmen Miranda – known for her fruit castle headdress and deliciously thick accent.

All this frivolity occurred under the gathering clouds of war. *The Saturday Evening Post* declared, "the situation is abnormal. The country is neither at war nor at peace. Not being at war, it is reluctant to embrace a war economy; and yet on the other hand, an emergency defense program in which time is the crucial factor, a program moreover that entails imperative expenditures comparable in magnitude to wartime expenditures cannot be carried through successfully under a peace economy."[9]

It was as though no one wanted to take the final step. Americans seemed to want to be pushed pulled or kicked into the war. In Washington men jostled and nudged, daring and egging one another on.[10]

Commentator and analyst Raymond Clapper said this:

> "We say goodbye now to the land we have known. Like lovers about to be separated by a long journey, we sit in this hour of mellow twilight, thinking fondly of the past wondering...It's been a grand life in America. We have had to work hard. But usually there was a good reward. Man has gained steadily in security and dignity in hours of leisure, in those things that made his family comfortable and gave lift to his spirit. Under his feet, no matter how rough the road, he felt the firm security of a nation fundamentally strong, safe from any enemy, able to live at peace by wishing to. In every one of us lived the promise of America. Now we see the distant fire rolling toward us...It is still some distance away, but the evil wind blows it towards us."[11]

As vigorous as the isolationists made their arguments, by 1940, the worsening global situation was impossible to ignore. Nazi Germany had annexed Austria and Czechoslovakia. They had conquered Poland, Belgium, the Netherlands, and overwhelmed France. Great Britain was the only major European power left standing against Hitler's war machine. The urgency of the situation intensified the debate in the United States over whether American interests were better served by staying out or getting involved. Even so, the CDA and the Red Cross raised $14,000,000 in one week in June 1940.

Americans were startled in September of 1940, more than a year before the attack on Pearl Harbor, when FDR, deeply concerned by the situation in Europe and by Japan's aggression in the Pacific, declared a state of national emergency. With only 175,000 men in uniform, the US had an army smaller than even Switzerland. To increase the size of the Army and National Guard, FDR alarmed the nation by instituting the Selective Training and Service Act, which required all men between the ages of 21 and 35 to register for the draft. This was the first peacetime draft in United States' history. The draft was approved by Congress with the condition that the first 800,000 men called up could serve only in the Western hemisphere. (The announcement of the draft prompted a surge in marriages.)

Impatient, some Americans were not waiting for the draft. Dozens of home-grown militias and defense groups sprang up. Home guard units ranged in size from Carson City Nevada's 25-man unit to Miami's 400-man McAllister Volunteers. One of the largest guard units was an all- female militia in Chapel Hill, North Carolina formed by Mrs Virginia Nowell and commanding nearly 1000 members. Another all-female guard named themselves The Molly Pitcher Rifle Brigade in honor of the Revolutionary female gunner. Their purpose was to pick off descending parachutists. Though not encouraged by the federal government, cities and towns funded, armed and drilled guard units. The Military Training Camp Association operated ten camps where participants paid $43.50 to be awakened at dawn, fed military rations, and be drilled all day as though they were in a military boot camp.[12]

FDR's announcement and the institution of the draft jogged Americans out of any lingering hope for peace. War was on the horizon. People began wearing patriotic pins and flags. In fact, flag makers enjoyed record breaking sales. Anything red, white and blue made cash registers ring. A real nationalistic unity settled in. A patriotic song "God Bless America" sung by Kate Smith became a best seller as did the wistful ballad "The Last Time I Saw Paris."

From this point until late 1945, Americans never put the war out of mind. It perhaps was this mood that pulled the president up from low poll numbers in his bid for a third term. Americans chose to go with FDR, the man who seemed most ready to re-arm America.

Other important actions were taken before Pearl Harbor:

- The Naval Expansion Act of 1938 demanded a 20% increase in naval strength.

- The 45th Infantry Division was activated from reserve to active status.
- Construction begins on the Pentagon.
- The government began issuing Defense Bonds which later became known as War Bonds.
- In June 1940, the Alien Registration Act, known as the Smith Act was passed. The act required that each alien living within the US go to their local post office and register their alien status with the government.
- On May 20, 1941, more than six months before the attack, FDR set up the Office of Civilian Defense (OCD) to coordinate state and federal measures to protect civilians in a war-related emergency. The OCD organized the United States Citizens Defense Corps to recruit and train volunteers to perform essential tasks. (More on Civil Defense in Chapter Three.)
- In October 1941, the US rejected offers by the Japanese government that would have ended the economic embargo. In a message dated November 26, 1941, the US further called for the unconditional pullback of Japanese forces in Indochina and the Far East, and the renunciation by Japan of the use of force in the region.
- The Tuskegee Airmen, the first African American soldiers, successfully complete their training and enter the Army Air Corps. Almost 1000 aviators will be produced as America's first African American military pilots.
- *The Fifth Column is Here*, by George Britt, a book declaring that more than a million people in the US were actively sympathetic to its enemies becomes a best seller. Espionage hysteria breaks out. In response the Dies Committee and the House Un-American Activities Committee are born. The FBI, under J. Edgar Hoover, becomes a spy-chasing apparatus. (More on this in Chapter Eight.)
- In November 1941, the 87th Mountain Division is formed with 3500 volunteers from the National Ski Patrol.

As the Germans began their thrust west and rolled over one city after another, a re-elected President Roosevelt delivered a fireside chat about events in Europe and about his plan for an extraordinary mobilization for war production. He prepared the American people for sacrifice. The chat became known as "the arsenal of democracy" speech.

The president felt that the only way for the US to stay out of the war was to arm and equip those fighting fascism. As a last-ditch effort to stay within the neutrality acts of the 1930s, the president announced what became termed Lend-Lease. Under this program the US would provide arms – war ships, planes, and munitions – in exchange for "repayment in kind"; often leases on the debtor county's land which could be used for US military bases. The material could not be transported on US flag ships. Through some very savvy political maneuvering, his program was passed by Congress early the following year.

Everyday Americans supported Lend-Lease. When the first of fifty destroyers left Boston Harbor, Bostonians lined bridges, blew car horns, and cheered. Americans were now all in for support of Britain. All over the country cities and towns held fund raisers for relief. Women made socks and sweaters for refugees and bandages for soldiers. Dozens of organizations, such as Allied Relief Fund and Bundles for Britain, collected money or other relief items. Bundles for Britain had more than a thousand chapters raising needed supplies.

In support of our allies and as an act of national defense, all German and Italian assets in the United States were frozen, their consulates were ordered to close, and their staff directed to leave the country. The actions hit Americans of Italian and German descent hard. They saw it as a sign of what was to come.

Some accounts of the era wrongly describe America as totally unprepared for war. Those accounts missed the already robust, though fitful, buildup of government conversion of civilian production to arms production. (Events will show that only six months after Pearl Harbor the US was outproducing all other nations in war material.) In 1940, Franklin Roosevelt, alarmed by Japan's expansionism into the rubber producing countries of Southeast Asia, called rubber a "strategic and critical material," and created the Rubber Reserve Company (RRC), to stockpile natural rubber and regulate synthetic rubber production. Firestone, B.P. Goodrich, Goodyear, and U.S. Rubber agreed to work together to solve the nation's wartime rubber needs.[13]

Japan's aggression further caused the president to abrogate the US trade agreement with Japan, imposing an embargo on scrap iron and oil, and freezing all Japanese assets in the US, essentially breaking relations with Japan.

For some American sailors, World War II began before December 7, 1941. During the latter part of 1941, US Navy ships provided escorts for convoys bound for Great Britain carrying war materials from our "Arsenal of Democracy." Because German U-boats considered all ships in the convoys fair game, it was only a matter of time before the US Navy became involved in a shooting war.

One such escort, the *USS Kearny* (DD-432) was escorting a convoy in the North Atlantic. On 16 October, three convoy merchant ships were torpedoed. The *Kearny* immediately began dropping depth charges and continued to barrage throughout the night. At the beginning of the midwatch, October 17, a torpedo struck *Kearny* on her starboard side. Regaining power in the forward fire room, *Kearny* steamed to Iceland at 10 knots, arriving October 19. The *USS Kearny* lost eleven sailors; Twenty-two others were injured in the attack.[14]

Disaster struck again in the early morning hours of October 31. While escorting convoy HX-156, the American destroyer *USS Reuben James* was torpedoed and sunk with the loss of 115 out of 160 crewmen, including all officers. Although not the first US Navy ship torpedoed before the war, the *Reuben James* was the first one lost. After the news of the sinking reached America, many concerned people wrote letters to the Navy to find out the fate of friends or loved ones. Sadly, most of the country ignored the sinking. One who did not was folk singer Woody Guthrie, who wrote his now famous song immediately after the incident:

> *Tell me, what were their names?*
> *Tell me, what were their names?*
> *Did you have a friend on the good Reuben James?*[15]

President Roosevelt declared in his Navy Day address, "We have wished to avoid shooting. But the shooting has started. And history has recorded who fired the first shot. In the long run, however, all that will matter is who fired the last shot."

Inside Washington's corridors, fierce political battles waged. On one side were those who foresaw war as imminent and the country's present capabilities, even for defense, as weak, and on the other stood those who championed the status quo and worried about corporate opportunism. Often the battle was between New Deal liberals and the business community.

Production capacity emerged as a political issue. Americans bought a record 3.6 million automobiles in 1941 as part of the post-Depression surge in market demand. But as the US economy was rebounding, demands for military production for our allies and our own defense also rose sharply. In May 1940, President Roosevelt called for Americans to produce 185,000 airplanes, 120,000 tanks, 55,000 anti-aircraft guns and 18 million tons of merchant shipping in two years.[16] To the country's benefit, the tough work of learning how to set priorities and allocate production capacities began well before December 7. Defense orders traditionally were placed with a heavy influence of politics. The new efforts got off to a slow and rocky start in 1940 with commissions, departments, bureaus, boards, and individuals jockeying for power as will be seen in Chapter Two.

The first round of spending to hit Americans, beginning in mid-1940, was the construction of military bases and defense plants. In addition to the facilities themselves were the infrastructure elements of support, businesses, and housing. Small towns became cities almost overnight with the expected disruptions, petty graft, and cultural upheaval. However, no one could deny the benefits of economic resurgence. By mid-1941 most Americans were better off than at any time including the 1920s. They had money and were looking for ways to spend it.

The ballooning demand triggered inflation, creating another issue for President Roosevelt and Washington to deal with. They chose to establish the Office of Price Administration (OPA) as the vehicle. It would come to be one of the two most far-reaching agencies of the war, regulating the rationing program and setting ceiling prices on goods, rents, and services as will be seen in Chapter Four.

SNAPSHOTS OF LIFE IN AMERICA IN 1941

January

The year began with the inauguration of President Roosevelt for a third term. Later that month, Lindbergh testified before Congress, pressing his views on a neutrality pact with Hitler.

US Ambassador to Japan, Joseph Grew, reported on a rumor overheard at a diplomatic reception about a planned surprise attack upon Pearl Harbor.

The White House in early 1941 was quite a tourist attraction. None of the four gates had guard houses. There were no guards, other than to direct traffic and urge that cameras be left in the check room. Thousands of visitors wandered through the formal rooms every day. Reporters filing into the president's office did not have to show ID unless they were unknown.[17]

February

Washington creates the United Services Organization (USO) to entertain American troops.

Winston Churchill, in a worldwide broadcast, asks the United States to show its support by sending arms to the British: "Give us the tools, and we will finish the job."

Admiral Kichisaburō Nomura begins his duties as Japanese ambassador to the United States.

Americans tune in to the 13th Academy Awards, hosted by Bob Hope, presenting at Biltmore Hotel in Los Angeles, with Alfred Hitchcock's *Rebecca* winning Outstanding Production. The film also received the most nominations with eleven, while *The Thief of Baghdad* wins the most awards with three. John Ford wins his second Best Director award for *The Grapes of Wrath*.

March

Captain America Comics #1 issues the first *Captain America & Bucky* comic.

Washington state's Grand Coulee Dam begins to generate electricity.

Japanese spy, Takeo Yoshikawa, arrives in Honolulu, Hawaii and begins to study the United States fleet at Pearl Harbor.

All German, Italian and Danish ships anchored in United States waters are taken into "protective custody."

April

The US acquires full military defense rights in Greenland.

The US destroyer *Niblack*, while picking up survivors from a sunken Dutch freighter, drops depth charges on a German U-boat (the first "shot in anger" fired by America against Germany).

The US begins shipping Lend-Lease military equipment to China.

The America First Committee holds its first mass rally in New York City, with Charles Lindbergh as keynote speaker.

President Franklin D. Roosevelt, at his regular press conference, criticizes Charles Lindbergh by comparing him to the Copperheads of the Civil War period. In response, Lindbergh resigns his commission in the US Army Air Corps Reserve on April 28.

May

President Roosevelt buys the first War Bond.

Orson Welles' film *Citizen Kane* premieres in New York City.

The first Series E "War Bonds" and Defense Savings Stamps go on sale in the United States, to help fund the greatly increased production of military equipment.

At California's March Field, entertainer Bob Hope performs his first USO Show.

Americans become baseball crazy as Joe DiMaggio's 56-game hitting streak begins. The New York Yankee center fielder goes 1 for 4 against the Chicago White Sox.

Meanwhile, Ted Williams of the Boston Red Sox starts slamming his way toward a record .406 batting average.

950 miles off the coast of Brazil, the freighter *SS Robin Moor* becomes the first United States (neutral) ship sunk by a German U-boat, after its crew have been allowed to disembark. Americans are reminded of the submarine sinking of the Lusitania and the US entry into WWI.

President Roosevelt proclaims an "unlimited national emergency."

June

All German and Italian assets in the United States are frozen.

All German and Italian consulates in the United States are ordered to close and their staff to leave the country by July 10.

The United States Army Air Forces comes into being, taking over the former United States Army Air Corps.

July
Commercial television is authorized by the Federal Communications Commission.

NBC Television begins commercial operation on WNBT, on Channel 1. The world's first legal TV commercial, for Bulova watches, occurs at 2:29 p.m. over WNBT, before a baseball game between the Brooklyn Dodgers and Philadelphia Phillies. The ten-second spot displays a picture of a clock superimposed on a map of the United States, accompanied by the voice-over "America runs on Bulova time." As a one-off special, the first quiz show called "Uncle Bee" is telecast on WNBT's inaugural broadcast day, followed later the same day by Ralph Edwards hosting the second game show broadcast on US television, *Truth or Consequences*, as simulcast on radio and TV and sponsored by Ivory Soap. Weekly broadcasts of the show commence in 1956, with Bob Barker.

CBS Television begins commercial operation on New York station WCBW (modern-day WCBS-TV), on Channel 2.

American forces take over the defense of Iceland from the British.

In response to the Japanese occupation of French Indochina, US President Franklin D. Roosevelt orders the seizure of all Japanese assets in the United States.

General Douglas MacArthur is named commander of all US forces in the Philippines; the Philippines Army is ordered to become nationalized by President Roosevelt.

The US gunboat *Tutuila* is attacked by Japanese aircraft while anchored in the Yangtze River at Chungking. Japan apologizes for the incident the following day.

The Lockheed P-38 Lightning fighter aircraft is introduced.

August
Between August 9 and 12, under the code name *Riviera*, President Roosevelt and Prime Minister Winston Churchill meet at the Naval Station in Argentia, Newfoundland, for what became known as the Atlantic Conference.

The product of the meeting is the *Atlantic Charter*.

The *Atlantic Charter* sets out American and British goals for the world after the end of World War II. The joint statement outlined the aims of the United States and the United Kingdom for the post-war world as follows: no territorial aggrandizement; no territorial changes made against the wishes of the people (self-determination); restoration of self-government to those deprived of it; reduction of trade restrictions; global co-operation to secure better economic and social conditions for all; freedom from fear and want; freedom of the seas; abandonment of the use of force; and disarmament of aggressor nations. (The charter's adherents will later, in January 1942, sign the *Declaration by United Nations* which became the basis for the modern United Nations.)

US President Roosevelt bans the export of US aviation fuel from the western hemisphere, except to Britain and Allies.

By one vote (203–202), the US House of Representatives passes legislation extending the draft period for selectees and the National Guard from one year to thirty months.

The Great Gildersleeve debuts on NBC Radio.

September

The *USS Greer* becomes the first United States Navy ship fired upon by a German submarine in the war, even though the United States is a neutral power. Tension heightens between the nations as a result.

Charles Lindbergh, at an America First Committee rally in Des Moines, Iowa, accuses "the British, the Jewish, and the Roosevelt administration" of leading the United States toward war. Widespread condemnation of Lindbergh follows.

The first liberty ship, the *SS Patrick Henry*, is launched at Baltimore.

The first Moscow Conference begins; US representative, Averell Harriman, and British representative, Lord Beaverbrook, meet with Soviet foreign minister, Molotov, to arrange urgent assistance for Russia.

The draft uncovers a disastrously low level of literacy among the incoming draftees. A shortage of teachers due to pitiful teachers' salaries in many parts of the country is held up as a cause.

October

The New York Yankees defeat the Brooklyn Dodgers, 4 games to 1, to win their 9th World Series Title.

The destroyer *USS Kearny* is torpedoed and damaged by German submarine *U-568* off Iceland, killing eleven sailors (the first American military casualties of the war).

Walt Disney's fourth animated film, *Dumbo*, is released to recoup the initial financial losses of both *Pinocchio* and *Fantasia* the previous year.

President Roosevelt approves US$1 billion in Lend-Lease aid to the Soviet Union.

After fourteen years, work ceases on sculpting Mount Rushmore National Memorial.

The destroyer USS *Reuben James* is torpedoed and sunk by German submarine *U-552* off Iceland, killing more than 100 US Navy sailors.

November

In a speech at the Mansion House, London, Winston Churchill promises, "should the United States become involved in war with Japan, the British declaration will follow within the hour."

Japanese diplomat, Saburō Kurusu, arrives in the United States to assist Ambassador Kichisaburō Nomura in peace negotiations.

Joseph Grew, the United States ambassador to Japan, cables a warning to Washington DC that Japan may strike suddenly and unexpectedly at any time.

The United States grants Lend-Lease to the Free French.

US President Roosevelt signs a bill establishing the fourth Thursday in November as Thanksgiving Day in the United States (this partly reverses a 1939 action by Roosevelt that changed the celebration of Thanksgiving to the third Thursday of November).

The Hull Note ultimatum is delivered to Japan by the United States. *The Hull Note*, consisting of nineteen very specific steps to be undertaken by the US and Japan, is a final effort to avert conflict. The Japanese never respond to the communiqué.

The Mayor of Port Orford, Oregon, declares that three Oregon counties should join with three California counties to form a new state, to be named

Jefferson. He claims that these heavily rural areas are underrepresented in state government, which tend to cater to more populous areas. On November 27 a group of young men gain national media attention when, brandishing rifles and pistols, they stop traffic on US Route 99 and handed out copies of a Proclamation of Independence, stating that the State of Jefferson was in "patriotic rebellion against the States of California and Oregon" and would continue to "secede every Thursday until further notice." The effort simply fades.

All US military forces in Asia and the Pacific are placed on war alert. America had broken the Japanese code. There is little doubt that Japan is on the attack but where? Unfortunately, US military officials believe Japan will attack Manilla or Hong Kong.

Fiorello La Guardia, Mayor of New York City and Director of the Office of Civilian Defense, signs Administrative Order 9, creating the Civil Air Patrol under the authority of the United States Army Air Forces.

December
FDR moves the lighting of the national tree inside the white house gates to give it a more "homey" feel. He is joined by Prime Minister, Winston Churchill.

On Saturday, December 6, with only fifteen shopping days left until Christmas, business was booming. Retail stores were selling out of some goods, especially war toys and maps. Early model 1942 cars were snatched up as soon as they could be found. Nightclubs and theaters were full. Americans were enjoying Hildegarde at The Savoy, dancing to *Chattanooga Shoe Shine Boy*, and *Elmer's Tune* while some were watching Bob Hope or Abbot and Costello at the movies. The nylon stocking had debuted, replacing hard to get silk and baggy cotton. Americans were reaching out to one another by phone and by record breaking mail.

On that same December 6, President Roosevelt wrote what became his final personal appeal to Emperor Hirohito to avoid war between the United States and Japan: "Developments are occurring in the Pacific area which threaten to deprive each of our Nations and all humanity of the beneficial influence of the long peace between our two countries," the president wrote. "Those developments contain tragic possibilities…I address myself to Your Majesty at this moment in the fervent hope that Your Majesty may, as I am doing, give thought in this definite emergency to ways of dispelling the dark clouds. I am confident that both of us, for the sake of the peoples not only of our own great countries but for the sake of humanity in neighboring territories, have a sacred duty to restore traditional amity and prevent further death and destruction in the world."

The response to the president's plea came the following day, Sunday, December 7 (07:48 Hawaiian Time; 12:48 EST; December 8 03:18 Japan Standard Time) when the Imperial Japanese Navy Air Service stages a military strike on the United States Navy fleet at Pearl Harbor in the Territory of Hawaii, thus drawing the US into World War II.

Chapter Two
The War Production Colossus

America was doing just fine until Sunday morning when word of the Pearl Harbor raid spread across the country. Americans spent most of the day glued to the radio. The untested Civil Defense teams' responses were spotty, but many managed to form up. The country reeled in shock. Long distance calls took hours to get through.

On Sunday evening, the president himself was deeply engaged with his advisors and so his wife, Eleanor, took to the air to talk to the American people. Her words conveyed empathy as she declaimed her confidence in the people of the United States.

On Monday, dazed Americans went about their day in disbelief as radio reports came in describing the carnage at Pearl Harbor and other Japanese actions. Some wondered how military defense was so lax, but most saw deceit and surprise as the cause. Some Americans wondered how a tiny island country could be so foolhardy to initiate such an attack. Many felt the US would quickly trounce Japan. Chinese Americans, in their own self-interest, were pleased to now know that Japan would be confronted.

At noon, the president addressed the largest radio audience in history as he delivered a short address and immortalized the phrase, "a day that will live in infamy."

Reports of enemy planes came in from both coasts. Civil Defense was called out. School children and workers were sent home, though some children chose to go and play rather than go indoors. Aircraft were dispatched to hunt the planes down, but no planes were found.

> The war came as great relief, like a reverse earthquake, that in one terrible jerk shook everything disjointed, distorted, askew back in place. Japanese bombs had finally brought national unity to the U.S.[1]

In a short time, the magnitude of the attack settled into the country's psyche. Americans were in a rage and restless. Crowds gathered all over Washington DC – in front of the White House, the war department, the Navy department – jamming the streets and clogging traffic. The same happened in New York and Chicago and other cities. The crowds wanted to be told something or be given something to do. Some armed forces recruiting stations were overwhelmed.

An incident in Los Angeles involving the great American chronicler-song writer, Woody Guthrie, captures the mood. Guthrie and a friend were entertaining in a bar when a group of patrons noticed a Japanese-owned business nearby. The crowd worked itself up into a mob frenzy and went after the business, first shattering its plate glass window and then confronting the owners, a man and wife. Guthrie, his friend, and some sailors who had been drinking in the bar got between the mob and the two Japanese people. It was drizzling. Guthrie began to sing an old union song:

> *We will fight together,*
> *we shall not be moved.*
> *We will fight together,*
> *we shall not be moved.*
> *Just like a tree*
> *That's planted by the water,*
> *We shall not be moved.*

Other people began to join Guthrie and his friends and soon outnumbered the mob. When the police arrived, they found a group of people, soaked from the rain, singing that old union song in front of the broken window as others slunk away. A riot had been prevented.[2]

The Illinois University archives recorded this regarding December 7:

From that day forward, there were constant crowds in the Union Building swarming around the radios, trying to soak up every last bit of news which came in from the war bulletins. Many students even carried portable radios to their classes with them. The IU system and its leaders made it a priority to discourage students from reacting with anger and retaliation and emphasized how education was even more important now in time of war than during peace. The message was simple; help and support your country by being the best prepared and most informed person you can possibly be. This message was delivered in many forums.

In Hollywood, an amateur baseball team of Paramount studio employees was playing the L.A. Nippons, an all-Japanese team, when the news about Pearl Harbor came over the radio. FBI agents allowed the game to finish (Paramount won 6–3) then rounded up the Japanese players.[3]

Within a week after the Pearl Harbor attack, the US declared war on Japan, Germany, and Italy. It was immediately clear that to meet the tasks of engaging in war, the complex bureaucracy of government required a complete reorganization. (A list of the new agencies and their roles can be found at the end of this chapter as *Note One*)

At the core of these agencies was the need for the three M's: Manpower, Materials, and Money.

MONEY

Money was perhaps the easiest need to deal with. The country had mostly recovered from the Depression and taxes were relatively low. Once the war started it was easier to raise taxes for existential programs, though conservatives fought for strict accountability and disdained any notion of progressive taxes.

War bonds presented an unusual situation. $180 billion was raised by bond drives but supporting the war effort was not the only reason the government pressed for sales as hard as they did. Bonds pulled money out of Americans' hands and helped keep almost certain inflation down as demand was exceeding rationed supply in many areas.

Only a small portion, about a quarter, came from individuals; the rest came from banks, insurance companies, and corporations. Propaganda posters were ubiquitous, and some were downright scary. School children were encouraged to line up and buy 25 cent war stamps which could later be pasted into a booklet until they reached the $18.75 needed to buy a

$25 bond. (This proved to be an embarrassment for children who could not afford to line up and make a purchase.)

Even though they could be bought on installment and payroll deduction plans, individual quotas were never met while corporate quotas were always oversubscribed. In fact, the retail sale of bonds may not have been necessary at all to pay for the war. But bonds gave Americans a concrete way to participate in the country's defense. Buying bonds became synonymous with patriotism and sacrifice, much-needed traits to maintain morale and commitment and it did dampen inflation.

People outfitted their town squares with large cardboard thermometers representing the goal for a town's bond drive. Towns competed to see which could sell the most bonds. Trucks with loudspeakers patrolled the streets.

Bond drives afforded lots of entertainment with auctions of celebrities' belongings such as Jack Benny's violin and Betty Grable's hosiery. Kate Smith performed what today would be called a telethon. She spent sixteen hours on the air and raised $40,000,000. The interest on those bonds would be repaid through taxation, assuring that the mass of Americans would be paying for the war for years. (But they would be rescued by the great post-war boom.)

A major factor in gaining business support involved an assortment of financial incentives composed of both tax relief and lessening regulations. The "cost plus" contract guaranteed that a company would not lose money working on needed war goods as had happened in WWI.

In 1942, a 5 percent Victory tax, essentially an income tax on all income over $624, was levied. Congress attempted to reduce the tax to 3 percent in the Revenue Act of 1943; that bill was vetoed by President Roosevelt, but his veto was overridden. Taxes became more complex as the first withholding regulations went into effect. The tax was eliminated in the Individual Income Tax Act of 1944.

War time spending not only provided the means to produce the materials to win the war but underwrote the economy by bringing full employment and full pocketbooks.

MANPOWER

Military

The most fundamental manpower need was the military. The 1940 draft and the Pearl Harbor attack were swift and powerful drivers to raise the number of people in the services from 458,000 to 1,800,000 in one year (a growth of 4 times), and to nearly 4 million (or 10 times), in 1942, after just two years.

Immediately after the attack, American men flocked to recruiting stations. Overwhelmed, many stayed open 24 hours a day. The growth continued throughout 1945 when the total was more than 12 million men and women in uniform.[4]

One little story about men joining up comes via the late Mr Roy Hoopes.

Newton T. of New Hampshire told journalist Roy Hoopes:

> I was interested in the State Guard, because I knew a lot of these young kids who had never gone through the sixth grade, and I thought "Jesus they'll get drafted and they don't know how to kill or drill; they don't know nothing." So I went all over the area, not only in my town, telling the young kids to get into the State Guard. They'd say, "What for?" And I'd say, "Well you're going to get drafted. Don't you know there's a war going on?"
>
> Well, I talked a lot of them into it. A fellow who was in here this morning got into the Marines. He has only one eye now. He had a terrible time, but he made it out. If he hadn't had this State Guard preliminary training, he wouldn't have. These guys could hardly read or write or anything, but they learned to drill, they learned the routine, principally the phony part of it but you have to learn it. Once a week we'd have encampments, and then we'd go out three or four nights and have sham battles in the woods and that kind of stuff. All the officers got drunk as hell. These kids remember that training to this day. I saw one yesterday who I hadn't seen in about fifteen years. He said, "You know, you saved my life with that State Guard thing."
>
> Credit: Roy Hoopes (1922–2009)
"Americans Remember the Home Front."

Civilian

Civilian manpower proved more difficult. (It quickly lost its gender identity as women were drawn into the workforce.) While the draft was calling up hundreds of thousands of men, those vacated civilian jobs and the new jobs in defense work drew more than 15 million people into the work force. A real problem emerged: how do those workers get to the most needed jobs? The War Manpower Commission (WMC) was given the task but enforcing compulsory job assignments was beyond its reach. Collaboration among industry, labor, and government was needed.

Because teachers were so indispensable, school districts began to allow teachers to be married. Retired teachers were sought out and urged to return to the classroom. Small schools and even some districts were merged. Districts trimmed curricula, removing some special courses. School systems made it easier for people to gain special teaching certificates.

Defense workers presented the biggest issue. Regulations on age were winked at as boys joined on the factory floor. Pressure was so great it broke down some, though not all, of the resistance to women and African Americans in the workplace. (More on women and African Americans in the workforce in Chapter Five.)

Farming and Farm Labor

When Congress passed the Lend-Lease Act of 1940, it provided for more than ships and planes. The program was also an export program for farmers. The government bought food commodities that had been in surplus before the war and shipped them to the Allies.

By the end of 1941, farm income was higher than at any time since 1929. Between 1940 and 1945, net cash income for farmers increased from $4.4 billion to $12.3 billion. The average farmer went from a net income of just over $700 to over $2,063 – yet farmers still earned only 57 percent of what their urban workers made.[5]

When the US officially entered the war, the need for food increased even more. Soldiers could fight only as long as they had food to fuel their bodies. So, farmers were exhorted to produce even more. For example, Hormel had introduced the canned meat product Spam in the 1930s. It proved to be an ideal combat ration because it could be shipped easily and wouldn't spoil for long periods of time. By mid-war, Hormel was producing 15 million cans of Spam for the troops each week. Net sales doubled. Hormel was buying 1.6 million hogs each year, and 90 percent of the canned goods were going to the military.[6]

Farmers were being asked to produce much more food with fewer workers, and in addition, they had to comply with a whole new set of regulations:

- To buy a tractor, the farmer dealt with the War Production Board; that was more interested in steel for tanks than steel for tractors.
- To ship products to market, there were regulations to be met from the Office of Defense Transportation.
- Farm labor problems were handled by the War Manpower Commission.
- The prices farmers got were set by Congress and the Office of Price Administration.
- The War Food Administration handled USDA programs.

What had begun in the Depression as modest price support programs were now institutionalized, and farmers were becoming more and more dependent on the federal government.[7]

Due to farm workers volunteering for service or taking higher paying defense jobs, they were in such short supply that growers began to recruit labor from Latin America. One special program resulted from an executive order called the Mexican Farm Labor Program establishing the *Bracero Program* in 1942. These agreements between Mexico and the United States permitted millions of Mexican men to work legally in the United States on short-term labor contracts, addressing a national agricultural labor shortage.

Farm communities advertised on the radio and in newspapers for help. To address the farm labor shortage the government created the Women's Land Army, (WLA) which trained thousands of non-farm women to work on farms. Some worked for a whole summer while others worked only on their summer vacation. Some commuted daily while others boarded with farm families. Others lived in barrack-like accommodation with other women workers. WLA reported that 400,000 women were placed.

In a holdover from WWI, some of these women were called Farmerettes. They could, at their own expense, purchase uniforms. The International Harvester Company promoted their "Tractorettes."

One woman farm worker remarked, "No matter how heavy the hay we pitched, how our backs ached from weeding, or how stubborn the team we were driving, we always had the secret joy that we were helping the war effort."[8]

A New England farm owner said. "They were wonderful workers, but they nearly ate us out of house and home."

Mass Migration

What may stand as the most transformative and the longest lasting effect of World War II on America's home front can be found in the huge migration of its people – both Black people and White people, from farms to cities, from south to north from everywhere to be adjacent to defense plants and the economies surrounding them. It was estimated that when the war ended in 1945, more than 15,000,000 people were living in a different county than they were in 1940.[9]

For those Americans who had been through the Depression, the vision of a high paying defense job presented reason enough to make the move. They sold off everything they owned to earn what they hoped would be enough money for them to make the journey and to hold them over until they found a job. The process of migration was fraught with emotion and risk. Most had never travelled beyond their hometowns.

The defense industry would pull workers from backwaters, tenant farms, mined-out hill country, farmed-out land, backwoods, piney woods, fishing boats, mill towns, wide places in the road, from the humdrum of retirement, and the housewife's kitchen.[10] Ford sponsored mass meetings in the south to recruit people to their Willow Run aircraft plant.

The story of Duncan Eisley of Oklahoma (b. 1935):

> I was eight when we made the move. My dad enlisted in the Army as soon as the war started so my mother and I lived with my grandfather. We lived in pretty poor conditions outside of Stillwater. We had no electricity or running water and we didn't exactly live off the land, but close to it – hunting, trapping and fishing. My grandfather was old, but strong and healthy. One day a member of our church told him and some others that if you could work a twelve-hour day, the

airplane factories in California were begging for men and paid big money. They even gave you a house to live in.

My mother was afraid for us to set off by ourselves in our old truck, so my grandfather talked to some other people, and we gathered up three families to go in a caravan. The trip wasn't too bad as others had given us tips on how to do it.

We ended up in Santa Monica and my grandfather got work right away at Clover Field working for Douglas. It was a big change for us. We got to live in a small trailer, but it had electricity and water. One thing I remember liking the most is that I could go to a store and buy food.

It was like a big camp and we all learned about each other and where everybody came from. Sometimes someone lost a family member in the war and people gathered to help out.

Mostly there was a good spirit because we knew we were all working for the war effort.[11]

Housing blew up into an acute and persistent problem. Americans who flocked to new defense factories for jobs often ended up living in terrible conditions, in tents or found themselves living two and three families together. Where housing was available, rents shot up to record levels. Property owners converted garages into apartments. Storefronts and even warehouses were converted with bed sheets acting as room dividers. Large houses became rooming houses where sometimes renters lived and slept in shifts. Unsanitary shanty towns sprang up with shacks and people sleeping in sleeping bags. Local people in some areas would not rent to the new arrivals, viewing them as rootless outsiders who would not really become members of the community.

An American living in Burbank, California, saw the city population grow from 12,000 to 60,000. Richmond, California, grew from 23,000 to 135,000, severely straining the education system. Norfolk grew 61 percent and other cities endured similar, crushing growth.[12]

The government did build new housing at a rapid clip but what they built was envisioned to be temporary. These were sometimes barracks-like, with a central building for toilets and showers to conserve on copper and other materials. Residents of communities where they were built thought that after the war they would be left with empty slums of "tempos."

Somewhat forgotten, the government developed a Share Your Home Program, with the slogan "move over." An estimated 1,500,000 families shared homes with relatives, friends and strangers.

Housing wasn't the only problem arising from this mass migration. When a new factory came to these defense boomtowns, the towns' services were often overwhelmed. Grocery stores restocked only to have their goods depleted. Schools, transportation, police, fire departments, and health facilities could not keep up. Health facilities faced the double whammy of a crush of patients and a shortage of doctors who were called up for military service. At Portsmouth, Virginia, the Navy brought in a hospital ship to help meet the shortage of health care. The issue of childcare for the children of defense workers is covered in Chapter Six.

The mass migration produced a culture shock for some. Those coming from segregated regions found the openness of California and the north beyond belief. Many migrants from poorer areas had never experienced running water or electricity. Children coming from rural regions, used to being shoeless and wearing homemade clothing, sometimes faced the cruel teasing of classmates. Their mothers endured similar treatment being taunted as "Okies" or "Arkies." The locals often failed to see what these migrants were enduring: inadequate food, unheated trailers, and unending fatigue.

One joke, adapted for any state where migrants were arriving, asked the question, "How many states are there in the union?" The rude answer was "There are now forty-five. Kentucky and Tennessee have moved to our state and our state has gone to hell."

But the disruptions were not just in the states that were receiving migrants, but in the states where migrants departed. Black vegetable pickers across the south left farmers unable to harvest crops.

Some of these migrants had been migrants for years. They were the Mexican farm workers in California and the Southwest. The war years opened huge opportunities for them not only to replace men going into the service or defense work, but to replace the 100,000 plus Japanese now interred in camps (see Chapter 7). In addition to farm work, they entered work in shipyards and aircraft plants. Under a 1942 agreement between the US and Mexico, Mexico, in the so-called *Bracero* program, would provide 168,000 workers to enter the US home front to work.[13]

A regrettable side effect was friction between these workers and the many sailors stationed in California. The frictions led to the "zoot suit" riots of June 1943, named for the long coats, "pegged" pants, thick soled shoes, flat hats, and long draped key chains worn by Mexican *pachucos*. Sailors claiming revenge battled Mexicans in a bloody conflict.[14]

Mexican Americans served honorably in the service; 350,000 were called up in 1942 and eventually 500,000 served. They were especially valuable in the Philippine battles where the native language was Spanish.

For those migrants who found work, the pay might be good, but the culture shock and the 10-plus hour days were trying, especially when the home they came to at the end of that long day was a temporary one or a trailer. More than a few went back home.

The House Naval Affairs Committee investigated conditions in affected areas and reported unsurprisingly: migrants encountered substandard housing and exorbitant rents; health hazards ranging from scabies, ringworm, impetigo, and other skin conditions to life threatening epidemics such as meningitis, rheumatic fever, and polio; open sewers; leaky septic tanks; refuse and garbage, and other sanitary deficiencies; shortages of fresh fruits, vegetables, meat, and milk; inadequate childcare facilities; crowded school rooms; teacher shortages; and upsurges in juvenile delinquency.[15]

Another wave of migration involved the wives and, in some cases, families as they followed their armed service husbands from base to base. They faced many of the same hardships as families moving for defense jobs with the added emotional pressure of knowing they would be left alone. More on this is covered in Chapter Five.

For Americans all over the home front, their way of life was coming apart.

MATERIAL

"I want to tell you what, from the Russian point of view, the president and the United States have done for victory in this war," Stalin said. "The most important things in this war are the machines…The

> United States is a country of machines. Without the machines we received through Lend-Lease, we would have lost the war."
> – Josef Stalin, Tehran Conference, 1943

In the course of the war the American production colossus produced 325,000 planes, 650,000 jeeps, nearly 10,000 ships, plus countless guns and tons of munitions. At peak, one plane an hour rolled off one assembly line.

How did all this happen? Many stories portray this as an almost magic occurrence that took the US smoothly from making cars to making tanks overnight. It was anything but smooth. It was chaotic, disruptive, contentious, and deadly. (More workers died in defense work than in combat.) But eventually the pieces came together, and the US production colossus did its job.

The Need for Change

The first step in effecting change is recognizing the need for change. In 1939 the US was slow in recognizing the need to change from peacetime to war time production. Even as the US ramped up arms production for Britain, France, and Russia the public heard from some that the country could have both butter and guns. The recovery from the great Depression had been interrupted by a thirteenth-month long recession ending in 1938, but now the public, flush in its surge in income and strong in its aversion to repeating WWI, accepted the guns and butter proposition. Isolationists told the public that ramping up defense was simply a pretext to entering the war.

President Roosevelt and others in his administration observed the actions of Germany and Japan in 1939 and 1940 and did recognize the need, though with considerable underestimation at first. Given the lack of appetite for war by the divided population and by Congress, FDR's political skills were to be put to the test to mobilize the country.

He began with his first of many organizational gambits. New departments, committees and boards proliferated. Some had a very short life span.

In one of his great political feats, FDR overcame the objections to arming our allies and implemented the Lend–Lease program outlined in Chapter One. The program took up any slack in production capacity that might have remained, whether in manufacturing capacity, manpower, logistics or materials.

The Willingness to Change

FDR's calls for huge increases in defense/military outlays included new factories. He asked US industry to build the new plants and expand capacity, but he met with resistance. Change also requires both a willingness and a readiness to change. Business was certainly patriotic and willing to change, but it was not ready to change. Companies remembered how they had expanded in WWI and were left without enough business to sustain their enlarged size. They also recalled how they had competed for government contracts and often produced the goods at a loss.

This time was to be different. With tax money now available, the government could build the new facilities or industry could build them with the guarantee that after the war the government would buy them at market value. As for the fear of bidding on losing contracts, the government created a system of 'cost plus', contracting that guaranteed a profit for the business it contracted. The provision allowed the business to overextend in expanding capacity knowing that its costs would be met by the government contracts with a plus for itself in profit. Even more importantly, the cost of expanding facilities would be supported by a low interest loan from the Reconstruction Finance Commission (RFC) or by a direct grant from the government.

The Readiness to Change

It's easy to predict how these incentives would affect business. They were able to expand with little or no money, they had a guaranteed buyer, and were guaranteed a built-in profit – a capitalist's dream! Hitler's Fascist dictatorship took nearly a decade to build war production capacity. Under capitalism the US would become "the arsenal of democracy" in months.

The president issued a series of executive orders that shaped the banking system's wartime roles. Executive Order 9112, issued on March 26, 1942, established a program of guaranteed loans to industry for war production. Executive Order 9336, issued on April 24, 1943, expanded the scope of the program. For this program, the Board devised the general policies, after consulting with the Reserve Banks as well as the War Department, Navy Department, Maritime Commission, Office of Lend-Lease Administration, and the War Shipping Administration.

The Reserve Banks and branches acted as fiscal agents for those organizations. The banks and branches analyzed the financial integrity of loan applicants, determined the types of financing best suited to meet the borrowers' needs, prepared the necessary documents, and, for all loans under $100,000 (i.e., more than half of all loans), expedited the process by handling the loan on the spot. This swift, decentralized procedure expedited operations for the government and loan applicant, speeding the rate of industrial expansion.[16]

The Ability to Change

The government and American business now had three of the four requirements for change to take place: recognition of the need to change, a willingness to change, and the readiness to make the change. What remained was the ability to change. But first the American people needed to be brought into the change objective. The guns and butter idea needed to become a disabused notion. Unfolding war events and a large dose of government propaganda would do the trick.

Where capacity reached its limit, inevitable and obvious inflation developed. Capacity for everyday items like bicycles was taken away because Lend-Lease and our own defense needed the rubber. Metal for appliances was needed for airplanes and tanks. The American consumer could easily recognize the source of these changes. Up until Pearl Harbor the government relied on natural market forces, jawboning, and propaganda messages to keep the lid on the situation. Very shortly after the December 7 attack, the government would implement formal rationing. (See Chapter Four.)

Now the test presented was clear: does the country have the ability to make the changes required to convert from consumer production to the needs of war production? In some cases, "conversion" would be insufficient and completely new capacities would be needed.

Remarkably, all these dynamics took place while the US faced no certainty of war. Most of the country's efforts were reactions to events elsewhere. Except perhaps for the two coastlines, war was not an everyday concern but more like a twilight time. People went to movies, watched ball games, and went about daily life. Fortunately, the government found the motivation of those overseas events sufficient for the preparedness actions in 1940 and 1941.

After several false starts the overall task of managing war production fell to the most powerful of all war-time organizations, the *War Production Board* (WPB), established by Roosevelt a month after Pearl Harbor by executive order. Its purpose was to regulate the production of materials. The WPB directed conversion of industries from peacetime work to war needs, allocated scarce materials, established priorities in the distribution of materials and services, and prohibited non-essential production.

The first epiphany the WPB experienced was the preternatural interconnectedness of production at that scale. Parts for an aircraft could not be made without machine tools such as drill presses, sanders, and lathes, so orders for machine tools took temporal priority in any production plan. Then they learned that the country had a shortage of machinists needed to build those machine tools. In another case, what use would a new production facility be if there were no qualified workers close enough to man it? And without housing where would those people live? If most of the available steel was allocated to the large contractors, how would the small subcontractors provide the needed components they were charged to produce? The interconnectedness was a spider's web of often unforeseen linkages. *Harper's* used its own vocabulary in its July 1940 edition:

> "The primary theme in industrial mobilization is that it is impossible to regulate or control the operation of one segment of our industrial economy without the concomitant supervision of all of the other factors with which that segment is joined."

Resources of all kinds – human, capital and physical – were limited. What was needed was a system of priorities and any such system had to be interactive with a planning process. If a plan could be developed for, say, a new tank for the Army, the plan would need to compete for priority resources with the needs of the Navy and Air Forces. Added to the complexity of production was the fact that each service wanted to handle its own procurement. The military services were slow to recognize their dependance on industry, though the model of Krupp in Germany or Vickers in England made such dependance obvious. Even worse, all military services are traditionally accused of "fighting the last war." This was to be a different kind of war. The French soldier was probably as able a fighter as the German soldier, but he never saw a German soldier; he saw German tanks, German aircraft, and German cannons.

From *Days of Sadness – Years of Triumph:*

> Perhaps there was a time when courage, daring, imagination and intelligence were the hinges on which wars turned. No longer. The new total wars of modern history give the decision to the side with the biggest factories. The economically inferior may win battles; they do not win the all-out wars.[17]

As this war will soon begin to show, it is not solely the size of the combatants' factories but the technology they employ that will win the war.

To harness the country's technological brainpower a new agency was formed: The National Roster of Scientific and Specialized Personnel. The NRSSP created an inventory of more than 500,000 scientists and specialist practitioners. This inventory could be searched using IBM's new punch card system.

Any plan must also have a goal, but the country was not even certain about which wartime eventuality it should prepare for: a naval war in the Pacific, a land war in Europe, or a naval war in the Atlantic; or all three with air power a new component.

An effective planning process begins with an analysis of the present situation. By almost all measures the US was in poor shape. A war game held on the border of Louisiana and Texas in 1940 revealed how badly prepared the Army was. No aircraft or anti-aircraft guns were involved. No paratroopers dropped from the sky. The tanks involved were old and were small compared to the German Panzers. One calvary brigade still consisted of horses (and trucks to haul them on long marches[18]). Germany had 136 divisions in the field and an estimated 200 total. The US had perhaps six.

The Navy was worse off. It did not even have so much as an inventory of its vessels or a catalog of its facilities. It had no planning or purchasing process but even if it did, it would not have known what to plan for or in which ocean.

The Army Air Corps was in bad shape. Germany had 650 first class airfields while the US had 20 military airfields, with another 200 available civilian fields. As for aircraft, including trainers and obsolete models, it had only 2755 planes and just 8000 pilots. Mechanics for the planes were also scarce. Of the 84 American plants producing aircraft, only 23 produced military planes. In one month in 1940 they produced 300 aircraft, while the president was calling for 4167 a month to meet the goal of 50,000 a year.

Three American industries that benefitted greatly from the war and WPB were the automotive, shipbuilding, and aircraft industries.

The aircraft industry, especially, began a period of unprecedented economic boom. In many respects the US was way behind its enemies, which had early on stepped up the production of fighters, bombers, transports, and other type of warplanes.

In 1941, the US aircraft industry was a "job shop" boutique business running on one shift a day, five days a week. Someone ordered an airplane. The manufacturer consulted the list of the parts needed and contracted with machine shops, engine builders and others for what it needed. Each component had to be built to the specifications the manufacturer required for that particular aircraft. The components arrived at the manufacturer's facility and that aircraft was built. The time taken was measured in months.

To meet FDR's goal of more than 4000 aircraft a month, the industry would need to undergo massive change and it did. The aircraft industry adopted the assembly line technique of the auto industry. Each plane and all its component parts were standardized to exacting tolerances. This permitted mass production and stocking of components from a larger number of suppliers. Components could be built into sub-assemblies, such as engines, further speeding the process of assembly on a moving platform. This standardization made it possible to employ less skilled people including women and Black workers.

The output of this new technique was astounding. Between Pearl Harbor and D-Day the US aircraft industry produced far more than the 4000 aircraft a month goal. It produced 171,000 planes – 5700 a month.

From January 1, 1940, to August 14, 1945, the United States produced 300,317 military aircraft. Beginning in early 1942, factories ran twenty-four hours a day, six to seven days a week. By the end of 1943 the industry labor force had swelled to a high of 2.1 million workers, including tens of thousands of women. The Ford Motor Company plant in Michigan alone turned out 5476 B-24 bombers in 1944–45. At its peak, Douglas Aircraft Company's production line built one C-47 military transport (the military version of the DC-3) every five hours. By the summer of 1944, 15 airframe builders were producing 23 types of combat aircraft.[19]

The perception that aircraft manufacture was centered in California is true, but there were many key plants elsewhere:

CALIFORNIA
Douglas (6 plants) C-47, B-17, B-24, B-47
Lockheed (3 plants) P-38, B-17
Consolidated (2 plants) B-24, PBY
North American B-25, P-51, A-36, B-29, PB4Y, B-24, B-25, AT-6 (SNJ) trainer
Northrup P-61
Hughes, The famous all wood Spruce Goose

WASHINGTON
Boeing (2 plants) B-17, B-29

NEW YORK /NEW JERSEY
Grumman F4F, F6F, F7F, F8F, TBF
General Motors FM-1, FM-2, TBM-1, TBM-3
Bell P-39
Republic P-47

The remainder were scattered around the country, the most (in)famous of which was the Ford plant in Willow Run, Michigan. Built thirty miles from the major employee market of Detroit, it was the largest aircraft plant in the world. Originally designed to be 100 percent integrated production, it became strictly an assembly plant turning out, at its best, one B-24 bomber every hour. Its problems involved difficulty attracting employees from the auto makers, labor disputes, employee retention, and the poor conditions in the 10,000 housing units in "Bomber City." The plant earned the nickname "Willit Run."[20, 21]

Willow Run made use of America's "little people." Little people helped produce B-24 Liberator bombers. They set rivets inside of the narrow center sections of wings, insulated the airplane's fuel cells, and inspected work done in other confined spaces that larger workers could not access.

Despite these issues, Willow Run was able to achieve remarkable production rates. At its peak in 1944, when it was producing a B-24 every hour, pilots and crew members slept on 1300 cots as they waited for their aircraft to roll out the door.

Germany and Japan had already been working hard for a decade producing military aircraft. America's allies were also working at a feverish pitch to produce planes to defend themselves.

But it was America's aircraft manufacturers that became engaged in the greatest military industrial effort in history. Aircraft companies went from building a handful of planes at a time to building them by the thousands on assembly lines. Production in WWII went from a distant 41st place among American industries to first place in less than five years. In 1939, total aircraft production for the US military was less than 3000 planes. By the end of the war, America produced 300,000 planes

The American aircraft industry was given impetus very early on by the demand from the British and French for aircraft to supplement their own domestic production. The 1939 Neutrality Act permitted belligerents to acquire armaments from US manufacturers provided they paid in cash and used their own transportation.

The American aircraft production in WWII did adapt to the demands of war. In 1939, contracts assumed single-shift production, but as the number of trained workers increased, and the industry opened its doors to women and Black workers, the factories moved first to two, and then a three-shift schedule. The government creatively aided development of capacity and skills by placing "Educational training orders" with manufacturers to cut their teeth on, and by providing new government-built plants for the private firms to use.

Perhaps the industry's greatest achievement after the sheer quantities produced was its ability to design, produce, and service new combat aircraft after the war had begun. The B-29 Superfortress, A-26 Invader, P-51 Mustang, P-61 Black Widow, F6F-Hellcat, and P-47 were newly designed and produced during the war. One example, the P-51 Mustang, resulted from a proposal by North American Aviation in 1940 for an entirely new plane designed to British specifications. And when the Merlin engine replaced the Allison engine, the plane became arguably the outstanding US fighter of the war.

To bolster morale, the government often arranged for pilots to visit the plants and talk to the workers, letting them know how important their work was. If a plant achieved an exceptional level of production, it would receive a visit from a dignitary who would award the plant with the Army Navy "E" award for productivity – a large red and blue flag with a white E in its center.

SOME STARTLING STATISTICS PROVIDED BY WIKI

Aircraft Production by Manufacturer

Manufacturer	US Army Air Forces	US Navy and US Marine Corps
North American	41,839	0
Douglas	25,569	5411
Consolidated-Vultee	27,634	3296
Curtiss	19,703	6934
Lockheed	17,148	1929
Boeing	17,231	291
Grumman	0	17,448
Republic	15,663	0
Eastern (General Motors)	0	13,449
Bell	12,941	1
Martin	7711	1272
Chance Vought	0	7896
Beech	7430	0

Manufacturer	US Army Air Forces	US Navy and US Marine Corps
Ford	6792	0
Fairchild	6080	300
Piper	5611	330
Cessna	5359	0
Goodyear	0	3940
Taylor	1940	0

World War II aircraft production

Country	1939	Total
US	2141	324,750
USSR	10,382	157,261
UK	7940	131,549
Germany	8295	119,371

All did not go smoothly. Labor felt that they were in a position of strength because of the need for their work and the solid financial position of the defense contractors. They decided to press the advantage to improve their wages. A strike at the North American plant in Inglewood, California, had FDR call out troops to break the strike. Wielding bayonets and backed up by tear gas the strike was broken. The Selective Service Director threatened future strikers in defense plants with the loss of their draft deferments.

Shipbuilding

A dazzling achievement occurred in shipbuilding. The table below illustrates the growth of nearly 6000 full warships in less than five years.

Type	7 December 1941	14 May 1945[22]
Battleships	17	23
Fleet Carrier	7	28
Escort Carrier	1	71
Cruiser	37	72
Destroyer	171	377
Frigate	0	361
Submarine	112	232
Amphibious Warfare	0	2547
Total active	790	6768

The assembly line production method had been a growing competence in American industry and was already being applied to weapons, tanks and planes. Its application to shipbuilding proved to be a boon. In both the Navy's own shipyards and the private yards, building methods were modified from "keel up" to parts assembly. To simplify and speed construction, standardized parts were used for each type of ship ensuring that the ships they produced would be virtually identical.

One type of ship designed for emergency construction was called the "Liberty" or "Victory" ship. More than 2700 of these work horses were built.

Shipyards and the US government learned invaluable lessons about shipbuilding during World War I. The United States began increasing the size of its merchant fleet in 1936, well before it entered the World War II. The goal quickly became building sturdy, reliable ships in a hurry – faster than German submarines could sink them. By 1943, American shipyards turned out three a day.

In 1941 there were 29 large ship emergency ship builders: 8 on the Atlantic coast; 5 on the Gulf coast; 6 on the Great Lakes; and 10 on the Pacific coast. The Navy had four public shipyards – Norfolk Naval Shipyard, Portsmouth Naval Shipyard, Puget Sound Naval Shipyard, and Pearl Harbor Naval Shipyard.

During World War II, the San Francisco Bay Area billed itself as the "greatest shipbuilding complex in the world." Shipbuilding was the Bay Area's main contribution to the war effort. Spread out around the Bay were more than thirty shipyards and many other machine shops and fabricators that worked together to build ships. Between 1940 and 1945, workers in the San Francisco Bay Area built more than 1400 ships.

Los Angeles liked to brag about its shipbuilding prowess, too. In a speech, the West Carnifax, yard manager said, "We believe that we have done our share in showing the nation just what Los Angeles enthusiasm and enterprise can do, and we can get behind the nation, no matter what our talk. Shipbuilding came to Los Angeles as a war measure, but it has come to stay, for Los Angeles is a world port from now on…"[23]

One key factor in this overwhelming feat was the loosening up of the restrictions against hiring women and Black workers. (More on this in Chapter Five.)

In shipbuilding, perhaps more than in any other defense endeavor, a single man stands out: Henry J. Kaiser. Americans came to look upon him as "the man who can get things done." The son of German immigrants, he became involved in construction as a young man and became enormously successful building roads in Cuba and building the Hoover and other dams. He opened his first shipyard in Richmond, California in 1942. His innovations were to use the model of the standardized auto assembly line and to substitute welding for riveting.

The first Liberty Ship, the *Patrick Henry*, was built in 245 days. The record was set with the *Robert E. Peary*, a ship completed in 4 days, 15 hours and 29 minutes. However, the average time to build a Liberty Ship in 1943, when construction of these vessels was at a peak, was 30 days. The average cost per vessel was $1.5 million.

When things were going badly in some area of defense, Americans would call out, "give the job to Henry J."[24]

Americans working in these shipyards were toiling in a dangerous environment, complicated by a high noise level. A study revealed that 173,000 or so shipyard workers suffered non-fatal disabling injuries with falls and "struck by" as the leading causes. Surprisingly, the number of fatalities recorded given the millions of manhours worked was statistically very small: 655, and yet, total injuries in factories exceeded those of the battlefield.[25]

For Grandad, WWII (and Fate) Put an End to the Depression
by Emil Stefanik (b. 1938):

My grandfather was from Cleveland. He owned a clothing store and held some stocks and lost everything in the Depression. He took a job in a small steel mill where he earned 50 cents an hour. He was too old for the war. He heard about the need for workers in the war plants, so he moved his family to Camden, New Jersey and got a job in the shipyard. His pay went from 50 cents an hour to a dollar an hour with plenty of overtime. Grandad, my grandmother, and my mother also got help to pay for some of the rent. He always told that it was fated for him to make that move because the first ship he worked on was the *USS Cleveland*.[26]

Americans building ships in these yards were very proud of their work. Identification badges were worn openly and visibly marked a person as someone helping to win the war. War themed posters hung on the walls. Workers painted humorous and patriotic messages on bulkheads and hatches. Every worker knew about the production records of other shipyards and took huge delight when their shipyard set or broke some production mark. Shipyards' crews had spirited ceremonies for each launch of a finished ship.[27]

As might be expected, a small number of workers engaged in the theft of parts and tools. In other situations, workers skimped on their work to make their quotas more easily. The FBI was very active in such cases resulting in 600 convictions.[28]

Concern about corporate fraud and waste led to the formation of the Truman Committee, Chaired by Senator Harry Truman from Missouri. (See *Note Two* at the end of this Chapter.)

The bottom line was that the US was able to build ships much faster than German subs could sink them. Liberty ships carried tons of aid to England and its allies. Convoys were protected by US destroyers. In the Pacific, US aircraft carriers proved to be the deciding factor in battles.

OTHER MATERIAL

Material production enjoyed spectacular success. The conversion of auto plants to truck and tank factories was rapid. New plants – and their machinery – sprung up at a torrid pace. The government made extraordinary efforts to get businesses to seek opportunities to become suppliers of needed materials. In late 1941 it assembled trains to crisscross the country, displaying a wide range of parts needed for defense and explaining how businesses, especially smaller businesses, could become defense contractors. The trains attracted lots of attention, painted as they were in red, white, and blue.

Regrettably, small businesses were often unable to secure needed material or workers and the home front suffered a loss of half a million small businesses between 1940 and 1945.[29]

The Jeep

With 60 horsepower and all-wheel drive, the Jeep was the ubiquitous vehicle of the armed services. General George Marshall, Chief of Staff of the US Army during the war, called the vehicle "America's greatest contribution to modern warfare."[30]

The government set up several competitions among three bidders: Bantam, Willys, and Ford. World War II government documents show Bantam bid $788.32 per Jeep, with Ford undercutting it at $782.59. The government couldn't ignore Willys' bid of $748.74. This was enough to buy a 1941 Chevy Master Deluxe town sedan, at $754.[31] Ford and Willys got the contracts and built more than 650,000 Jeeps. Willys produced 360,000 in Toledo while Ford produced 280,000 in five plants.

Higgins Boats (Landing craft)

In the late 1930s, the US military began developing small boats that could carry troops from ships to open beaches. Andrew Jackson Higgins of New Orleans, who had been manufacturing shallow-water work boats to support oil and gas exploration in the Louisiana bayous, adapted his Eureka Boat to meet the military's specifications for a landing craft. Designated the Landing Craft Personnel (Large), or LCP(L), it was used in the invasions of Guadalcanal and North Africa in 1942.

Initially, separate landing craft were used for troops and vehicles, the LCP(L)s and the LCVs (Landing Craft Vehicle). The LCP(L) was designed without a ramp. Troops unloaded from the LCP(L) by jumping over the side, which proved unsatisfactory because climbing over the side exposed the men to hostile fire. Higgins solved this shortcoming by combining the LCP(L) and LCV's designs into the Landing Craft Vehicle and Personnel or LCVP. This craft, which is now the most famous of Higgins's designs and is often referred to as the Higgins Boat, allowed infantry or small vehicles to exit through a front ramp.

Higgins Boats changed the way that war was fought. Previously, navies would have to attack ports, which were usually heavily defended. By using Higgins Boats, armies could unload across an open beach and have more options in choosing their attack points. This also stretched the defending armies. Instead of concentrating on only a few entry points, defenders had to cover more shoreline. In both the Pacific and European Theaters of World War II, Higgins Boats allowed Allied armies to move ashore.

The success of these boats ensured that Higgins Industries would be a major employer during the War. A small workforce of only 75 workers in 1938 grew to over 20,000 by 1943. The Higgins workforce was the first in New Orleans to be racially integrated. His employees included undrafted White males, women, African Americans, the elderly and disabled people. All were paid equal wages according to their job rating. They responded by shattering production records, turning out more than 20,000 boats by the end of the war.[32]

The Big Inch and Little Inch Pipelines

As discussed later in Chapter Four, an extraordinary engineering (and political) feat created two pipelines from the southern oil producing regions to the production regions of the north, bypassing Nazi submarines.

Munitions – Bullets, Explosives and Shells

As a first order of business, Congress authorized $3 billion to build explosive and propellant plants in 1939. There were only a half dozen companies in the US with experienced personnel to produce explosives, and the capacity of smokeless powder production had fallen to only 30 tons a day and TNT was lower at 12 tons a day. Therefore, a large proportion of Ordnance funding obligated during the latter half of 1940 went to new powder and explosives plants and for plants that loaded, assembled and packed (LAP) artillery.

The Ordnance Department signed its first contract with DuPont for construction of a smokeless powder works (Indiana Ordnance Works). Another contract was approved for the construction of Radford Ordnance Works in Virginia with Hercules Powder Company as the operating contractor. By December 1940, a full year before Pearl Harbor, twenty-two new facilities were under way for shell loading and production of chemicals and explosives.

By October 1941, several ammunition complexes were producing ammunition. By the end of 1941 there was at least one of every essential type of government owned ammunition plant incorporated into the industrial base to include TNT, DNT, tetryl, toluene, anhydrous ammonia, smokeless powder, bag loading, and shell loading plants. After Pearl Harbor, an additional twenty-five facilities were authorized almost immediately, and construction began between January and August 1942. A total of 112 plants were authorized and 84 were constructed in only a few years.

Women in munitions plants started an organization called Women Ordnance Workers, or WOW. All it took to join was perfect attendance on the job and at chapter meetings for three months. The reward was a WOW insignia and a special WOW uniform.[33]

A Story from an arsenal
Anonymous (b. 1936):

My brother, Raymond, the oldest, went into the Army as soon as the war started. My sister Phyllis went to work at the Watertown Arsenal. The arsenal was a huge collection of old brick buildings with its own railroad. They tried to keep it secret, but everybody knew they made weapons. Phyllis probably wasn't supposed to tell me, but she said they made big anti-aircraft guns. She told me because she wanted to tell me about what she and the women did to the guns.

The women called themselves "WOW" – women ordinance workers – and made jokes about that, but the most fun they had was writing on the barrels of the big guns in lipstick. Mostly they wrote notes to the soldiers like "Go get 'em G. I Joe" and sometimes they wrote fresh things, but some, like Phyllis wrote the names of family members and friends. Phyllis wrote "This one is for you Raymond" and other messages.

Everything was about the war back then.

A Story from another Arsenal
from Julia W:

Here is a story about what some in my family experienced during World War II as residents of Niles, Michigan. This story is neither exceptional nor unique. It is just the result of me talking to my grandma. My grandmother worked in the Kingsbury munitions plant in LaPorte, Indiana, during WWII. Her job was making bombs. Born a true Victorian lady, she never wore trousers, not even to make bombs.

She told me they sometimes wrote notes on the bombs to support the soldiers who would use them. Often, they would put on bright lipstick and give the bombs a big red kiss. Somebody else put ink on an old pair of high heel shoes and stamped footprints across the casing of a bomb. A note to the enemy (we stomp on you with our pretty little shoe) or a note to the soldiers (we'll be here when you get home, Hon, and we will be lookin' good.)

Grandma O said the money at the Kingsbury plant was great, plus they also got free housing and food. She told me they were required to smoke Kool menthol cigarettes during breaks and lunchtime to "clear the lungs." So, what if her hair turned green and her complexion yellow? She was a single mother of a very large family and desperately needed the work. Plus, she was serving her country.

In spite of all the toxins, the birth of 12 children, and the stress of widowhood and loss, Grandma O lived past her hundredth birthday. I make no claim to historical accuracy in the details of this story. I am just recounting what my grandmother told me. We love her story just the way she told it and we don't need anything more.

I encourage everyone to talk to the Greatest Generation. They have much to teach us and will not be here long. Just ask for stories. You will be amazed. But hurry. *You've got to hurry.*

Parachutes

Up until the outbreak of WWII, most parachutes were made of silk, but pre-war preparations cut off supplies from Japan. After Adeline Gray made the first jump using a nylon parachute in June 1942, the industry switched to nylon. The following is a story about the Pioneer Parachute Company where Adeline worked.

Parachutes for Their Sons

At Pioneer Parachute it was really possible to pack a parachute for your son by Claire Stafford (b. 1936):

My Aunt Marie worked at the Pioneer Parachute Company in Manchester, Connecticut. Pioneer was the first company to use nylon instead of silk for parachutes. It was an important factory for the war effort. Mostly women worked there making and packing parachutes that paratroopers would use.

A woman named Adeline Gray who worked there tested the first nylon parachute by jumping out of a plane.

My Aunt Marie told me that women had to put their name and identification number on the chutes they worked on, and that one woman's chute actually got to her own son. She wasn't sure it was true, but it didn't matter because every woman felt she had to do her best because somebody's son's life depended on her.

Rubber

Another example of the country's formidable capabilities involved rubber, vital for the war effort. With supplies from Asia cut off, the industry turned to synthetic rubber. At this time, the United States had a stockpile of about one million tons of natural rubber, a consumption rate of about 600,000 tons per year, and no commercial process to produce a general purpose synthetic rubber. Conserving, reclaiming, and stockpiling activities could not fill the gap in rubber consumption.

Under the guidance of the Rubber Committee the government invested $700 million to build fifty-one plants. Firestone produced the program's first bale of synthetic rubber on April 26, 1942, followed by Goodyear on May 18, United States Rubber Company on September 4, and Goodrich on November 27. In 1942, these four plants produced 2241 tons of synthetic rubber. By 1945, the United States was producing about 920,000 tons per year of synthetic rubber, 85 percent of which was GR-S rubber. Of that 85 percent, the four major companies were producing 547,500 tons per year (70 percent).[34]

A plant in Institute, West Virginia, made its first shipment of Buna-S synthetic rubber on March 31, 1943. By May 31, only two months later, one million pounds of Buna-S had been produced. On June 10, government and industry dignitaries visited Institute to see the miracle plant.

Synthetic rubber was not the only technology Americans worked on. Blood plasma transfusions, the magnetron (microwave) radar, and computers were all moved forward.

Roadblocks and stumbles

America didn't create this production miracle without difficulty. Organizations and people jockeyed for power. The learning curve was too steep at times. Even the best intentions failed such as the nationwide aluminum drive in 1941. Families piled tons of pots and pans and anything else made of aluminum at depots. Unfortunately, recycled aluminum could not be used for aircraft or other war production. The tons of collected aluminum went back to recycling plants where it returned to store shelves once again as pots and pans. The effect of these scrap metal drives on actual war production was marginal at best. Their true value was in galvanizing citizen morale and a sense of patriotic unity, making everyone feel a part of the war effort.

Labor strife and the threat of it hovered around the war effort for the whole duration. Most actions were not crippling but some drew government action. One of the biggest to cause intervention was the coal miners' strike of 1941 led by a titanic figure, union president John L. Lewis. A coal strike would have crippled steel production. Lewis called the miners out on strike and the issue went before the National Defense Mediation Board (NDMB) where Lewis got what he wanted – easier rules for union membership – and returned the miners to work. The NDMB was rendered ineffective.

Lewis finally overreached himself in May 1943, when the United Mine Workers went off the job for three days. Furious, Roosevelt ordered the army to seize the mines and threatened to withdraw the miners' draft deferments. The miners went back to work, but Congress had had enough, and in June passed the Smith-Connally bill which didn't actually ban strikes but required a sixty-day notice beforehand. Roosevelt vetoed the bill; it took the Senate exactly eleven minutes to override him.[35]

Strikes antagonized many Americans who viewed the unions as self-serving, taking advantage of the wartime labor shortage and being unpatriotic.

FDR declared daylight saving time to be adopted in February of 1942. It was believed that adding daylight at the end of the day would cause people to spend more time outside and even if they were inside, they would use less electricity thus saving coal use. Post-war analysis showed that the idea was, at best, harmless.

The US outproduced all of its enemies in every aspect of warfare. No war was more industrialized than World War II. It was a war won as much by machine shops as by machine guns.

NOTE ONE
War Time Agencies

The following is a list of the organizational agencies which President Roosevelt and Congress put into place to manage the government in wartime. The first two, OPA and WPB, wielded the most power. Later chapters will demonstrate how these entities affected Americans.

OPA — The Office of Price Administration was established on August 28, 1941. The OPA's main responsibility was to place a ceiling on the prices of most goods and rents, and later, to limit consumption by rationing. Americans received their first ration cards in May 1942.

WPB — The War Production Board was established by Roosevelt a month after Pearl Harbor by executive order. This powerful board was to regulate the production of materials. The WPB directed conversion of industries from peacetime work to war needs, allocated scarce materials, established priorities in the distribution of materials and services, and prohibited nonessential production.

WPA — The Works Progress Administration was an agency designed to combat unemployment by employing millions of jobseekers (mostly men who were not formally educated) to carry out public works projects, including the construction of public buildings and roads.

NHA — The National Housing Act's original charter was to improve housing standards and conditions, provide a method of mutual mortgage insurance, and reduce foreclosures on family homes. The housing market was in dire need of intervention during the Great Depression. The NHA played a vital role in organizing war time housing near production factories.

OWI The Office of War Information. The purpose was to conduct information programs to promote, in the United States and abroad, understanding of the status and progress of the war effort and of war policies, activities, and aims of the US government. Some labeled it a propaganda effort.

FEPC The Fair Employment Practices Committee was established by FDR to help prevent discrimination against African Americans in defense and government jobs.

WRA The War Relocation Authority was established to handle the internment of Japanese Americans during World War II. It also operated the Fort Ontario Emergency Refugee Shelter in Oswego, New York, which was the only refugee camp set up in the United States for refugees from Europe.

NWLB The National War Labor Board was constructed to arbitrate labor disputes during World War II. Members included four labor leaders (from both the American Federation of Labor and the Congress of Industrial Organizations), four corporate executives, and four public representatives,

OWM The Office of War Mobilization was essentially charged with refereeing differences among agencies.

OSRD Office of Scientific Research and Development to initiate and coordinate defense research and development.

ACS (American Chemical Society) The industry group representing most of the large chemical manufacturers.

Not all the organizational entities fared well in Congress where conservatives pushed back against spending and overreach. The National Resources Planning Board (NRPB) charged with post-war planning was dropped. The Farm Security Administration (FSA) designed to help poor farmers buy land, the Rural Electrical Administration (REA), and the Civilian Conservation Corp (CCC) were all cut.

NOTE TWO
The Truman Committee

What follows from the Levin Center portrays how America conducted itself on the home front. News accounts of Truman's committee hearings built trust, helped morale, and provided ongoing assurance that things were under control. Harry S. Truman, though best known as the 33rd President of the United States, gained initial prominence in national politics as a Missouri senator from 1935 to 1945. His fame arose from his oversight efforts related to World War II.

Billions of dollars in taxpayer money were flowing like a river into government contractors' coffers. Senator Truman spotted waste and suspected there was more to be found. He became the head of a committee charged with investigating the procurement and construction of supplies, materials, munitions, vehicles, aircraft, vessels, plants, camps, and other articles and facilities in connection with national defense.

Senator Truman insisted upon a fact-based approach to the committee's work. "There is no substitute for facts," Senator Truman often repeated in committee meetings. Here is more of what he said:

> "This committee is a bipartisan one and has adopted a policy of making a thorough inquiry of the subjects it undertakes to investigate without prejudice or bias. There will be no attempt to muckrake the defense program, neither will the unsavory things be avoided. The welfare of the whole country is at stake in the successful conclusion of our national defense policy. Where there has been so much haste in the expenditure of such enormous sums there are bound to be leaks and mistakes of judgment. Many people believe in both patriotism and profits, but sometimes, unfortunately, profits come first with them. My experience with the public contractors is that they must be carefully checked on Government construction."

Spending less than $1 million on its investigations over seven years, it is believed that the Truman Committee:

- Saved the government $10 – 15 billion;
- Provided citizens a reason to believe that the defense program was under control;
- Saved thousands of lives by uncovering defective equipment and materials that were to be used by troops, and unsafe conditions at plants where wartime materials were being manufactured; and
- Shortened WWII by streamlining federal contracting practices.[36]

In a 1968 interview, Wilbur Sparks, who served as a lawyer on the Truman Committee, offered this assessment of its oversight work: "History may very well show that never before or since has there been a congressional committee which conducted itself in such a nonpartisan manner."

Chapter Three
Civil Defense and Blackouts

Americans Get into the Fight

On May 20, 1941, seven months before Pearl Harbor, President Roosevelt signed an executive order creating the Office of Civilian Defense (OCD). As the name states, civilians would play a major role in defense against enemy attacks. OCD would free up the military for its special mission. Americans on the home front would feel safer and would see themselves directly involved in the war effort.

FDR appointed Fiorello LaGuardia, the colorful and pugnacious mayor of New York City, to oversee OCD. LaGuardia saw his narrow charge to be the defense of America from attack, including preparation for such an occurrence. First Lady, Eleanor Roosevelt, however, felt that public health and welfare should also be included in the department in hopes of allowing women to become involved. LaGuardia, not wanting to deal with those aspects, hired Eleanor as his assistant.

LaGuardia had enough to address fire watchers, auxiliary police, auxiliary fire, decontamination squads, rescue squads, medical corps, messengers, utility repair squads, road repair squads, bomb squads, emergency food and housing. Mrs Roosevelt attempted to include the arts, physical fitness, and other somewhat vague and less direct activities under OCD's charge.

This article from the February 16, 1942, issue of *Time* Magazine sums up their view of her efforts.

> Most U.S. citizens would agree that Eleanor Roosevelt is a fine woman; but even a fine woman can go too far. And last week it began to look as if the First Lady had gone too far.
>
> As OCDiva to Fiorello LaGuardia's OCDemon of the Office of Civilian Defense, she had contributed the lioness' share to the air of bustling nonsense which has characterized OCD. This week Mayor

LaGuardia, by promising to resign as head man of OCD, somewhat cleared the air and quietened the room. But no sooner had he done so than Eleanor Roosevelt set the shouts and murmurs going again louder than ever. The suspicion that the OCDiva regarded OCD as her particular plaything was deepened by the appearance of her newly summoned playmates.

The playmate-protégé who roused the first angry shouts was personable, politically ambitious, cinema actor Melvyn Douglas (real name: Melvyn Hasselberg). First it was announced that he was going to be in charge of information for OCD. Then OCD said Mr. Douglas was actually going to look after OCD's art division, at the rate of $8,000 a year (when he worked at it; he is still in the movies). Straightway Congress sounded off. He's a Red, cried California's Leland Ford. He isn't, either, cried California's Jerry Voorhies. This hue & cry flushed another playmate-protégé from OCD's covert: one Maris Chaney, a toothsome blonde dancer who in 1938 had made up a dance which she gratefully called the "Eleanor Glide." Miss Chaney was in charge of the children's section of OCD's physical fitness division. Salary: $4,600 a year.

With Miss Chaney thus in view, the House really gave tongue. For four hours Congressman after Congressman lit into Miss Chaney, Friend Eleanor and OCD. Bayed Missouri's Philip Bennett: "If [she] is worth $4,600 a year, then Sally Rand, strip-tease artist from my own Congressional district, ought to be employed at once because she would, on this scale, be worth at least $25,000 a year to civilian defense." In full-throated chorus, the House voted to forbid the use of civilian defense funds for "instructions in physical fitness by dancers, fan dancing, street shows, theatrical performances or other public entertainment," amended a $100,000,000 appropriation bill to make sure that no dancer would get any of it.

Though Congress needed no encouraging voices, the press joined in with rousing view halloos. The usually mild-mannered Columnist Raymond Clapper set the pace. Said he: "Half the trouble around [OCD] could be got rid of if the President would haul [Mrs. Roosevelt] out of the place...There is hesitation in Congress about saying much because nobody wants to criticize the wife of the President. But this is public business and very important public business…It is incredible that President Roosevelt will allow this situation to continue much longer. It has become a public scandal. How can you have any kind of morale with a subordinate employe, who happens to be the wife of the President of the United States, flitting in and out between lecture engagements to toss a few more pets into nice jobs?"

The hunt flushed many another protégé of Mrs Roosevelt's from the thickets of OCD. One was Betty Lindley, wife of New Dealing Newshawk, Ernest K. Lindley, who used to handle Mrs Roosevelt's radio programs. Mrs Lindley was "principal civilian participation adviser," at $5,600 a year. Another was Jonathan W. Daniels, novelist and editor-son of an editor-father. This man of letters was "director of program planning." For "operations director" the OCD named a New York social worker called Hugh Jackson, and as survey director, Mary Dublin, formerly with the Tolan Committee.

Few doubted Eleanor Roosevelt's good intentions. And many a citizen thought it likely that James McCauley Landis, OCD's executive director, might be able to straighten out OCD's compound confusion if he were given a free hand – which meant, if Mrs Roosevelt would step out. All over the US everyone prayed that Mrs Roosevelt's admirable energy would find some less dangerous plaything. Mrs. Roosevelt soon declared her work complete and resigned.

As the article makes plain, LaGuardia (the OCDemon) was not on any more solid ground than Mrs Roosevelt (the OCDiva). Many predicted that his attempt to manage the multi-million-dollar OCD program, which would involve millions of Americans, while at the same time acting as mayor of the nation's largest city would prove to be too much for him. James Landis was moved in to head OCD and LaGuardia was given a face-saving ex-officio role.

America was plunged into a panic in December 1941. The whole country wondered what would happen next. Might the Japanese bomb Los Angeles or San Francisco? Or might they or the Germans come from the other direction and bombard the most densely populated city in the world, New York? No one knew for sure. "I lived in Clinton [New York] during World

War II," Barbara Williams Roberts wrote at the website www.clintonhistory. org. "It was scary. I was still in grade school and I remember hearing an airplane and looking up to see what it was. I think I expected the Japanese to bomb Clinton."

The pre-war existence of OCD is best described as chaotic. As usual, cities and states wanted to run their own shows while LaGuardia wanted a tight top-down federal program. Eventually the states and cities exerted their local power and influence. Americans' patriotic fervor overcame the administrative failings of the short (ten month) LaGuardia tenure and at full force 11,000 local defense councils were in operation with nearly 10,000,000 volunteers signed up.[1]

> During the war years, my aunt and uncle lived in downtown Miami. I remember how proud my uncle was being an air raid warden, patrolling the streets with his special hat and arm band, ensuring there were no lights shining during blackouts. Mom and Dad would take me along visiting friends in Miami Beach to play cards. I think the game was Canasta back then. They would have these long black curtains over the windows facing the ocean. German submarines apparently could use any lights on shore as a backdrop in sighting any ships between them and any lights on shore. Coast Guardsmen walked along the beach in patrol.[2]

Like any new organization, OCD had growing pains. Some cities like Detroit could not enlist enough people to serve as wardens. On the other hand, many small cities and towns with exaggerated views of their own importance viewed themselves as Target #1. Training such a large number of people, from top to bottom, under time constraints, and with very little equipment, took a strong effort from the small core of early managers. The OCD published a handbook, *The United States Citizens Defense Corps*, to explain the duties and responsibilities of various positions. The country even lacked warning sirens and those that were in place were inadequate for the purpose. In irony, OCD did design a standard siren for all to use but the Victory Siren, as it was named, proved to be too loud. In another irony which caught Americans' fancy, many of the whistles supplied to volunteers were made in Japan!

Like the military, civilian defense councils were segregated. So, for example, a local defense council sometimes had two completely separate health and safety committees, one working only with White citizens, the other only Black citizens.

After screams to locate the ubiquitous white OCD helmets for New York City's OCD corps, they were found, but while they were being fitted with their liners it was discovered that they were three-quarters of an inch too small.

In Maryland, the Maryland State Guard was sent out to Rod and Gun clubs, trap shooting clubs and shooting ranges to recruit men to be a part of this militia force because they owned their own weapons and knew how to shoot. Because these men utilized whatever weapons they had, arms ranged from shotguns to rifles to muskets. Following recruitment, the Maryland State Guard and/or retired military personnel would provide basic field training on small arms (weapons use and maintenance, shooting positions, rapid shooting techniques) and field training (basic drilling techniques, study of terrain from military standpoint, and setup and maintenance of communications).[3]

OCD also organized the scrap drives (discussed in Chapter Four), through the thousands of local scrap committees. It provided educational material. OCD's key brochure, *What to Do in an Air Raid* had a printing of fifty-seven million copies and was augmented with reprints in hundreds of newspapers. (The bestselling book of 1942, at 8,000,000 copies, was the Official Red Cross Handbook on first aid.[4])

On December 9, due to a (false) report of planes heading for the city, New York had its first air raid alarm. New Yorkers appeared more confused than frightened.

Through OCD, Americans volunteered for a variety of activities including blood donations, acting as block captains, becoming shore patrollers and aircraft spotters.

Watching for enemy aircraft was an important defense task. Men and women of all ages —even children – volunteered their time to sit atop roofs, watchtowers, and other structures to look for airplanes. Ground observers, as they were called, were supposed to identify each plane they saw and report them by telephone to a control center, which would use the information to track the plane's movement. In an age when radar was only just coming into use, this was a vital job.

In military conflicts prior to World War II there were no aircraft capable of long-range flights so up until then there was no concern with airborne attacks to American soil. However, between 1919 and the start of World War II, great accomplishments in aeronautics occurred and the long-range bomber was created. This meant that an air attack from an overseas enemy could very well become a reality. To protect the American public from such a threat, a warning system needed to be developed.

The American East and West Coasts were especially vulnerable to attacks from German or Japanese bombers. Available mechanical technology at the time was limited to sound detectors which were felt to be inadequate and utilizing the military as lookouts and spotters was seen as an inefficient use of soldier time. Therefore, it was determined that the American people could help fill this gap and play a role in aircraft detection by serving as aircraft spotters. The American legion helped organize volunteers in 1941 and the Aircraft Warning Service (AWS), a civilian arm of the military's ground observance corps, was created.

Next, observation posts, information centers and call filter centers were established on both coastlines. As the war escalated, thousands of observation posts were established on the East Coast from the top of Maine to the tip of Florida, and roughly inland as far as the western slopes of the Appalachian Mountains. On the West Coast, posts ranged from upper Washington to lower California. Men and women who were determined 4F status, meaning they were unfit to serve in the military, were recruited to the AWS to be aircraft spotters. These volunteers were given extensive training in aircraft recognition and provided materials such as aircraft spotter dials, aircraft recognition playing cards, aircraft identification cards and hard rubber aircraft models to help them learn how to identify American, British, German, and Japanese planes based on wings, engines, and aircraft shape. There were even aircraft recognition bees to test the knowledge of the spotters.

At the peak of the war over 750,000 individuals were involved in the AWS throughout the country. Spotter towers and call centers were manned 24 hours a day, 7 days a week. These volunteers were extremely vigilant and would report any aircraft spotted. Often, reports would be called from multiple observation posts, allowing for triangulation and accurate tracking of aircraft. Fortunately, no enemy bombers ever made their way to the US and the AWS was deactivated in May 1945. However, the many hours of time spent by the spotters and call center operators were not in vain and proved helpful in other ways to the military.[5]

One far reaching OCD program allowed Americans on the home front, older Americans, women, and others who could not serve in the armed services, to suit up in uniform and conduct themselves in a quasi-military fashion: The Civil Air Patrol (CAP).

German Submarines became a real threat to America's East Coast, sinking valuable oil cargo in plain view and costing many lives. As a result, OCD activated the Civil Air Patrol, a voluntary corps which grew to 80,000 men and women along with 20,000 air cadets, boys and girls aged between 15 and 18, who undertook preflight training.[6]

The first CAP base #1 was established near Atlantic City, New Jersey and flew patrols from New York to Cape May. Within a few months CAP patrols were flying from twenty-six bases all along the Atlantic coast. The program was a success. The CAP patrols freed Army and Naval aircraft to fly longer range surveillance. In a few months CAP aircraft were armed with bombs and actually engaged fifty-seven German subs.

The following story tells of how CAP planes became armed:

Pilot Thomas Manning and observer Marshall Rinker, flying from the Lantana, Florida, base in May 1942, spotted a submarine just off Cape Canaveral. The German U-boat crew saw the aircraft and dove to escape but ended up ramming the sub's nose into a mud bank and getting stuck. For 42 minutes, the CAP plane circled the sub, calling the base and begging someone to come and attack the Germans. But neither the army nor the navy could respond quickly enough. The U-boat got free and escaped, leaving two frustrated CAP volunteers in its wake. When news of that incident reached Hap Arnold, head of the Army Air Corps, he made sure that CAP planes were armed with either a single 100-pound bomb or a 300-pound depth charge. Which weapon a plane carried depended on its size and horsepower. The CAP is officially credited with sinking or damaging two of the German submarines it attacked.[7]

CAP pilot, Bob Mosely, the brother of Zack Mosely the cartoonist, who created the popular war time strip "Smilin" Jack, tells this story about his time flying with the CAP on the American home front:

> The Civil Air Patrol (CAP) had been given a mission by the US Army Air Forces to perform shore patrol duties off the Fla. coast from Palm Beach up north to Cape Canaveral (about 130 miles of coast) and then there was another CAP unit out of Miami for the area south of us and others on up the north coasts, all the way to Maine (as I remember it). German submarines by that time were sinking many cargo ships along the east coast. The Gulf Stream is a current of water about 50 miles wide (just a guess) and moves at about 10 to 15 knots and flows around the bottom of Fla. out of the Gulf of Mexico and north along the coast and then on out into the Atlantic.
>
> The US ships moving south would often get in very close to shore, to get inside the Gulf Stream and avoid the current so as to not lose that 10 to 15 knots of speed. At this time the Army Air Forces were short on planes and could not provide much in the way of patrol coverage. And if a submarine was spotted by some other source, a call would have to be made through channels and a very slow observation plane could then be dispatched, but if the observation plane did not happen to be in that particular area at that time it might have to come all the way down from Savannah Georgia. This was obviously no threat to the Germans so they were having a field day out there sinking merchant ships. When the ships were in so close to land, inside the Gulf Stream, the Germans would silhouette them against the lights of Palm Beach at night and blaze away at them (this led to more strict blackout rules). They were in so close we were awakened several nights (living in West Palm Beach) by torpedo explosions sinking ships. Some of the broken

hulls stayed around for a long time; one in particular hull off of Vero Beach was visible for as much as 20 years later.

These sinkings led to a bunch of things; one being a lot of oil on the beaches, one being a total black out at nights (we had to tape up the head lights of our cars and leave only a little slit of light for night driving, but with gas rationing there wasn't all that much driving going on anyhow) and another thing it brought about was the change in the mission of the CAP being upgraded from an observation/rescue role to a more aggressive role, to try to help out with the German submarine menace. The idea was to put 100-pound bombs on the little Stinson 10 A, 90 HP planes we flew. Now we really did not expect to do a lot of damage with those little planes, although they could possibly inflict some damage. But mainly it was figured that the Germans had some kind of electronic gear to detect an airplane was over head, and it might deter an attack.

With the advent of the war, that sleepy little airport in West Palm Beach that I had fallen in love with when I arrived in West Palm Beach in 1940, became Morrison Field and a beehive of activity with military planes of all sorts parked everywhere. Thus, there was no room for any civilian operations like there had been for the original Florida Air Patrol and early CAP operations, so the CAP operations had to be moved to the new Lantana airport, about 5 miles to the south of West Palm Beach.

It was at this time, thanks to my brother, Zack, that I got into the CAP as a pilot because I had my pilot's license. I went from a grunt working 10 hours a day, 6 days a week, for $10 dollars – washing, fueling and hangering airplanes – to a Second Lieutenant in the CAP, where they paid me $8 dollars a day and I could get all of the flying time I wanted. They called that pay Per Diem; a word I became very familiar with later on in my career. I had definitely moved up in the world and I was beginning to realize that my decision to become a military pilot; i.e., work for the Government, was not a bad idea from a monetary stand point as well as getting to fly their beautiful airplanes.

I really loved that CAP experience. Nearly all of those Civil Air Patrol pilots were of Zack's age or older (a couple of them had even been in World War One). They were successful people by my standards in that they had made enough money to buy their own planes, and they were very experienced pilots. I had enormous respect for them and it was an honor to get to fly with such men. They seemed to respect me also even though I had done nothing to prove myself except that I did have a pilot's license. Part of their respect for me, I'm sure, came from the fact that I was Zack's brother. But I suspect it also was the fact that they knew I was going to be getting in the real shooting war very soon and they were too old and would not be able to get to do that. That is a strange thing to think about as I write this, in that people really wanted to go to war which could mean getting killed. But a person needed to have lived at that time, when your country was really in danger of being taken over by the Germans and the Japanese, to understand how Americans wanted to get in the fight. It was an extremely threatening period and almost everyone wanted to do their part.

Thousands of American civilian pilots on the home front joined the Civil Air Patrol (CAP) and flew millions of hours as couriers, woodland fire spotters, and anti-submarine patrollers. They also towed gunnery targets and even acted as decoy enemy aircraft in drills.

Other civilian organizations were considered. In Wisconsin, the American Legion proposed mustering thousands of deer hunters in a guerilla army. Georgia considered a militia, as did a city in Oregon. No doubt many other home front guard schemes were plotted.

But the heart of OCD's work centered around the Air Raid Warden and the administration of blackouts and drills. One source provides this dramatic description of the Air Raid Wardens' role:

"The most well-known element, however, is the Air Raid Warden. These are men and women tasked with protecting the lives of their fellow neighbors. By day, the Air Raid warden visits his neighbors and educates them about blackouts and what to do if an air raid were to occur – turn out lights, hang black out curtains, don't drive or use the telephone and teaches them how to fight an incendiary bomb fire should one fall through their attic. By night, these same wardens will don their helmet, flashlight, gas mask, medical kit, air raid siren, gas alarm, whistle and maybe a stirrup pump fire extinguisher and patrol their neighborhoods enforcing blackout and air raid drills. These wardens take their roles quite seriously, sometimes even going to the extent of shooting out a light bulb if one is left on and no one is home, as he is well aware that any source of light could direct enemy bombers to his neighborhood resulting in public harm and potential destruction of the neighborhood or war material plants."[8]

In another equally intense description we are told, "Around the air raid warden revolves the whole of Civilian Defense protection. It is upon his shoulders that the responsibilities of all phases of protection rest. He is the man – and the only man – who can call upon emergency services during a bombing. He is the boss of your block during an emergency. He is the man to whom you might owe your life when and if we are bombed by the enemy."

That was from Robert Smith of the Oregon State Defense Council on April 1942 on a KGW radio show entitled "Before the Bombers Come." Each week the thirty-minute show hosted experts who covered civilian defense topics such as where to go and what to do in case of an air raid. There was plenty to learn.

Military and civilian defense officials on the American home front learned a great deal about how to organize and train for air raids from the British. German air raids over London in 1940 killed and injured thousands and left large areas of the city in ruins. Facing ongoing attacks, the British responded by teaching citizens how to cope with fires from incendiary bombs and how to take shelter. While the raids continued, loss of life diminished. Oregon officials played sound clips of a London raid to try to impress the potential horror to radio listeners with the added comment: "These are the sounds of a hell that I hope we in the United States will never experience."[9]

Blackouts
While air raid drills were an occasional disruption, blackouts were a frequent condition. Blackouts required Americans to cover windows and doors with

heavy drapes or other material to block out all light each night by 11:00 p.m. Street lights were extinguished, and hoods covered the tops of traffic lights that are still made that way today. Automobile headlights were covered or used new lamps that had been approved by the War Department. These lights were designed by US Army engineers and mass-produced by General Electric and were equivalent to one-sixth of the light cast by a full moon on a clear night. This dim light could not be seen from the air and still allowed traffic to move at 12 mph. The incidence of auto accidents still increased, and cities were plagued with traffic jams.

During drills, along with dousing lights Americans were required to shut off appliances, disconnect electricity, turn off gas and water, and might include moving to a shelter or basement until the drill ended. Cars were required to pull over, turn off their vehicles, and find shelter.

Dimouts differed from blackouts. Blackouts, which attempted to extinguish or shield light sources completely, usually were called for a relatively short period in relation to a possible imminent air raid. Dimouts, on the other hand, were put in place every night but were less restrictive measures. The intent was to shield light from being seen from above or from the sea. Dimouts remained in effect for the duration in coastal regions. Blackout and dimout preparedness varied for inland America. Key cities and defense sites engaged in the process.

School children were also required to practice air raid drills at school. Boys and girls lined up and marched to basements or hallways, gathered in assigned areas, and often were instructed to bow their heads to protect them from debris in case the school was hit by a bomb.

There were also blackout drills that forced people to practice their response to the air-raid alarm signal – a series of intermittent siren blasts. Air-raid wardens supervised the blackout drills, cruising up and down neighborhood streets to make sure no light escaped the houses.

Some American communities took these drills very seriously. They arranged for mock bombings with flares, firecrackers, and flour-filled bombs which left the streets littered with boy scouts, their pantlegs and sleeves oozing ketchup – small towns and ordinary people wanting to do their part.

Sherill Jankowski Cunning of Long Beach California and her sister had an unorthodox drill activity:

We had a back closet that we figured was the safest place in the house to hide in case of invasion. My mother stored all her old clothes in there in big rubber garment bags. We figured that nobody would find us behind those bags. But just in case they did, we kept a bottle of ketchup in the closet. We were going to douse ourselves with it and lie there as if we had already been bloodied and killed, so that they would walk away and not stick their bayonets into us.[10]

Businesses were required to turn off all signs and lights. Charles Lindbergh notes in his war time journal of a trip to New York City, "The entire city was blacked out but some resourceful stores had screens hanging just inside the glass. You could see fairly well when looking directly but the screens shut off the light completely at an angle." Factories that were running three shifts in order to produce much-needed war materials needed to keep their lights on without interruption. But these were considered prime targets for attack; so many companies installed huge window and door coverings to protect them from being seen.[11]

Blackout drills were planned and advertised, scheduled to avoid panic, and announced in newspapers and radio broadcasts. While large cities erected huge sirens – New York City had 409 sirens – smaller towns might ring church bells to alert residents of a drill. Alarms normally sounded for thirty minutes until the drill was completed. Once the alarm was sounded a large squadron of volunteer air wardens drove around America's roads and streets to ensure no light was visible. If a resident didn't comply the air warden would approach the house or shout "Put out the lights!"

Street lights were turned off at the scheduled time. Anyone outside was to take cover inside. Those in their homes were instructed to pull down the blinds on their windows and keep the light inside to a minimum. People in cars were to pull over and find shelter in the nearest building. The idea was that enemy planes couldn't target what they couldn't see, and that any light visible from above could attract bombs and gunfire. Because of the risk of car accidents in the dark, the speed limit was reduced to 20 mph. To help drivers and pedestrians, white lines were painted on roads, which are still there today.

The Empire State Building and the giant RCA sign in New York city went dark. Vigilantes roamed some cities smashing lighted stores.

The federal government sponsored public service announcements to promote participation in the drills and make sure people knew what to do. Among the more unusual of these promotions was the 1942 song by Tony Pastor and his Orchestra "Obey Your Air Raid Warden," which instructed listeners, "Don't get in a huff. / Our aim today is to call their bluff. / Follow these rules and that is enough. / Obey your air-raid warden." Posters were more common.

Technically, people who didn't comply with the blackout orders and keep the required supplies on hand could be arrested, though arrests on these grounds were rare. On his education website, *The Doyle Report*, Denis P. Doyle, who was a young child during the war whose father was in service overseas, noted several things he remembered from the WWII days. "My most vivid single memory, however, was the visit of a helmeted air raid warden to our apartment in Shaker Heights, Ohio," Doyle wrote. "My mother was out for the evening and our grandmother was caring for my little sister and me. She spoke not a word of English. A knock on the door announced an air raid warden trying to explain that an air raid drill was underway, and she must either turn off all the lights or lower the curtains. At three years of age, it fell to me to translate, and we pulled down the living room shades."[12]

Each home was given enough blackout material, which was usually a dark cotton fabric. Putting up and taking down the material quickly became a boring and unwanted daily task for most households. Windows were covered in the dark material. Car headlamps were also blacked out, causing many accidents, and people were not allowed to smoke cigarettes or cigars outdoors.

Many small shops had to have an extra door fitted, to stop light from showing when people came in and out of the shop. Some large factories with glass roofs had to paint their entire roof black.

In coastal areas, ships were also blacked out to prevent them from being seen against the shore. It made them less of an obvious target for German submarines.

Training manuals were issued that instructed citizens to have emergency supplies in case of an air raid. Necessary supplies included 50 feet of garden hose with a spray nozzle, 100 pounds of sand divided into four containers, three 3-gallon metal buckets (one with sand and two filled with water), a long-handled shovel with a square edge, a hoe or rake, an ax or hatchet, a ladder, leather gloves, and dark glasses. Stores such as Kresge's, Hammacher Schlemmer, and Bloomingdales were only too happy to "be your blackout headquarters." Americans were discouraged from purchasing black fabric, an obvious choice for black outs, because it was needed by the military. At the extreme, defense measures were home bomb shelters either constructed by the home owner (a trench with a metal cover) or purchased for $500. Cellars could be converted for as little as $200.[13]

Louisiana thought that prisons would make good shelters and planned to double up prisoners to make room. They even asked prisoners to volunteer to share quarters with civilians.

Some measures were dubious. New York City Civil Defense managers advised city residents to fill their bathtubs and sinks with water. The result would have been a drastic, even catastrophic, drop in the city's water pressure. Another ill conceived (and never implemented) idea was to turn off all gas pilot lights. Seeking refuge in lighted subways was not a great idea as New York's subways were not deep enough to offer full protection. One thing the blackout did in New York City was to foster re-socializing. People got to know their neighbors as they milled about questioning each other about what was going on.

Posters appeared imploring Americans to "Look Out in a Black Out" as many accidents and fatalities resulted from trips and falls. People were to carry a flashlight but with blue tissue covering the lens.

One part of the American home front behaved differently, at least early on. Most Alaskan communities did not plan for blackout eventualities. On November 21, 1941, the Petersburg Press ran a poem with the following lines:

> We don't have to dodge a bomb,
> Or grope in blackouts here,
> The night is peaceful, still and calm,
> There is no trace of fear,
> The only blackout we go through,
> Is when brother blows a fuse.[14]

On March 8, 1941, Seattle became the first major American city to test its blackout procedures. Author and fighter pilot, Samuel Hynes, was in Seattle during its first blackout. He later wrote:

> "On the night of the city's first blackout I left the apartment in the early dark and walked to the top of the hill, where there was a wide space without buildings or trees. An overcast night, neither moon nor stars; only the lights of the city made the darkness visible. Then the sirens began to keen, some near, some far-off, and the lights on the seven hills went out, neighborhood by neighborhood; out beyond Lake Washington where the university was, south toward Tacoma, along the Sound places disappeared, fell out of light into darkness like falling angels. Now the night was entirely dark and featureless, cloud and earth one black emptiness."

Right after Pearl Harbor, on the evening of December 8, more than 1000 residents of Seattle gathered after the 11:00 p.m. blackout deadline in front of a downtown clothing store. Unlike many of the buildings in the city, the clothing store's signage was still lit up and clearly visible. To achieve total darkness, the crowd threw rocks at the sign's light bulbs hoping to extinguish the glow. This continued for an hour, until a store employee showed up to turn off the lights, though there were other store fronts still illuminating the streets. The mob continued to break into local businesses to turn off any lights, stopping for a moment to sing "God Bless America" before returning to what they felt was justified vandalism.[15]

Shortly after Pearl Harbor the tanker Montebello was attacked and sunk by a Japanese submarine while in sight of the California coastline. People on the shore dragged survivors and bodies from the sea.

Americans on the home front did get to see the effectiveness of the blackouts on June 21, 1942, when a Japanese submarine, *I-25*, surfaced near Fort Stevens, Oregon. The Japanese sub was able to inflict minor damage before a complete blackout was instituted. With no visible target, *I-25* fired blindly on the area for fifteen minutes before giving up. It was the first and only attack on a military installation on US soil in WWII.

No one was injured, and the only result was a handful of craters in the fort's baseball field.

A few months before the Fort Stevens shelling, another enemy submarine, number *I-17*, captained by Kozo Nishino, entered the Santa Barbara Channel and began firing on the Ellwood Oil Field, just ten miles north of Santa Barbara, causing no real damage.[16]

Perhaps the most galvanizing event on the West Coast was "The Battle of Los Angeles," a full-throated shooting response to a false alarm. What most likely was a weather balloon was spotted by primitive radar. On February 25, in the wee hours of the morning, the air raid alarm sounded and anti-aircraft firing began. By daylight, the all-clear was sounded and firing had stopped, but not until more than 1400 rounds had been fired at the invading "target." The incident resulted in five casualties, due to car accidents that happened during the blackout and heart attacks caused by shock.[17]

The two bombardments and the invasion scare gave credence to all the blackout warnings and preparations and stoked a sense of paranoia felt by Americans on the home front that a Japanese invasion or bombing run could be imminent. Americans on the West Coast were now more likely to follow blackout regulations after such incidences.

In addition to the nightly dimouts, defense councils along the Florida coast organized blackouts to make it harder for enemy submarines to attack Allied ships at night. The dark silhouettes of ships were easy to see against a background of bright lights, but with all the lights turned off it was harder for enemy submarines to know where they should fire their torpedoes. Business buildings near the coast were equipped with light traps – double doors. Street lights were shielded on the ocean sides. Even with the blackouts, German submarines still sank twenty-four ships off the Florida coast during the war.

In January and February of 1942, German submarines were operating openly off the East Coast. Flashes and explosions could be heard, and beaches became strewn with terrible litter – empty life jackets, charred lifeboats and even bodies. Americans' reactions ranged from fear to undiluted curiosity. Here is one report.

A Front Row Seat for the War
by Michael Cranston (b. 1936):

My family ran a small beachfront resort – today you would call it a motel – near Newport Rhode Island. We thought the war would shut us down, but soon after the war started business was just about back to normal. People had money they couldn't spend on things like cars and they did want some recreation. With gas rationed, people often came in a group, piled into one car.

Being on the water we had special blackout regulations. We invented our own ways to keep the light from shining out to sea. We built frames the size of a door and hung them with black oilcloth. At sunset we put them in front of the doors so that people could go in and out, but no light could be seen from the sea. We fitted all our outdoor lights with tin cans that we cut the bottom out of so that the light would shine only to the ground. We had wardens who patrolled in boats to check to be sure no lights could be seen from off shore. Sometimes we had to make changes.

When a boat got sunk or someone saw a German sub we thought people would be too afraid to come, but it turned out they were excited to think that they might see some war action close up. We set up chairs outside where they could sit and watch. Many nights we could hear them talking, "Did you see that?" "Was that a boat?" "I thought I heard voices…"

I don't know what would have happened if we really did see a sub!

A lighter side to the nightly blackout requirements during WWII was a "Blackout Kit," produced by the Vernon Company of Newton, Ohio. The kit included five rolls of Blackout material [luminous paper]; an official Blackout test tube; "Voodoo Man" mask sheet; and a great instruction/ideas booklet. The elaborate instruction book was packed with info and wonderful illustrations (traceable civil defense insignias, blackout party ideas, glow-in-the-dark novelties, etc.). This may have been designed to lighten the mood as well as entertain the children in the house during the dark times of war.[18]

Blackout Drills
by Robert LaRue (b. 1937):

December 7, 1941 may have been "a date which will live in infamy" for President Roosevelt, but it was the beginning of all kinds of strange and scary events for a four-year-old. The wailing sirens and darkness of blackout drills stand out in my mind.

We lived on a dairy in Baldwin Park, California. Baldwin Park is located only 20 miles from downtown Los Angeles. In the days before supermarkets, it was not uncommon for dairies to be located near population centers. On site retail marketing was a common practice. After the attack on Pearl Harbor, what had been considered a good location for dairy product retailing also came to be considered a prime target for a Japanese attack.

Before radar bomb sights, bombardiers relied on what they could see on the ground to figure out where to release their devastation. A primary means of civil defense against night attack was the blackout. If there was no light on the ground, the attackers could not identify their targets. The sound of blackout sirens in the night became a fact of life for us.

Rationing also became a fact of life. Living on a dairy, we had plenty of milk to drink, but meat was rationed even for us. To supplement our diet, Dad built some hutches and raised rabbits. He shared the fryers with the dairy's owners, a Dutch family named Cohn, in exchange for alfalfa and grain. Mrs Cohn also helped with caring for the animals.

One dark night, I was out by the hutches helping Mrs Cohn when the sirens wailed and the lights went out. She had come prepared for such an event with a flashlight. She handed the flashlight to me to hold while she finished the chores. Like any kid of four, I proceeded to flash the light around and point it at the sky. Sweet, gentle Mrs Cohn came unglued. She grabbed the offending torch from my little hands and explained to me in no uncertain terms that I could have caused us to be bombed. I suppose she was somewhat oversensitive about bombing since she still had family in Holland who had recently experienced the Blitzkrieg. But she scared the heck out of me. I quickly changed from being a carefree child piercing the night sky with a harmless flashlight to being a beacon for falling explosives.

To this day, I feel a stab of fright any time I allow a flashlight's beam to wander above the horizon at night!

The rest of the nation became involved with these regulations in the winter of 1944. It was a winter of record-breaking cold causing a heating fuel shortage. The shortage was amplified by railroad outages, snowstorms, and labor shortages. To save fuel, a nationwide brownout was ordered. Lighted signs were prohibited and stores were ordered to close before dark. In many parts of America schools were closed for lack of fuel and businesses went on short hours.[19]

Chapter Four

Rationing

"Use it up/Wear it out/Make it do/Or do without"

Rationing did not burst into full blown effect on December 7. Months before the war, in mid-1940, President Roosevelt recognized that the prosperity coming out of the Depression plus the huge influx of factory orders for arms placed by war torn Britain, were driving prices up and causing inflation and in some cases profiteering. With some factories converted to the manufacture of war goods, Americans found shortages of cars, refrigerators, stoves and other appliances. President Roosevelt chose to reinstate a World War I advisory board and reshaped it as OPAC (Office of Price Administration and Civilian Supply) later simply called OPA, as the vehicle to regulate the economy, now boasting 10 percent inflation.

The government's pre-war actions were erratic and amounted to simply strong jawboning as it tried to control prices voluntarily on raw materials, rents, and groceries. Americans were enjoying the economic good times and pretty much ignored the efforts of the OPA. However, these pre-war actions permitted the OPA to find its footing and notch a few successes, making it more prepared for the real thing.

Soon after the Japanese attack on Pearl Harbor it became apparent that voluntary conservation on the home front was not going to suffice. Americans felt the pinch of shortages coming on slowly. There were already restrictions on imported foods and limitations on the transportation of goods due to a shortage of rubber tires. Added to that was the diversion of agricultural harvests to soldiers overseas. All of this contributed to the government's decision to ration certain essential items. On January 30, 1942, the Emergency Price Control Act granted the OPA the authority "to set price limits and ration food and other commodities in order to discourage hoarding and ensure the equitable distribution of scarce resources."

Price limits or "ceiling prices" were set, limiting the price that stores could charge for items. Stores could not raise prices above what the price was in March of 1942.

In a task that would be difficult even today with computer resources, rationing boards were set up in every county in the US. The government wanted the American people to understand the reasons for rationing and so it cranked up a huge propaganda machine.

Americans on the home front had the uneasy feeling of what was to come and encountered rationing in full force in the spring of 1942. In simple terms, two ration books were distributed to "every eligible man, woman, child, and baby in the United States." One contained blue coupons for processed goods while the other contained red coupons for meat, fish, and dairy products. Each person started with 48 blue points and 64 red points each month.

Americans did not purchase items with ration coupons alone, the coupons had no monetary value. Cash was still required.

The ration books contained removable certificates for some special items like tires, as well as stamps that could be used for certain other rationed items, such as shoes, sugar, and coffee, and points that were good for a variety of items. A person could not buy a rationed item without giving the seller the right ration coupon.

Institutions such as restaurants, hotels, and hospitals were instructed to apply for their ration books at the high schools. Restaurants were allocated between 20–30 percent more ration coupons than private citizens were for sugar, flour, processed foods, canned goods, and meat. Receiving more sugar, flour, and meat was important because it meant they could keep on making their signature dishes and baked goods. The length of time the coupons were valid changed every three to four months, to prevent any counterfeiting. When the new ration book coupons appeared, then everyone went back to the OPA authority to officially sign up for the new coupons and restaurant owners would then restock their supplies.

The instructions that came with the first ration book are as follows:

Your first ration book has been issued to you, originally containing 28 war ration stamps. Other books may be issued at later dates. The following instructions apply to your first book and will apply to any later books, unless otherwise ordered by the Office of Price Administration. In order to obtain a later book, the first book must be turned in. You should preserve War Rations Books with the greatest possible care.

1 – From the time the Office of Price Administration may issue orders rationing certain products. After the dates indicated by such orders, these products can be purchased only through the use of War rations Books containing valid War Ration Stamps.
2 – The orders of the Office of Price Administration will designate the stamps to be used for the purchase of a particular rationed product, the period during which each of these stamps may be used, and the amounts which may be bought with each stamp.
3 – Stamps become valid for use only when and as directed by the Orders of the Office of Price Administration.
4 – Unless otherwise announced, the Ration Week is from Saturday midnight to the following Saturday midnight.
5 – War Ration stamps may be used in any retail store in the United States.
6 – War Ration Stamps may be used only by or for the person named and described in the War Ration Book.
7 – Every person must see that this War Ration Book is kept in a safe place and properly used. Parents are responsible for the safekeeping and use of their children's War Ration Book.
8 – When you buy any rationed product, the proper stamp must be detached in the presence of the storekeeper, his employee, or the person making the delivery on his behalf. If a stamp is torn out of the War Ration Book in any other way than above indicated, it becomes void. If a stamp is partly torn or mutilated and more than one half of it remains in the book, it is valid. Otherwise it becomes void.
9 – If your War Ration Book is lost, destroyed, stolen or mutilated, you should report that fact to the local Ration Board.
10 – If you enter a hospital, or other institution, and expect to be there for more than 10 days, you must turn your War Ration Book

over to the person in charge. It will be returned to you upon your request when you leave.

11 – When a person dies, his War Ration Book must be returned to the local Ration Board, in accordance with the regulations.

12 – If you have any complaints, questions, or difficulties regarding your War Ration Book, consult your local Ration Board.

NOTE

The first stamps in War Ration Book One will be used for the purchase of sugar. When this book was issued, the registrar asked you, or the person who applied for your book, how much sugar you owned on that date. If you had any sugar, you were allowed to keep it, but stamps representing this quantity were torn from your group (except for a small amount which you were allowed to keep without losing any stamps). If your War Ration Book one was issued to you on application by a member of your family, the number of stamps torn from the books of the family was based on the amount of sugar owned by the family and was divided as equally as possible among all the books.

To enable change from ration stamps, the government issued "red point" tokens to be given as change for red stamps, and "blue point" tokens as change for blue stamps. These dime-sized tokens were made of thin compressed wood fiber material, because metals were in short supply.

The OPA allotted a certain number of points to each food item based on its availability. For example, customers were allowed to use 48 "blue points" to buy canned, bottled or dried foods, and 64 "red points" to buy meat, fish and dairy each month – that is, if the items were in stock. Due to changes in the supply and demand of various goods, the OPA periodically adjusted point values, which often further complicated an already complex system that required shoppers to plan well in advance to prepare meals.

The middle-class household of pre-war America had a strong focus on meals and mealtimes. It began with almost daily grocery shopping required by the small refrigerators of the day. Presentation at mealtime included china dishes and full place settings. Working men and schoolchildren often came home for lunch, which meant that the housewife was expected to spend several hours preparing three full meals a day.

With the advent of the war and women joining the workforce, home front America underwent a change. Time for meal preparation grew tight. The housewife no longer had the time to shop every day and learned how to use the refrigerator more efficiently and cut her trips to the store. Cereal breakfasts and bag lunches became the norm. Some companies arranged for markets to send representatives into their factory to take orders which women could pick up at the end of their shift.

The pressure cooker entered the scene, originally for use at high altitudes, to shorten food preparation time. They were made of metal and hard to obtain. In addition, they required some instruction for use to avoid accidents.

Americans faced a flood of new cookbooks based on rationing with recipes for meatless Tuesdays, endless ways to substitute eggs, mock fish, rice and flour combinations, and more. Cooking soups and casseroles helped stretch food and leftovers. Molasses, corn syrup, and honey substituted for sugar. (The pressure of the shortages caused black market thieves to ransack beehives for the honey.)

Newspapers Become a Rationing Resource
Each ration stamp had a generic drawing of an airplane, gun, tank, aircraft carrier, ear of wheat, fruit, etc. and a serial number. Some stamps also had alphabetic lettering. The stamps did not define any specific commodity or value. Americans learned what the stamps could buy from announcements in the newspapers. For example, the paper might announce that next Tuesday one airplane stamp was required (in addition to cash) to buy one pair of shoes and one stamp number 30 from ration book four was required to buy five pounds of sugar. The commodity amounts changed from time to time depending on availability. Red stamps were used to ration meat and butter, and blue stamps were used to ration processed foods.

With the rapid changes in food availability, newspapers were an important resource for home cooks as they tried to navigate the new world of rationing. Consider the workload of the typical American home front shopper. First, she had to set her food budget. Next, she had to plan her menu and create her shopping list. Working with information from the newspaper, she tried to budget the ration stamps she would need. She might then spend time trying to swap stamps with family or neighbors to get the type of stamps she needed. It was with great frustration that after all that work, she might find that the store was out of stock on items she had planned on – and may have had to wait in line to find out!

Newspapers also published a wide variety of tips for cooking under rationing. They published column after column about how to cook with reduced amounts of rationed ingredients and educated readers about which ingredients could be used as substitutes. Honey and corn syrup, for instance, were commonly suggested replacements for sugar. Wartime recipes were in high demand, so many newspapers asked readers to send in their favorite recipes or even held contests for the best wartime dishes. Food companies jumped on the bandwagon as well, publishing ads that included rationing recipes using their products. Many learned about Kraft's macaroni and cheese.

Food Co-ops

A special response to the meat shortages had enterprising American neighbors forming food growing co-ops. The following is one example.

Pig Clubs
Dovey Sommers (b. 1936):

I grew up near Delmar, NY, south of Albany. We weren't a poor village, but we weren't well off. My mother and the other women around spent a lot of time trying to keep food in the house using ration coupons and scrimping with what we had. We shifted over to margarine or salted lard instead of butter sometimes and one neighbor's son could get us powered eggs.

Most important was we couldn't waste anything. It was a minister in town who came up with the idea of "pig clubs," which were just like it sounds. Three or four families would get together and buy a pig and fatten it up with everyone's leftover scraps. When the pig grew to size the families butchered it and shared the meat.

Our pig club would start a second pig a month or so before the first one was grown. Some people had "chicken clubs," too, with hutches in their backyards.

It seems funny to talk about that now, but at the time it seemed like just something you had to do to help win the war.[1]

The co-op idea included labor, too. A group of women would divide up tasks such as shopping and childcare and thus free up much needed time for household tasks and volunteering.

A very American response to these shortages was the victory garden. After initial resistance by the Department of Agriculture, who feared "radishy" gardens, and calls for coffee seeds, the government called for 18 million Victory Gardens and churned out a full blown patriotic promotional program to encourage Americans to plant vegetables. In schools throughout the country children were encouraged to knock on doors and sell packages of seeds. Contests and prizes energized the junior sales people. Nearly 20 million Americans answered the call. They planted gardens in backyards, empty lots and even city rooftops. Neighbors pooled their resources, planted different kinds of foods and formed cooperatives, all in the name of patriotism. With the call up of agricultural labor, victory gardens offset millions of tons of food for the American home front.[2]

Chicago Victory Gardens
by Jim Kelly (b. 1936):

My memory was raiding the Victory Gardens. Most of the empty lots in Chicago were converted to vegetable gardens because of shortages caused by the war and were called Victory Gardens. We kids would sneak into the gardens at night and eat radishes, carrots and kohlrabies. We saved the tomatoes to throw at street cars!

Canning the vegetables grown in the Victory Gardens became a way of life for some families. The government sponsored more than 6000 community canning centers though out the country. Women were encouraged to support their families and the nation by canning produce grown in their Victory

Garden. Canning, like gardening, was presented in official propaganda as a patriotic and unifying act, linking soldiers' activities to women's roles in the kitchen. No other war time endeavor, except perhaps war bonds, received so much push from propaganda as did Victory Gardens and canning. Hundreds of posters were commissioned, radio scripts developed, movie shorts produced, pamphlets printed, and advertisements placed. It seemed to work.

Government officials asked individuals to organize their garden activities in conjunction with the canning outcomes that they envisioned, urging them to "plan your canning budget when you order your garden seeds." The interconnectivity of the two activities ensured that just as Victory Garden yields reached their peak in 1943, so too did canning levels. The USDA estimates that approximately 4 billion cans and jars of food, both sweet and savory, were produced that year. Community canning centers aided in the process of reaching record levels of preserved food in the United States during the war.[3]

While ration books were, by law, intended for the person who received it, many systems arose to sell and barter the stamps, which by the way, were not supposed to be removed until making a purchase. Some schemes were simply neighbors swapping or buying stamps from one another. Others involved the storekeeper acting as a bank and receiving unwanted or excess coupons and trading or selling them with buyers. For the poor, rationing, with its "make it last, wear it out, make do or do without" was just a continuation of the shortages of the Depression. Americans chafed under rationing now that they had money to spend, but overall accepted it as a way to provide fairness and support the war effort.

Scrap Drives
Perhaps nothing represents the response to shortages and the patriotism of the US home front in World War II better than the scrap drive.

The following is from *An Emergency Statement to the People of the United States* published by the US War Production Board in the Des Moines Register on April 20, 1942:

> The steel industry has been rapidly stepping up its production…but we need to get production up to the industry's full capacity of 90,000,000

tons – a total equal to the output of the rest of the world combined. This volume of production cannot be attained or increased unless an additional 6,000,000 tons of scrap iron and steel is obtained promptly. We are faced with the fact that some steel furnaces have been allowed to cool down and that many of them are operating from day to day and hand to mouth, due only to the lack of scrap.

The rubber situation is also critical. In spite of the recent rubber drive, there is a continuing need for large quantities of scrap rubber. We are collecting every possible pound from the factories, arsenals and shipyards; we are speeding up the flow of material from automobile graveyards; we are tearing up abandoned railroad tracks and bridges, but unless we dig out an additional 6,000,000 tons of steel and great quantities of rubber, copper, brass, zinc and tin, our boys may not get all the fighting weapons they need in time…Even one old shovel will help make 4 hand grenades.

Enemy conquests cut off supplies of crucial raw materials such as tin and rubber, and the need for products made from these materials skyrocketed due to the war. Since useful materials often ended up in the trash can or languished unused in homes and on farms, the War Production Board encouraged scrap drives throughout the war. Drives were held for metal, tin cans, rags, tires, and paper.

Metal shortages especially posed a threat to the war effort. The government launched a "Salvage for Victory" program. Americans scoured their homes, farms, and businesses for metal. Housewives donated pots and pans, farmers turned in farm equipment, and children even sacrificed their metal toys.

Scrap Day – No School!
by Janet O (b. 1932):

I'm glad to talk about a memory I have of those years. We were all so patriotic back then. My special memory is about the day my town, Springfield, closed all the schools and told the kids to go collect scrap for the war effort. First we cleaned out our own houses and farms. But then we started going alongside the roads and found so much stuff like tires, cans and even old stoves. We had so much fun yelling to each other about what we found. Adults helped us haul stuff to the central collection place. We stayed out all day until dark. We wanted to do it again the next day, but we had to go back to school. Besides, we had collected a mountain of scrap. I only remember doing it once.[4]

Many people removed bumpers and fenders from their cars for the war effort. Communities melted down Civil War cannons and tore down wrought iron fences. These drives were often great community events, with performers, speeches, and opportunities to throw your scrap metal at a bust of Hitler.

Competitions were held to see which town, county, and state produced the most scrap, and the winners boasted of their feats. However, these drives had mixed results. Used aluminum was found to be useless for aircraft, but used tin, steel, and copper were easily melted down and reused. One unlikely source came from prisoners in the Great Falls, Montana jail who offered the bars on their cells.[5]

By June 1942 companies stopped manufacturing metal office furniture, radios, television sets, phonographs, refrigerators, vacuum cleaners, washing machines, and sewing machines for civilians.[6]

The use of tin packaging was greatly reduced during the war, due to the use of alternative packaging materials and to the rationing of canned goods. However, consumer use of tin continued throughout the war, and this irreplaceable resource needed to be recovered. Starting in March of 1942, dog food could no longer be sold in tin cans, and manufacturers switched to dehydrated versions. Beginning in April 1942, anyone wishing to purchase a new toothpaste tube, then made from tin, had to turn in an empty one.

Most communities collected tin cans once a month. In some towns, people placed boxes of cleaned and crushed tin cans by the curb for collection, and other towns had central collection sites. Youth groups, especially the Boy Scouts, were highly involved in these drives.

One of the most remembered parts of these drives was the peeling and collection of the silvery paper on gum wrappers. The material was rolled into a ball and brought for collection at schools and stores where it was rolled into a bigger ball and then…well it turned out the stuff was of no value in war production, but the effort remained a good prop for patriotism.

A lot of the scrap collected proved to be worth very little. One very worthwhile collection was for reclaimed fats and oils. The residue was useful in manufacturing glycerin. Americans were diligent about saving and collecting household fat.

Tight paper allocations meant that Americans found fewer pages in their papers and magazines and thinner pages in books that also employed wider page margins. The shortage of paper fostered one of the most comprehensive home front shortage programs of the war: the paper drive. These drives were often conducted like a milk route in reverse. Americans would bundle up their paper and place it for collection along the road (or elsewhere) and a truck would regularly collect the paper and bring it to the recycling center.

It's interesting to note that regardless of the rationing situation, books enjoyed explosive growth. Restricted in their activities, Americans turned to housebound activities including books. Buoyed by the introduction of compact "pocketbooks," sales rose from just several hundred thousand to more than 10,000,000 in 1941 and to 40,000,000 in 1943. All those books took 100,000 tons of paper while advertising managed to lay claim to 1,000,000 tons.[7]

A Different Kind of Drive
During WWII, the Japanese cut off America's access to Java plantations where "kapok" was grown. Typically, kapok was the material used as filler for life jackets. When it was no longer available, an alternate fiber was desperately needed. How else could we keep a downed aviator or soaking-wet sailor from drowning?

A Chicago physician and inventor named Dr Boris Berkman proposed that milkweed floss would be even better than kapok for the job. The US Navy then conducted extensive tests, proving that a pound of the floss (equivalent to two open-mesh bushel sacks) could keep a 150-pound man floating in the water for more than forty hours. And so it was that the common milkweed lost its lowly "weed" status and was elevated to being a strategic wartime material.

When Petoskey, Michigan's first official milkweed crop, was ready for picking by Sept 16, 1942, the call went out to families, community organizations, and schoolchildren, and that call was answered with gusto.

It is reported that at least 1000 bags were picked before rain ended the day. Local fairgrounds were used as drying stations where bags of pods were hung over every available fence and building.

The pod-picking operation relied heavily on the labor of children as well as adults and was testament to a civilian army encompassing people in twenty-five states and two Canadian provinces. The government's slogan "Two Bags Save One Life" provided a simple message to all involved: that they were doing their part for the war effort. And most of them understood this.[8]

The Impact on Clothing and Fashion
Clothing fashions underwent drastic changes to conserve cloth needed for the military. The government put forth detailed standards and restrictions, though rationing was not imposed except for shoes.

American men could suit up in the Victory Suit, a single-breasted model with no lapels, no patch pockets, no vest, no cuffs, and an adjustable waist band. He could also feel like a hero in the new, short Eisenhower jacket.

For women, the War Production Board produced a poster that became ubiquitous, if somewhat ridiculed, showing the new standards for dresses, coats, jackets, suits, blouses, and skirts. Under the WPB standards, wide shoulders were out, replaced by natural shoulders or bare arms. Long evening dresses vanished while one piece jump suits made their appearance. Turbans became popular, particularly with women working in factories. Shoe styles became simpler, almost slipper-like. The girdle-free dress hit the market.

Americans were advised to purchase or make warmer and more durable clothes. Knitting made a strong comeback on the home front with mothers and wives knitting for a loved one overseas. The government promoted sewing and went so far as to sponsor regional and national contests for clothes sewn at home. Young people in 4H clubs could earn awards. Scouts had merit badges based on sewing.

The uniforms for WACS and WAVES attracted the attention of top designers. Mainboucher provided the WAVES with stylish uniforms while WACS uniforms were cut by Russell Patterson and Philip Mangone. Fashion shows introduced the new military couture to the American public.

Coco Chanel closed her studio in Paris and the fashion industry moved to New York where it took on an American look. Claire McCardell, for example, made use of fabrics that were not in demand by the military such as cotton denim, jersey, striped mattress ticking, gingham, and calico.

The fashion showings of New York offered these 100 percent American fabrics in styles influenced by the military including the colors Navy blue and Marine green. Along with the military influence went assorted patriotic badges, pins, and flags.

Hair was worn long and curled at the ends for a soft, feminine look. Beauty salons were expensive and American women saved money by having their hair cut less often. As so many women enlisted in the military or took factory jobs, it was easy to tie long hair back for safety. Then, the long hair could be worn down for casual or dress occasions.

Women in America often knitted or crocheted snoods which were a combination of a hair net and a veil. Some American women wore corsages made of artificial flowers or gathered netting.

Girdles were out as the rubber was needed for the war effort. Skirts and dresses were often fitted with adjustable waistlines. Shoe heels were lower and shoe designers thought to add interest with the introduction of the wedge shoe. Many women wore flat heeled shoes for safety and comfort in the workplace.

Pants gained widespread acceptance for wear at defense work, for casual wear, and for work at home in the garden. Katherine Hepburn helped make trousers popular by appearing in several movies wearing elegant, wide-legged trousers. College girls quickly copied the style.

One of the most publicized impacts involved nylon stockings. They were a relatively new fashion item introduced by DuPont at the World's Fair in 1939. Demand skyrocketed when Japan cut off supplies of silk early in 1940. The boom for DuPont did not last long. On the day after Pearl Harbor the government declared that DuPont would produce nylon strictly for government purposes. Nylon would go into parachutes, surgical sutures, and other military necessities. The price of nylon stockings immediately jumped from about $1.25 a pair to $25 on the black market. One of the few stores that had nylons hired guards to prevent trouble.

The home front American woman, now absolutely sold on nylons and dissatisfied with several fabric alternatives, found a simple solution: she put tan liquid make up on her legs and took an eyebrow pencil and scribed a line down the back of her legs. The scheme required a steady hand and created a big fashion gaffe in the rain.

Women treated their remaining stockings with great care, often reserving them for special occasions. Rayon or cotton stockings were worn, but not fondly, as they tended to sag around the knees and ankles.

Rubber Rationing

Rubber products, including tires, were the first items to be rationed. They deserve special mention because of the far-reaching impact they have on so many other products and activities.

"Just get it Done!"
George A. (b. 1932):

I grew up between Charlton and Huntington, WVA, and my home front changed in a big way because of rubber, which was needed for the war.

All of us in West Virginia, like everywhere I guess, were getting used to the news about all the new programs and plans to mobilize for the war effort. Rubber was one of the things the government really needed. In our town we could turn in old tires for a penny a pound at the gas station. My cousin William and his friends used to go up and down alongside the roads looking for old tires.

When the government said they were going to build a rubber plant near us we couldn't imagine why. It turned out it was for synthetic rubber and I figured the coal was important.

All our local boys and men who weren't in the service got hired in lots of different jobs to help build the factory. Women, too, got hired on, and not just for secretary jobs. Some people worried that it would take too long to build the factory and we needed rubber right away.

But what happened is what I like most to remember – and that is that everybody pulled together to get it built. "Just get it done!" everybody said. The United States Rubber Company opened the factory less than a year after construction started. I was about 10 years old.

We were proud to make such a big contribution to the war effort. It was a good feeling. I still feel pride when I think back on it.

By mid-1941 the Japanese had cut off rubber supplies from the Far East. Our cargo ships were needed for military purposes making importation from South America difficult. Fortunately, the prescient synthetic rubber program had already begun but didn't yet produce enough to meet either civilian or military needs.

The administration, hungry for substitutes, entertained suggestions ranging from inefficient to downright crazy but chose to continue to rely on oil-based technology. (Even though housewives complained that the oil-based synthetic left black marks on their floors!)

Stockpiling was attempted, but the on-hand inventory of crude rubber was barely enough to last a year. In addition to tires, rubber was being used for other civilian goods – boots and shoes, gloves, raincoats, girdles, garden hoses, and even toys. Now the military required rubber for truck, Jeep, and aircraft tires and a host of military supplies.

To ensure rubber supplies for military and vital civilian purposes, a freeze on tires and recapping tires was slapped on almost immediately. Americans were allowed to have only five tires per owned car and were to turn in all others.

Americans had to go through yet another new process and apply to their local tire rationing boards for an application to get a tire or to get a tire recapped. Approvals for new tires were kept to medical, fire, police, garbage, and mail services, trucking (for food, ice, fuel), and for public transportation.

Men's rubber boots and work shoes were soon rationed while other non-military products were simply no longer produced. The now ubiquitous "make it last, wear it out, make do or do without" applied. Americans simply had to make do.

The government martialed major public service announcements directed at the rubber shortage. Americans read and heard about ways to properly care for rubber products – protecting them from heat and cold, proper cleaning, proper inflation, and avoiding contact with chemicals.

People saw posters and heard radio announcements to drive slower. They were told to drive at the "Victory Speed" of 35 mph. They were also told to drive less by using public transportation and by carpooling. They were told to check tire pressure and alignment to prolong tire life.

One well intentioned effort was a national rubber collection drive nicknamed "the penny a pound drive." The drive collected old tires, boots, raincoats and even hot water bottles. Unfortunately, the 400,000 tons of used scrap rubber that Americans brought in was unusable. Rubber was just too complex a material to recycle.

Due to one side effect of the ban on rubber, Americans could no longer view auto racing, now banned for the duration.

A truly iconic image of the home front in America was that of the automobile up on blocks in the driveway for the duration. On January 1, 1942, all sales of cars, as well as the delivery of cars to customers who had previously contracted for them, were frozen by the government's Office of Production Management. The result was a huge rise in auto repair businesses.

The tire situation, with such blatant opportunities for illegal gain, attracted hoarders, black marketeers, and out and out criminals. Tire bearing wheels were stolen off cars in broad daylight. Several states elevated tire theft to be a felony with prison terms of more than five years. Firestone offered to "brand" their tires with the owner's initials, much as cattle were branded in the old West.[9]

Another result was the beginning of waiting lists which every car dealer would maintain throughout the war.

Gas Rationing

Even more than rubber rationing, gas shortages and gas rationing made deep impacts on everyday life for Americans.

Much of America's crude oil was produced along the gulf coast and sent by oil tanker ships to the refineries in the northeast. But early in 1942 German submarines began attacking these oil tankers as they made way up the East Coast and supplies of crude were cut sharply.

According to historian, Michael Gannon, in his book *Operation Drumbeat: The Dramatic True Story of Germany's First U-Boat Attacks Along the American*

Coast in World War II, "The U-boat assault on merchant shipping in United States waters during 1942 constituted a greater strategic setback for the Allied war effort than the attack at Pearl Harbor."

With Nazi submarines now targeting tankers off the Atlantic coast, sea shipping routes became vulnerable. To make up for the lost tankers, oil from Texas was sent to the northeast using trains and river barges. But those modes could not replace the large volume of petroleum that had been shipped by tanker. East Coast refiners had been receiving roughly 300,000 barrels of oil daily by ship. Trains and barges were only able to deliver about half of that.

To address the problem Washington, after monumental political wrangling, directed the construction of the longest pipeline ever built up to that time. It was named the War Emergency Pipeline. It passed through ten states and connected Baytown, Texas, on the Gulf of Mexico, with Linden, New Jersey. The pipeline was actually two pipelines running parallel. One was 24 inches in diameter and carried crude oil while the other was 20 inches in diameter and carried refined products. Because of its size, the War Emergency Pipeline was named "the Big Inch." (The 20-inch line was dubbed "the Little Big Inch.")

In an incredible feat of engineering and political collaboration, the line was completed in only one year; from June 1942 to June 1943. Americans followed the progress of the construction closely in newspapers and in short features at the movies. The pipelines delivered more than 500,000 barrels of oil per day, far more than the 300,000 barrels a day the tankers had been delivering and all of it safe from Nazi submarines.

The early shortages of crude quickly translated to shortages of gasoline and rationing was installed for seventeen eastern states. From the beginning, this special rationing effort caused confusion among Americans and lit a political firestorm. As gasoline was being restricted to the East Coast, the US was still shipping oil to Japan – more oil than was being sent to Britain. FDR stated he wanted to have some bargaining power with Japan, but the whole matter of rationing caused a policy change and exports to Japan were closed off.[10]

The fact that only eastern states were rationed chafed Americans who lived there. Adding to the resentment was the very complicated and, many thought, unfair rationing categories, trumpeted by colored stickers pasted on car windshields.

- A: most motorists – 3 gallons/week, reduced to 2 gal/week March 22, 1944
- B: for war workers who shared rides with 3 or more passengers — 8 gal/week
- C: essential occupational use, such as physicians, clergy, and mail carriers
- D: motorcycles
- E: emergency vehicles such as ambulances, police, fire – unlimited
- R: non-highway use, such as farm vehicles — unlimited
- T: truckers, instituted January 1, 1944 — unlimited
- X: a controversial sticker for VIPs – unlimited

Americans received gas ration cards which they presented at the pump where the card was punched to denote gas was purchased.

Home front Americans were not above misrepresenting themselves and their needs in order to upgrade their stickers from A to B, C or X. Doctors asked for X stickers for their wives. Station wagons were presented as ambulances. Cheating became so widespread that officials feared rationing was producing a nation of liars. Prompted by fears that local rationing boards practiced favoritism, FDR opened all rationing records to public inspection. OPA authorities warned that they would investigate gas ration application forms for false statements.[11]

All the typical behavior surrounding the rationing of food quickly carried over to gasoline. Americans waited in lines (sometimes lines of fifty or more cars), followed tanker trucks, and schemed to barter their rations. Siphoning was common enough that some Americans sought locking gas caps.

Because gas was so vital to so many, illegal schemes involving the theft of government coupons and even the paper on which they were printed were reported. The government sought and gained fraud and theft convictions. One black marketeer of gasoline made national headlines in *Colliers* magazine. He drove from Texas to the Canadian border without one ration coupon. In fact, he was able to barter for extra coupons along the way. (The OPA revoked his 1944 ration book and gave him a warning.)

Because gasoline had no easy substitute (wood burning cars and compressed natural gas were not practical on a mass basis) Americans resorted to mass transportation, carpooling, bicycling, walking, and finally just staying home.

One substitute existed for those living near natural gas wells. Those wells were fixed with condensation lines and the liquid that condensed was called drip. Drip could be used in cars if it was strained and mixed with regular gasoline. Those using drip were easily identified by the smoky exhaust.

Heating fuel oil rationing arrived in late 1942. The war effort demanded fuel oil as did the railroad industry where the oil was converted to diesel. The rationing formula was very complicated and ended up just being a percentage of a homeowner's 1941 usage. The northwestern states were faced with more than just oil rationing, they were also to be rationed for firewood and coal.[12]

But even with oil stocks restored in the east, gas rationing was to become nationwide. The event that started the movement to nationwide rationing was *The Baruch Rubber Report* presented to President Roosevelt in September of 1942. It decried the rubber shortage and called out the need for rubber by the military. The report demanded drastically reducing non-essential civilian driving as crucial to conserve tire wear and rubber consumption.

So, it was not the shortage of gasoline, but the national shortage of rubber that led to nationwide gas rationing in December of 1942. In fact, the US remained a major oil exporter all through the war.

Americans in the Midwest, Southwest and on the West Coast – and their representatives in Washington – sent up a howl. They had oil fields and refining capacity and no shortage of gasoline. Whether they never read the Rubber Report or whether they just didn't share its findings, they felt put upon for the great inconveniences.

In addition to reducing Americans' rubber consumption, gas rationing had other effects. Tax revenues from sales fell dramatically as did traffic accidents and fatalities. Dating underwent changes. A young man planning a date had to be certain he had enough gas to make it back to his date's house. Long drives in the country were given over to short trips to the corner movie house. Though gas was only 19 cents a gallon, most cars got barely 15 miles a gallon, even at the 35 MPH Victory speed.

The importance of US oil went beyond the home front. "Without the prodigious delivery of oil from the U.S.," stated historian Keith Miller, "this global war [WWII], quite frankly, could never have been won."[13]

Adapting to Rationing

Most Americans adapted to rationing and, except for sporadic shelf-clearing hoarding and some minor stamp trading, complied with the intent of the effort. Retailers bent the rules just a bit too. They sometimes offered scarce goods in "tie-in sales" where the buyers had to purchase something the seller wanted to offload in order to purchase what they really wanted to buy.

However, some did engage in genuine fraud. Counterfeiting was the nemesis of the OPA and its 3100 investigators. The OPA would issue different colored books hoping to stick the counterfeiters with books of the voided color, at least until they caught up to the new color.

Many businesses couldn't legally raise prices, and "skimpflation" seems to have been one way they tried to maintain profitability. For example, meatpackers began filling sausages and hot dogs with soybeans, potatoes, or cracker meal. Meatpackers and butchers added more fat to hamburgers. They sold steaks with extra bone. They began selling horse meat, muskrat meat, and other alternative meats. Other manufacturers went to smaller packages and cheaper ingredients but still sold at the ceiling prices.

The largest illegal enterprise was the black market. The term black market covered sales of goods at higher prices, sales with no ration certificates, short weighting to obtain higher prices for less goods, and sales of stolen goods. (Hijacking trucks and pilfering rail cars attracted professional criminals.) While the black market was widespread, it was essentially a local affair. Many Americans felt it was OK to wiggle around regulations to get some cigarettes or some beef or gasoline.

One person who did not think it was OK was Mrs E.W. St. Pierre of the Oregon State Defense Council. She wrote:

> The American public is being rationed on sugar and rubber today, and tomorrow many more things may be added to this list...From this

situation has arisen a genie which may undermine our whole war effort, unless an understanding American people lend a hand. It is obvious that there are not sufficient law enforcement officers in the land to detect all evasions of these regulations. A "black market" has sprung up, bootlegging these materials to persons willing to pay the price. Buyer and seller are equally guilty; they are both disloyal, dishonest, and traitorous to their country. Great hidden stocks of materials, undeclared by their owners when the Government made its check of essential materials, are now finding their way into these markets.

Only a person secretly in sympathy with Hitler or Hirohito would knowingly buy from such a source, for dealers in such hidden supplies are part of a great fifth column movement of the Axis powers. Every loyal American must be aware of this situation. Report at once any suspected infringement of these regulations. "I know where you can get a tire"…well, find out where and report it at once to your nearest Office of Price Administration or War Production Board. The American people must keep eyes and ears open to defeat this attempt to undermine the war effort of our country.[14]

In 1943, when analysts predicted a close end to the war, a selection of items – canned goods and meat – was taken off the rationed list. This move was very unpopular as Americans feared a rise in stockpiling would take place and that would lead to the terrible scarcities seen during World War I. This worry lasted only a short time, however, as the war did not end, and the items were rationed again a few months later.

Scarce medicines such as penicillin were rationed by triage officers in the US military during World War II. Civilian hospitals received only small amounts of penicillin during the war, because it was not mass-produced for civilian use until after the war. A triage panel at each hospital decided which patients would receive the penicillin.

Some Rationing Oddities:
- Ration coupons became gift items, especially for weddings.
- The Army ran short of chicken.
- A new phrase entered the American lexicon: *For the duration.*

- Trucks carrying cattle, pigs, or chicken were subject to "stop and search" looking for black marketeers.
- The government pressured retailers to stop using phrases like "Buy Now" in their advertising.
- Horse racing was cancelled because it was felt it required too much unneeded transportation.
- Macy's canceled their traditional Thanksgiving Day parade from 1942 through 1944 to conserve rubber and helium. In November 1942, Macy's ceremonially handed over their rubber balloons for the war effort.
- Horsemeat, rabbit, and game ended up on some American dinner plates.
- In 1943, 50 million boxes of Kraft Macaroni & Cheese were purchased because only one food ration stamp was required for two boxes. Kraft inserted contest calls for "mac and cheese" menu ideas in each box.
- Phonograph records relied on difficult to get resin for shellack from India and so went to recycling. People were offered 2 cents for every old record turned in. The quality of the recycled recording was affected (scratchy) but most record players of the day were not good enough to pick it up. Later, records became a subject of scrap drives where both consumers and record companies pitched out their old records. (To the sorrow of later collectors.)
- Employers, battling a shortage of workers, developed employee cafeterias as an attraction.
- Coca Cola managed to convince rationing board members that Coke was essential for soldiers and sailors and so received large sugar rations. Wrigley's gum did the same. Lucky Strike replaced its iconic dark-green signature pack with a white pack in 1942. American Tobacco claimed the change was made because copper was needed for the war effort. Their ads at the time proudly boasted, "Lucky Strike Green has Gone to War!" The green ink was actually made from chromium, though the gold trim was made from copper. At any rate, supplies of both were limited, and substitute materials made the package appear less appealing.[15]
- The sugar shortage had a cascading effect putting hardships on bakeries and restaurants.
- Although Great Plains farmers produced an abundance of sugar beets, much of the sugar went from the processing plants to the munitions

industry where it was converted into alcohol for the making of smokeless powder. Soon sugar supplies for consumers dwindled. Normally well-behaved diners could be seen slipping an extra sugar cube or two into their pockets.
- Sugar bowls disappeared from restaurants.
- "Café Sugar Bowls to Vanish Thursday Until War is Ended," reported the Denver Post, February 10, 1942.
- Butchers had to follow the dizzying 40,000-word wholesale beef regulations. Some workers, such as miners and lumberjacks, went on strike to get higher meat allocations.
- Meat rationing carried a class perversion. The well to do ate three times as much meat as the poor. When meat became rationed at two- and one-half pounds per person, it meant that more than half the population would be entitled to more meat than they currently bought.[17]
- Labor shortages brought about a sharp contraction in domestic servant availability as maids and others flooded into the higher paying defense jobs. This was of particular benefit to African Americans as well as women.
- Whiskey and cigarettes went unscathed by regulations, although shortages appeared from time to time. Canned beer disappeared because of the tin shortage. Americans rejected most of the foul-tasting beer and alcohol imports and substitutes brought to market.
- Americans endured the same taste situation with coffee. Pamphlets recommended chicory as an extender, an idea rejected by the public, as was the suggestion to use soybeans. A not-so-popular alternative drink was called Postum, a mixture of wheat bran, wheat, molasses, and malt. A crew of door-to-door salespeople offered a powdered coffee substitute – it was pretty bad. FDR himself suggested that Americans reuse their coffee grounds to a second cup. The coffee lobby disabused him of that recommendation.
- A curious case revolved around the substitution of margarine for butter. Margarine makers could easily have colored their margarine yellow, but the dairy industry protested and so margarine had to be packaged white. But the margarine makers got around the situation by packaging margarine in plastic bags which included within a small round yellow dye capsule. The housewife would knead the package, break the dye

capsule, and knead the package until it was yellow! Children in the family clambered to have the chore.
- To save both rubber and gasoline, horse-drawn milk wagons reappeared with every other day deliveries. The author's mother delivered milk in a horse drawn wagon.
- Sales of sliced bread were banned supposedly to conserve steel used in industrial slicing machines. Not surprisingly, the ban produced a buying run on steel kitchen knives. The ban proved so unpopular that it was lifted after two months.
- Americans dealt with an unusual buying dynamic as rationing took hold. During the Depression with little money to spend, shoppers worked diligently to find the least expensive item that would meet their needs. Now, with plenty of cash to spend and few choices to make, Americans were scrambling after higher quality goods that would have been far beyond their means just a short time ago.

A Positive Impact
Rationing was not without an important, though narrow, positive side. Poor Americans were already enduring shortages and had since the Depression. Now they faced market discrimination. Without rationing and in a free market, they would have easily been out bid for the scarce food and other goods. Rationing put a lid on prices in a way that allowed these poorer, often minority Americans, to have at least somewhat more equal buying power.

Rationing was designed to distribute scarce goods fairly. OPA official, E.W. Eggen, put the issue in practical terms while he was a guest on a 1943 KGW radio show in Portland: "Suppose the demand for coffee exceeded the supply (which it does) and there were no rationing. What would happen then is that the woman who got [to] the grocery store first would get coffee and the woman who arrived late would get none. That means that the woman working in a defense plant, with not much time for shopping around, would be coffee-less so that the woman who has little else to do but shop would have more. It means that the woman who has no children to tie her home would have plenty of time to stand in line and get coffee, whereas the mother of a family would not. The same principle would apply to towels, sheets, shoes, dresses, any other type of commodity in which shortages might develop."

Mrs. E.W. St. Pierre of the Oregon State Defense Council, put it another way: "Rationing is essentially democratic…[it] protects the 'little man' who is unable to pay exorbitant prices for articles of which limited quantities exist."

The OPA had a base of consumer support that included different socio-economic classes and racial groups who supported the agency because of their belief it would bring about a post-war vision of "broad popular participation and consumer rights." The OPA worked to defend consumers from exploitation by businesses while also acting as a space for citizens to become involved in politics.

Rationing was billed as a time of sacrifice, but how much was really being sacrificed? More Americans were earning more money and living better than they had in years. Many kinds of consumer goods could no longer be had, but enough remained to make daily life more comfortable than it had been during the recent Depression. John Kenneth Galbraith concluded that "never in the long history of human combat have so many talked so much about sacrifice with so little deprivation as in the United States during WWII."

It may be true that Americans were, in some sense, living better, but having only one pair of shoes a year for your child, or scrambling to conform to myriad regulations while at the same time worrying about a family member at the front could feel heavy. Perhaps the idea of sacrifice arose from the fact that rationing and all the wartime regulations created a very un-American feeling not so much of sacrifice, but of impotence. Americans were simply not used to being told what to do. In any event, they rose to the task with overwhelming spirit. The mantra of the times was, "Use it up/Wear it out/Make it do/Or do without."

Rationing extended its powerful influence into post-war America by creating a population with money piled up and with the eagerness to spend it to satisfy its huge pent-up demand.

Chapter Five

The War's Impact on Black People and Women

The Impact on Black Americans

African Americans did derive benefits from the demands of war, but it certainly was not a solution to the injustices they faced. At the start of the struggle, systemic segregation shackled Black people in employment, the armed services, and in the general conduct of their lives. Their unemployment rate was twice that of White Americans, and the majority of the jobs they held were unskilled.

Perhaps the central gains for Black Americans came from the migration itself. Millions of Black families left the rural south and moved north and west. No matter what the next few years would bring, they were not going back to the poverty and oppression they were escaping.

The onset of the war brought the civil rights of Black Americans into center stage. US industry developed a voracious appetite for labor and Black workers wanted in on those (mostly) good paying jobs. The problem was segregation. Even where companies were willing to hire Black workers, the employed White labor force was resistant to the point of refusing to work.

In December of 1940, FDR was approached by Black labor leader A. Philip Randolph, with an appeal to end discrimination in the new defense employment. FDR rebuffed Randolph's request. Americans were still divided on the issue of race, but the tide was moving in favor of inclusion. The pressure was building in the spring of 1941 when several Black leaders joined Randolph and again approach FDR, this time with the threat of a 100,000-person march in Washington, DC.

FDR's calculations doubtless involved racial equity, fear of riots, international embarrassment, and the practical need for the defense output that required these workers. On June 25, just five days before the July

1 scheduled march, FDR issued Executive Order 8802 which forbade discrimination of any worker because of race, creed, color, or national origin in employment of government contracts. The Fair Employment Practices Committee (FEPC) was established to investigate and monitor hiring, though it was never completely effective. The large unions did not provide any but spotty support.

EO 8802 was widely debated by the Black community. Some saw it as a huge victory and others saw it as an appeasement measure by FDR. While it cracked open the locked gate of defense opportunities, it could not completely overcome ingrained discrimination. In addition to ineffective enforcement, the order did not include the armed forces and lacked any protection against discrimination for women of any color.

In spurts, employment resistance gave way in defense plants and other employment. The jobs were often the undesirable jobs and promotions were few, but Black employees were making progress. It could be termed an "on the one hand" kind of situation. Black women were less benefitted.

Americans' attention was drawn to Philadelphia where the Philadelphia Transit Company, acting to upgrade Black porters to drivers, was confronted with a strike of its White drivers opposed to working with Black drivers. FDR, holding that the strike was illegal and that in view of the nation's manpower shortage Black workers were needed, ordered the US Army to take over the company. The strikers returned to work and the Black operators remained in their jobs. This was a victory not only for the FEPC, but for Black workers in general. Philadelphia opened more jobs for Black employees rather than risk more confrontations.

The unfairness in employment and resistance of White employees to work with Black employees, both in civilian work and in the military, led to a series of riots and near riots on the home front.

Detroit's Bell Isle Amusement Park riot in June of 1943 may have been the worst, but not the only one. In 1943 more than 240 racial incidents – ranging from hate strikes and industrial conflicts to full scale race riots – occurred in 47 towns and cities. Americans read the Pittsburg Courier's headline on June 26, 1943: "Race Riots Sweep Nation."[1]

The foolishness of segregation could be seen in the situation with Washington DC streetcars where Black and White riders could sit together until the streetcar entered the state of Virginia, where Black riders were then required to move to the rear. More foolishness could be found in the rumors of "Eleanor Clubs" in which the president's wife was purported to be to encouraging rebellion among Black maids.

In its worst form, one war-time practice was particularly hurtful. German prisoners of war were used in the south to work on farms. They were transported by train from whatever detention center held them to the farm owners' locations by train. The German prisoners were escorted in their own rail car up front, while the era's Jim Crow rules forbade Black passengers from even riding in the same car as the white prisoners, so they had to ride in cars behind them.

Such treatment of Black soldiers was not restricted to the South. It existed in other parts of the home front.

> As we entered, the counterman hurried to the rear to get the owner, who hurried out front to tell us with urgent politeness: "You boys know we don't serve colored here." Of course we knew it. They didn't serve "colored" anywhere in town…The best movie house did not admit Negroes and the other one admitted them only on the balcony. There was no room at the inn for any black visitor, and there was no place in town where we could get a cup of coffee. "You know we don't serve colored here," the man repeated…We ignored him, and just stood there inside of the door, staring at what we had come to see – the German prisoners of war who were having lunch at the counter. There were about ten of them…No guard was with them…We continued to stare. This was really happening. It was no jive talk. It was the Gospel truth. The people of Salina would serve these enemy soldiers and turn away black American G. I.'s…If we were untermenschen in Nazi Germany, they would break our bones. As "colored" men in Salina, they only break our hearts.[2]

On April 3, 1942, The *New York Times* called out "a sinister hypocrisy for fighting abroad for what it is not willing to accept at home."

The situation in the armed services was dismal for Black servicemen and women. Shortly before the war, in the regular Army of nearly a half-million men, there were only 4700 Black soldiers, 2 Black officers, and 3 Black chaplains. There was not a single serving Black person in the Marine Corps or the Army Air Corps. The Navy relegated Black sailors to be messmen for officers. In the Army they were segregated from White soldiers, and they were bothered by constant slights.[3]

More than one and a half million African Americans served in the United States military forces during World War II. They fought in the Pacific, Mediterranean, and European war zones, including the Battle of the Bulge and the D-Day invasion. These African American service men and women constituted the largest number enlisted in the Army and Navy, and the first to serve in the Marine Corp after 1798.

However, as members of the United States military, this greatest African American generation, encountered unequal treatment and limited opportunities for promotion and transfer due to the practice of racial segregation adhered to by the US military. Black soldiers conducted their work assignments separately from White soldiers, received medical treatment from separate blood banks, hospitals, and medical staff, and socialized only in segregated settings.

If they left their stateside bases, they often experienced hostility from local White civilian communities. Moreover, the authority of African American officers was restricted to African American units only and, if there were White officers in these units, the African American officers were not allowed to have higher positions. In addition, pernicious beliefs of "race" often stalled the use of African American troops in combat units and excluded them from receiving recognition for their World War II service. It was not until 1993 that the first Medal of Honor was awarded to an African American World War II veteran.[4]

The rigidly segregated army into which more than a million Black men and women were inducted reflected at all levels the dominant racial attitudes of White America, including the doctrine maintained throughout the war that Black citizens were inferior to White citizens. Secretary of War, Henry Stimson, vowed that the US Army was not about to be turned into a "sociological laboratory," General George Marshall (a Virginian) insisted that desegregation of the Army violated American customs and habit and would destroy morale. Both agreed that "leadership" was not "embedded in the Negro race."

Yet, most Americans on the home front read with great admiration the stories of the Tuskegee Airman, the all-Black 332nd Fighter Group as it distinguished itself in Europe. That it was segregated passed notice.

This obvious irony of a Jim Crow Army fighting against racism overseas but enduring it at home sparked one much-read letter in the *Pittsburgh Courier* shortly after Pearl Harbor on January 31, 1942. The following is an excerpt from *"Should I Sacrifice to Live 'Half-American'"* by James G. Thompson:

> Being an American of dark complexion and some 26 years, these questions flash through my mind: "Should I sacrifice my life to live half American? Will things be better for the next generation in the peace to follow? Would it be demanding too much to demand full citizenship rights in exchange for the sacrificing of my life? Is the kind of America I know worth defending? Will America be a true and pure democracy after this war? Will Colored Americans suffer still the indignities that have been heaped upon them in the past? These and other questions need answering; I want to know, and I believe every colored American, who is thinking, wants to know."[5]

When the *Pittsburgh Courier* published his letter, it launched the Double V campaign in collaboration with several other Black newspapers across the nation. One "V" stood for victory in the war against the Axis powers and the other "V" for victory over the fight against discrimination in the United States.

Two Black women led actions that produced changes for Black Americans. Singer, Lena Horne, after an event at a military base where POWs were given better seating than Black soldiers, raised the issue all the way to the top of the USO hierarchy and then quit and toured on her own assuring that Black servicemen would receive equal treatment. The academy award winning actress, Hattie McDaniel, led a battle to change discriminatory racial covenants in Los Angeles real estate transactions. Her case went all the way to the Supreme Court where those covenants were struck down.[6]

The use of demonstrations along with political and economic pressure plus the Double V movement would become the new means which Black Americans would use to dismantle segregation and inequality.

One piece of the war's legacy changed everything for Black servicemen and women: The Servicemen's Readjustment Act of 1944, better known as the G.I. Bill. The Veterans' Administration vowed to give Black servicemen the full benefits of the Bill which included education and home loans.

The G.I. Bill, the migration of Black families out of the South, and good jobs in defense work brought a permanent change in the status of Black Americans. No other segment of American society was as confident as Black communities now were that their young men (and women) now had a better chance to get ahead than their fathers had had.[7] The recollection of one particular Black American is recounted below.

An interview with Mr Samuel Hyman, Civil Rights Activist (b. 1938):

Were the war time experiences of black people different from those of whites? The basis for the interview was to examine that question, at least from the viewpoint of one individual.

Sam felt that at the all-encompassing level – war, separation, rationing, fear, making do and so on – experiences were probably no different. However, he saw important differences in impact, especially in the post-war era and beyond.

For Sam, who grew up on a farm in North Carolina, one war time practice did remain vivid. German prisoners of war were used in the south to work on farms. They were transported by train from whatever detention center held them to the farm owners' locations by train. The German prisoners were escorted in their own rail car, while the era's Jim Crow rules forbid blacks from even riding in the same car as the white prisoners and had to ride in cars behind them.

On the civilian front, political and labor struggles for black rights kicked into high gear as the war effort wound up. The demand for labor worked as a force for gaining better conditions. Many steps forward were taken during the war.

The young black men who volunteered served in all phases of the war, but often were assigned jobs as drivers, cooks, truck drivers and even grave diggers. While some of the skills, such as cooking, working with vehicles, and cargo handling were useful in civilian life, few gained technical or administrative skills. None the less, these young men had seen new and different ways of life and their expectations and goals had been altered. The G. I. Bill gave the returnees a means to seek out other futures that they had never considered.

Many went back to high school and then moved, most often at night, to the new spate of technical and trade schools that sprang up to meet demand – and respond to the government paid tuition.

The trade schools played an important role because it led many of the veterans into trade roles as plumbers, carpenters and builders and eventually into their own businesses. Sam believes this extension into entrepreneurship simply wouldn't have happened as quickly without the G.I. Bill.

Many black veterans who Sam remembers, used the benefits to attend college and often chose careers as teachers or in government, particularly in the post office. Many other careers still remained closed to them. The pursuit of government jobs often meant a migration to Washington DC, forming the basis of today's heavy black population in that city.

The VA loan program that accompanied the G. I. Bill provided the funds for the veterans to become first time home owners. This higher demand, coupled with the growth in black construction and entrepreneurship, along with the VA loan program, helped to create a new community of ownership. "Without the VA loan program this would not have happened for another generation," Sam said.

There were other spillover effects of the war on black veterans which resulted from the country's huge surge in demand for goods and services. Many veterans were drawn to Detroit's auto plants and to the manufacturing factories clustered around cities in the Mid-west and Northeast, adding to a general black migration already underway.

Sam explained a special by-product of blacks' war time service – pride. "The veterans demonstrated their pride in their service by wearing their uniforms around town. They had played their role in winning the war. They felt honor in their victory. The community shared that pride just like communities all over the country. Their earned pride expanded into earned expectations to be treated just like other communities."

"The history and impact of this era on all of us should not be forgotten," Sam said.

The War's Impact on Women
Rationing, as mentioned in Chapter Four, provided a universal impact on women. A shortage of heating oil meant that her household was constantly chilly during cold times. The shortage of sugar, coffee, spices, and meat meant that women had to search around from store to store. While there was a level of hoarding, shoes included, rationing did work. Part of the reason was that the big supermarkets had yet to appear, and shopping was still a personal activity between the woman shopper and the local grocer who packed the shopping bags and who would know who was following the rules and who was attempting to cheat.

Newsweek, on September 6, 1943, stated "This week the call was clear – the nation still wants more women at work…In the next two months alone at least 3,200,000 new workers are vitally needed for industry – principally munitions work. And most of these will have to be women."[8]

Washington put forth a great effort to attract women into the work force. The centerpiece evolved to be a painting of a character called "Rosie the Riveter". Rosie first appeared in a song written in 1942 by Redd Evans and John Jacob Loeb.

> While other girls attend a favorite cocktail bar,
> Sipping dry martinis, munching caviar,
> There's a girl who's really putting them to shame —
> Rosie is her name.
>
> All day long, whether rain or shine,
> She's part of the assembly line.
> She's making history working for victory.
> Rosie, Rosie, Rosie, Rosie, Rosie, Rosie the riveter.

Later that year the Westinghouse company hired artist, J. Howard Miller, to paint posters to support the war effort of its workers. Basing his painting on the song, one of his posters became the "We Can Do It" poster which much later became the red bandana-clad "Rosie the Riveter." At the time, Miller's poster was not widely circulated outside of Westinghouse plants.

The image the American people most associated with Rosie was the May 29, 1943, Norman Rockwell cover on *The Saturday Evening Post*. The post loaned the cover of the slightly burly tool-toting Rosie to the government, and it became the Rosie the Riveter icon of several propaganda efforts to attract women to defense work and the workforce generally.[9]

Recruiting women employed a two-pronged approach. One was the powerful, but unmentioned, appeal of money. While women were paid less than men, they were nonetheless paid far more than in former women's jobs such as waitresses or cleaners. The other was an appeal to patriotism. A strong, slogan-filled promotional program filled the media with calls such as "Do the Job He Left Behind," and "Longing Won't Bring Him Back Sooner...Get a War Job."

This below came courtesy of the Office for Emergency Management, War Manpower Commission.

If Hitler came to Mobile, Alabama
Every woman would defend her home with a knife, a gun, or her bare fingers...
BUT

Hitler and his hordes will not come if women help to build ships, more ships to transport our men, tanks, planes and munitions to the battle line on other continents – or if women take other jobs directly aiding the war effort. This folder tells every Mobile woman not now in a war job how she may help win the war. Read it carefully and pass it to your neighbor. It is an official statement from the War Manpower Commission.

The American home front underwent an earth-shaking change that would last long after the war.

More than 5 million women joined the workforce during WWII. Many of the women had children to care for and so providing childcare became necessary to support their war time efforts. Other than private nurseries, day care as we know it today did not exist. To provide a subsidized system of care the government called on provisions of the Lanham Act. Officially, it was the Defense Housing and Community Facilities and Services Act, that gave the Federal Works Agency the authority to fund the construction of houses, schools and other infrastructure for laborers in the growing defense industry. More than 4000 Lanham-funded centers served approximately 600,000 children. Some of the defense plants provided childcare for their workers on their own. Separately, Eleanor Roosevelt had urged President Roosevelt to approve US government childcare facilities under the Community Facilities Act of 1942. Seven centers servicing 105,000 children were built. With all this, there was under-utilization due to transportation issues and cost.[10]

The most elaborate example of company-provided childcare was instituted by, not surprisingly, Henry Kaiser at his Portland shipyard. Under some urging by Eleanor Roosevelt, Kaiser built a huge, totally modern facility with the newest play equipment and staffed with education professionals and a nutritionist. It also contained an infirmary for minor illnesses. (Later he built and staffed a complete hospital which grew into the giant health care institution Kaiser Permanente.)

At full tilt Kaiser's center was open 6 days a week, 24 hours a day. It was also open to non-employees for 75 cents a day – which included food. Under Eleanor's influence Kaiser offered, at cost, fully cooked meals for his tired workers to take home.[11]

An American standing at the gate of an aircraft factory in 1943 would see that most of the workers showing their entry badges were women. Most aircraft workers were women; however, the majority of women did not go into defense work but into other jobs vacated by men. They became truck drivers, train conductors, welders, newspaper reporters, and stockbrokers. Some entered the armed service or went into farming, which was also desperate for workers.[12]

All this immersion into the male dominated world of work was not accomplished without pain. Women were sometimes given the worst jobs, coupled with slow promotion. Harassment was common. Many cried themselves to sleep on their first nights. Some employers engaged "matrons" to help women adjust to the work environment, including how to deal with sexual harassment. Pay was usually less than that of male workers. Managing a household and caring for children while holding a job was even more difficult when the husband was serving at the front.

The sudden and dramatic need for women caused a sea change in society's view of women's ability to function under adverse conditions. Laws existed forbidding women to work nights and weekends. These were swept away. Most likely not because women deserved more equal treatment but because they were needed.

But at the same time, there were appeals for women to be proud of their work in the home, as illustrated in this ad from Swift Brands in *Good Housekeeping* in January 1944.

"Her Seven Jobs All Help Win the War"

1. WIFE! She knows that her husband can carry on the war pace of his job only if she keeps his home a peaceful, happy place. She's a loving and lovable person, doing a fine job of home-making. A salute for being that kind of wife.
2. MOTHER! She guards her youngsters' health, body and mind. She sees they get foods from the "Basic 7" Nutritional Groups daily. Sensing their shock from wartime headlines, she calmly explains why American men go off to fight.
3. PURCHASING AGENT! She realizes rationing means fair sharing. She sympathizes with dealers – understands why she often cannot get just the cut she wants, or the Swift's brands of beef or other meats she'd prefer to have.
4. COOK! She cooks with care to save nutritive values. She makes the most of meat; reduces shrinkage by cooking at low temperature; prepares attractive dishes from leftovers; learns to cook every kind of cut so it will taste its very best.
5. SALVAGE EXPERT! She wastes nothing, for she knows that Food Fights for Freedom. She uses every bit of leftovers, even bones are saved for soup. She regularly takes to her dealer the drippings of fat that have no further cooking use.

6. WAR WORKER! She joins wholeheartedly in the community projects of civilian defense. She sends neat bandages on far errands of mercy. And (to her it is a matter of special pride) the honor list of blood donors includes her name.
7. WAR BONDS BUYER! She does without things she wants so our men will have the things they need. Over 10% of her husband's pay goes for war bonds, plus dollars she saves in her household budget.

Swift salutes Mrs America, Patriot!

Swift wasn't the only one appealing to Mrs America. The government had a department dedicated to influencing the home front woman. The department issued a monthly publication called *Magazine War Guide* which it sent to hundreds of women's magazine editors suggesting how their magazine's content, focus, articles, and photographs could support the war effort. Editors were urged to show women coping with the war and its shortages and challenges.

At the outbreak of the war American women faced discrimination in the job market. They found many positions simply closed to them and in the jobs they could find, the work was less desirable, and they earned less than men. They chafed under this inequality. Their break came in 1940 as the US geared up defense production and millions of men entered the military service.

Under the old saying, "Be careful what you wish for," women found that some Americans felt there was no reason why our women shouldn't be equally as patriotic as our men. Dramatic headlines appeared. "Draft for Women," proclaimed *Business Week*. "There Must be No Idle Women," *Independent Woman* announced. "Shall We Draft Women?" proposed *The Nation;* even *Woman's Home Companion* frightened its audience with "Should Women be Drafted?"[13]

The need for women workers was perceived as a national priority to the point where several bills were promoted in Congress, principally by conservative senators, to institute a draft of women. They failed, leading both government and industry to wage a concerted multi-media campaign to register women and get them to work in the factories, and, slowly, they did – in huge numbers. The number of working women rose from

14,600,000 in 1941 to 19,370,000 in 1944. These numbers include not only factory work but office work, the professions and agriculture as they replaced men in many jobs. (Chapter Ten offers more details on the iconic character *Rosie the Riveter* and the successful propaganda to attract women into defense work.)

As the war years went by, more than one third of all adult women were in the labor force. Conversely, women constituted more than one third of the civilian work force. The composition of women workers underwent a transformation in the early 1940s as well. Working women had been single and young, but during the war years married women came to make up nearly three quarters of the total number of female employees, and by the end of the war, half of all female workers were over thirty-five.

American women during the war did not use the modern term work-life balance, but they labored under a staggering load. The work week was six days long and the workday averaged nine hours. With the gas shortage, and overloaded public transportation, commuting required extra thought and effort. Rationing made food shopping and meal preparation a time-consuming exercise in creativity. Childcare as we know it did not exist, forcing women to cobble together friends and family to look after their children. And all this compounded life even more for home front women who worked on the off shifts! Children became very aware of the workload their mothers were shouldering. For children of the home front their mothers were an inspiration.

It isn't often reported, but absenteeism due to these dual roles was excessive, and women left their jobs in large numbers. The turnover rate was understandably and incredibly high, in some locations exceeding 50 percent.[14]

Because of reports through the years about women entering the work force during the war, a false narrative about women's preferences has arisen. Regardless of the new flow of women into the workplace, the preferred role of women as stated in a 1943 survey of both men and women, was the role of housewife.[15]

But the women who did work loved the work. Since economic stability breeds independence, the war acted as a profound catalyst in shaping new roles for women. Many agreed with a Baltimore advertisement that told them that working in a war plant was "a lot more exciting than polishing the family furniture." They remained frustrated at unfair pay differentials but wanted to continue working after the war. However, some recognized, as one woman in Tacoma noted, "My husband wants a wife, not a career woman," and complied with the propaganda campaign as the war drew to an end, to get them out of the factories so that returning servicemen could take back their jobs. Social pressure was levied on working women to do so, though many did so with reluctance. Still, their experience helped lay the groundwork for the women's movement in later years and the war was an important step on the road to equal rights.[16]

Nursing, a traditional employment for women, was just as desperate to fill vacancies. By 1944 the US needed 66,000 nurses for the military and nearly 300,000 for civilian duty – 100,000 more than were available.[17] The high pay of defense work put nursing jobs, with their long, unpaid training period, at a severe disadvantage. A program of training nurses' aides offered some help, but the unglamorous nature and low pay of the work meant that quotas went unfilled.

Americans were exposed to several days of debate on bills in Congress aimed at drafting nurses, who already had shown exemplary patriotism, only to see the bills defeated.

Women in the Armed Services
Beginning in December 1941, 350,000 women served in the United States Armed Forces during WWII. They had their own branches of services, including:

- Women's Army Auxiliary Corps (later the Women's Army Corps or WAC).
- Women Accepted for Volunteer Military Services (WAVES).
- Women served in a branch of the Coast Guard called (SPARS) for Semper Paratus.
- Women Airforce Service Pilots (WASP).
- Women also served in the Marines.[18]

WACs – US Army

In July 1943, an important step was taken when the Women's Army Auxiliary Corps became the Women's Army Corps (WAC) and officially became part of the US Army. This enabled WACs to serve overseas, as they could be given proper benefits should they be wounded or killed in service. WAC members receive rank, benefits, or even pay equivalent to men in the Regular Army.

The first WAC Director was Oveta Culp Hobby. Her greatest challenge was to convince the American public that a woman could join the Army, but still be "a lady." Despite cultural misgivings about women in uniform, by November 1942 the initial recruitment goal of 25,000 had been exceeded. A cap was set at 150,000 for WACs, which was met by the end of the war. Once the transition to WAC service was complete, African American women were accepted for service. The 6888th Central Postal Directory Battalion was the only all-Black female unit to serve in Europe during the war. They provided a vital service – sorting through a mail backlog of millions of letters that were important for maintaining morale at the front.

WAVES – US Navy

The establishment of the WAVES was not the first time women had served in the US Navy. During World War I, thousands of women had served as Yeomen through a loophole which opened naval service to all Americans, omitting gender as a requirement for service. Known as Yeomanettes, they were phased out after the war, and women were not able to join the US Navy until the creation of the WAVES. Under the direction of Lieutenant Colonel Mildred McAfee, the WAVES grew to 27,000 in number in the first year, eventually numbering over 8,000 officers and 80,000 enlisted WAVES.

SPARS – US Coast Guard

Following the lead of the other branches, the US Coast Guard's own women reserve force was authorized in late 1942. They too had a need for women to fill roles currently filled by men, allowing those men to go to sea. The first director came from the WAVES, Lieutenant Commander Dorothy Stratton. The initial recruitment drive was successful, but recruiting for the least-known service was always a challenge. African American women were not allowed to enlist until October 1944.

Smaller than the other service branches, the SPARS as they were known, had just 10,000 women in service from 1942–1946. By the end of 1944, recruiting had stopped, save for replacements or to fill positions requiring specialized skills. Although the Coast Guard fell under the jurisdiction of the US Navy during the war, SPARS, like their male counterparts, were trained in Coast Guard camps.

WASP – Women Airforce Service Pilots

Led by pilot Jacqueline Cochran, WASP were officially federal employees, and though they worked with the US Army Air Forces, were not members of any US military organization.

This group of female pilots, numbering just over 1100, was responsible for ferrying aircraft from factories to airbases, towing aerial targets for gunnery practice, and testing aircraft. They flew everything from B-17s to P-51s. WASP pilots ferried over 12,000 aircraft, even flying some to distant theaters. Two women, Dorothea Johnson and Dora Daugherty Strother, tested the B-29 Super Fortress when some male pilots refused to do so. The WASP were disbanded in 1944 due to a surplus of male pilots who were demanding their old jobs back and public pressure to do so. A bill in Congress to provide equity for the WASPS failed by nineteen votes.[19]

'Black Rosies' African American Women on the Homefront

From shipyards to factories to government administrative offices, Black women also worked to battle racism abroad and on the home front. For African American women, becoming a Rosie (war worker) was not only an opportunity to aid in the war effort, but also a chance for economic empowerment. Already on the move as part of the great migration, they sought to leave behind dead-end, often demeaning work as domestics and sharecroppers. "Black people were leaving the south anyway and fanning out across the country," says Gregory S. Cooke, director of Invisible Warriors, a documentary on the Black Rosies. "The war gave the women a more pointed motivation for leaving and an opportunity to make money in ways Black women had never dreamed before."[20]

Away from the home front, Black women soldiers won respect for rapidly unsnarling the huge backlog in servicemen's mail in Europe and in other war theaters. "The war represented this incredible opportunity, but black women really had to rally and fight for the opportunity to even be considered," says Dr. Maureen Honey, author of Bitter Fruit: African American Women in World War II and Emeritus Professor of Women's and Gender Studies at the University of Nebraska–Lincoln. "Many employers held out, attempting to only hire white women or white men, until they were forced to do otherwise." That coercion came in the summer of 1941 when Executive Order 8802, described above, banned racial discrimination in the defense industry. The order boosted Black women's entry into the war effort; of the one million African Americans who entered employment for the first time following 8802's signing, 600,000 were women.

These efforts foreshadowed the protest campaign strategy of the modern Civil Rights Movement.

Volunteering

American women's role as volunteers was never in doubt. The combination of women's good hearted will and the specter of war sparked a virtual avalanche of volunteer organizations. Dutiful rationing, victory gardening, and saving fats and tin were not enough for patriotic American women. They sought to volunteer to do more. To match their desires, more than fifty cities organized volunteer defense bureaus to register women's names to match them to needs. In some areas of the home front dozens of organizations were formed and were getting in each other's way and doing little. Some women even joined uniformed paramilitary organizations with little chance of ever encountering the enemy.

Of course, the vast majority of women gravitated to worthwhile organizations such as the Red Cross, the USO and local Civil Defense units. One large voluntary organization, modeled after a similar one in Britain, was the American Women's Voluntary Services, AWVS. At one point it claimed 350,000 members in 350 units. It's training focused on direct needs of wartime: ambulance driving, fire firefighting, map reading, air raid drills and more. As time wore on and the likelihood of attacks on the home front grew remote, the AWVS found other roles, particularly in healthcare and bond sales.

American women volunteers generously gave more than just their time. They paid for their transportation, donated money and supplies, and often were required to pay dues. Women volunteers became a visible hallmark of the home front during war time.

Newlyweds
Women who had been married before the war began, especially those who had children, had their own special problems, such as raising their children alone. But they experienced many of the same problems as the newlywed, albeit for the most part married women had a home and a degree of stability. The war years brought on a marriage boom that produced the largest number of families in the nation's history. But these were unconventional, wartime marriages with special tribulations for both partners. The partners, instead of sharing and building a solid relationship, were facing life's experiences separately. But where men had companionship and daily purpose, women faced the world on their own, many for the first time. Some had never had to budget money for a household, pay rent, or maintain a car. Some went protected by their father to their husband. Many had never been alone.

Some chose to follow their husbands from camp to camp until the husband shipped out overseas. They faced hardships that tried their spirit. Just finding transportation was an ordeal in the crush of war time traffic now overloaded with service men and migrating war workers. What housing was available was often poor and high priced. Connections were missed, cars broke down, and orders got changed. The August 30, 1943, edition of *Time* magazine described, "a strange unorganized home front battle being fought all over the US by a vast, unorganized army of women. They are the wives, mothers, sweethearts, or fiancés of servicemen. Their only plan of campaign, with the valor of ignorance, is to follow their men."

Relief agencies such as the Red Cross, Travelers' Aid, and Army and Navy relief funds felt a huge surge in calls for help, but they could not help the huge number of camp followers. The temporary nature of training bases meant that seldom were meaningful relationships built with other women. Women who gave birth in these camp towns had no one to support them.

Still, some chose to stay in the last place they had been with their husbands and to await their return in the company of others like themselves. This choice required determination. Rentals were hard to find and the rents were exorbitant. Services such as medical care were often meager. The armed services were not overly sympathetic, and wives found little help from them, though there were exceptions.

Many women chose to go into jobs that were opened up by men vacating to service. More than just defense jobs, they also took other jobs which were left open. This is covered more in Chapter Two.

Other women chose to move back home, back into a home that was no longer really theirs. The emotional adjustment to be under another woman's roof was difficult. The woman's position in the home had changed. Now that she was married the dynamics were different; she wasn't a family member as she had been, but on the other hand she wasn't a guest either.[21] One solution saw war wives living together sharing costs and experiences and proving support for each other.

Who's Sorry Now?
Albert S. (b. 1936):

My sister, Alice Mary, had a boyfriend who joined the army. Before he went in, he bought her an engagement ring. Alice Mary didn't want to be engaged, but she felt bad because he was going off to war. In 1945 her boyfriend was coming home and she was worried about how she was going to break the news that she didn't want to marry him. She felt sorry for him, but that's how she felt.

She met him at a restaurant downtown near the train station. My parents, my brother and I were all waiting for her when she came home that night. "How did he take the news?" we all asked. "I never gave him the news," she said. "He gave me the news that he was engaged to some girl he met when he was on leave in New York. He said he was very sorry."

Alice Mary felt she should be happy that he no longer wanted to marry her, but she felt jilted nonetheless and cried all night. The next day she was fine and was glad her pretending to him was over.

A special home front woman emerged out of the frenetic pace of wartime relationships. She was dubbed, "Allotment Annie." She would seek out especially lonely service men and respond to their wooing, pledging a love that would last them through the war. The proof of this pledge was marriage. Along with the marriage certificate came the serviceman's allotment check, usually $20 to $50 and a $10,000 payment if the husband was killed in action. There is no record of how many "Allotment Annies" were in operation, but the record for how many men one Annie married seemed to be seven.[22]

Furloughs and Leaves

No set of expectations could be higher than those of the home front woman waiting for her man to come home on leave. And, like all extraordinary expectations, many were cause for disappointment and some were sadly, devastating. You will find more on this in Chapter Eleven.

The Loneliness, the Letters and the Telegram

Nothing defines home front women more than their loneliness. No matter how busy the day juggling work or dealing with rationing or single parenting, they were lonely.

> **Left Alone as Soon as the War Started**
> by Claire Mc. (b. 1938):

My dad volunteered for the Navy right away because he didn't want to fight in the mud like his father had done in the Army. We didn't live way out in the country, but we were up the coast, pretty far from town. You couldn't call it a real farm, but my dad liked to raise our own chickens and tend a big vegetable garden.

Taking care of our place pretty much by herself was a big job, and she was not a big woman. On top of that, I used to see how hard she had to work to figure out how much gasoline she had to get around and how many ration stickers she needed for this and that.

With no end to the war in sight, she became weary, but not discouraged. "Lots of people have it worse than we do," she would repeat. I had my chores and tried to help, but a five or six-year-old can only do so much.

A memory I have is when I once found her sound asleep, with her head resting on her arms at the kitchen table. She tried to look perky when I woke her, but to me she looked so tired. That's what I remember from the war.

PS My dad came home safely.

Letters! Whether writing letters or waiting for one in the mail, letters meant everything. Two wonderful books contain dozens of those letters sent and received.[23]

The government developed a special form and format for writing letters: V-mail. To use V-mail the woman would use a special form. On one side she could write her letter and on the other she would write the address. There were three giant postal centers in New York, San Francisco, and Chicago. All of the mail was funneled through these centers. At the centers the letters would be censored, if needed, and photographed on microfilm. The film would be sent to microfilm equipped stations overseas and printed at 60 percent of the original size and delivered. V-mail saved thousands of tons of space for needed military transport.[24]

The Postal Service mounted a full campaign, complete with posters, ads, and radio spots encouraging letter writing to servicemen. Magazines and newspapers offered tips on how to write to husbands in the service. Most of the advice came down to "Keep him up to date on what you are doing but be positive and don't lay problems on him." A mother should talk about the children, their progress, their funny sayings and antics, and talk about the future.

One great puzzlement was what to tell home front children. Of course, age made a big difference. For very young children, "Daddy's gone away for a while." was sufficient. For older children "gentle truth" was prescribed: "No, we don't know how long Daddy will be gone. Yes, we hope Daddy will come back safe and sound. Yes, people on our side get killed in war, but not everybody gets killed. No, you will not be alone. I'll take care of you." Older children would hear about the war outside the home so it paid for mothers to be up to date on the war's progress so that her assurances would have the ring of credibility.[25]

It was important to keep the father as a presence in the child's life. If the child was old enough, he or she might write to the father themselves or help compose an answer to him. Birthdays and holidays should be celebrated. Tell the child that he should look forward to playing ball (or some activity) with Daddy when he returns. Having a young child mail the letter could mean a lot.

Here is how one home front child remembers the mail.

R. Sharon (b. 1935):

One thing I remember when I was very young is waiting for the mailman. Once I saw him going up the other side of our street I knew it would be 20 minutes or so before he came down our side. Some days I would run across the street and ask for our mail, but my mother said she didn't want me crossing the street alone and besides it made extra work for Mr. Graves, our mailman. Mr. Graves didn't seem to mind at first, but then one day he said I should wait on my side of the street. It always seemed like a lot more than 20 minutes some days. Mr. Graves would tease me by taking a piece of mail and pretend he was trying to find out who it was for. He would hold it up to read the address and say, "No, that's not for you. No, this is for the Lawtons down the street. Oh! Wait here's one! Yep, it's for you."

I remember how my day would revolve around meeting the mailman. When I started to go to school my first stop when I got home was the kitchen where the mail always got put. Some days I would be happy and some days I would feel sad.

The telegram. Every service family feared the telegram that began "The Department of the (Navy, Army, Air Force) regrets…" No family suffered more from that terse news than the Sullivan family of Waterloo, Iowa. All five sons of the Sullivan family had rushed to join the Navy. Within a year they were killed when the ship in which all five were serving was sunk in the pacific. All of America mourned them. Hollywood made a feature film. And the Sullivan's only daughter joined the Women's Army Corps. (She survived.)

Too late for the Sullivan family, the Navy implemented a policy that family members were not to serve together.

A 1944 campaign portrait of Franklin D. Roosevelt. (*Public domain image, via Wikimedia Commons*)

The USS Reuben James was sunk by a German U-boat on October 21, 1941. The sinking failed to bring the US into the war. (*Image courtesy of The National Archives and Records Administration*)

Joe DiMaggio.

Ted Williams.

Ted Williams and Joe DiMaggio both set records that still stand. (*Public domain images, via Wikimedia Commons*)

The US Times

WAR EXTRA

ESTABLISHED 1856 | NO. 35,247 | 56 PAGES | MONDAY DEC 8, 1941 | PRICE 5 CENTS

HUNDREDS KILLED IN HAWAII ATTACK
CONGRESS DECLARES WAR

ROOSEVELT TO ADDRESS CONGRESS

Reporter Frank J. Delaney

Washington, Dec. 8 President Roosevelt will address a joint session of Congress, to
discuss steps to be made after the attack in the Pacific.
The President will appear personally at 12.30pm; whether

CHURCHILL DECLARES WAR ON JAPAN IN ALLIANCE WITH U.S.

By C.M. Jones

The unexpected attacks in the Pacific yesterday, Sun. Dec. 7, by the Japanese Air Force and Navy have plunged the U.S and its Allies into active war with Japan. The UK Prime Minister, Sir

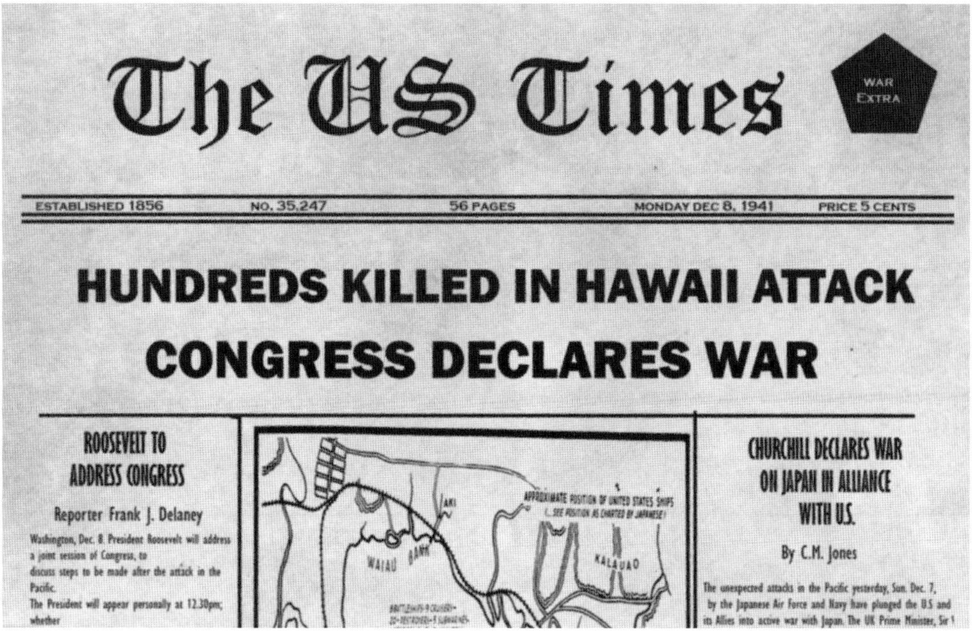

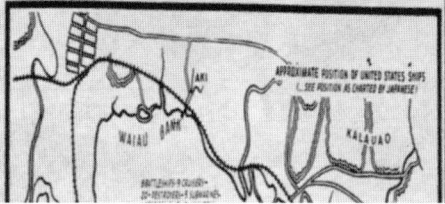

A mock-up of the various headlines that appeared on newspapers across the US after the 7 December bombing on Pearl Harbor. (*Image: author's own*)

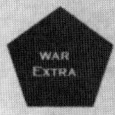

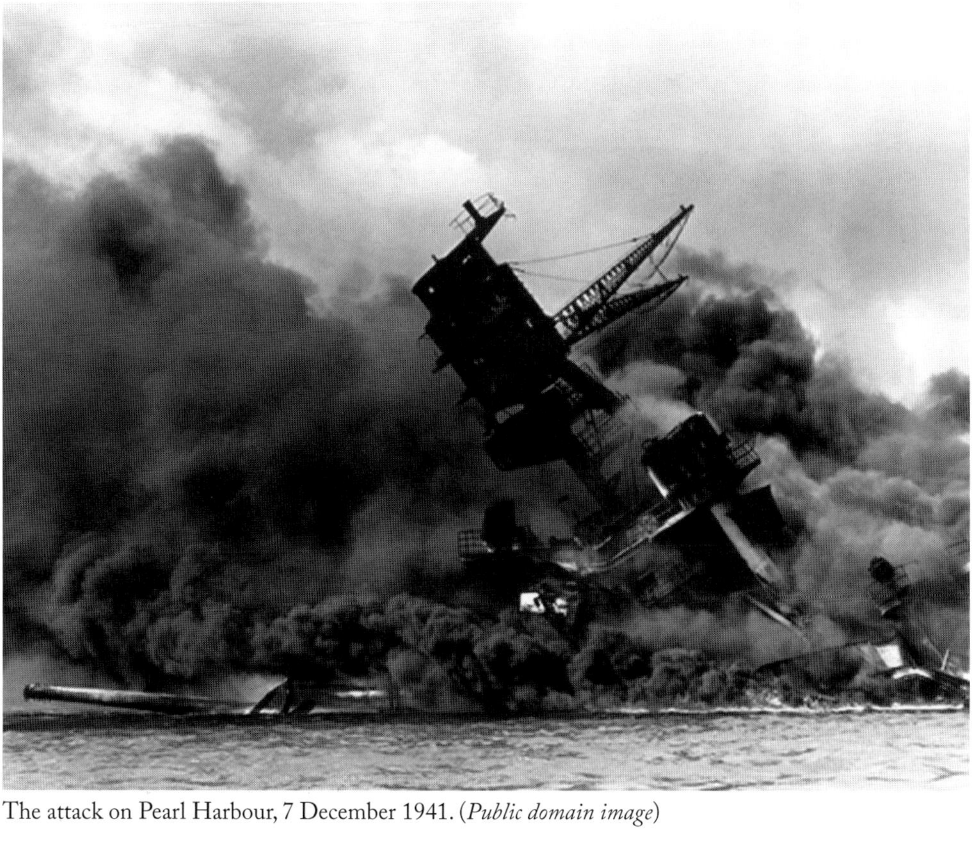

The attack on Pearl Harbour, 7 December 1941. (*Public domain image*)

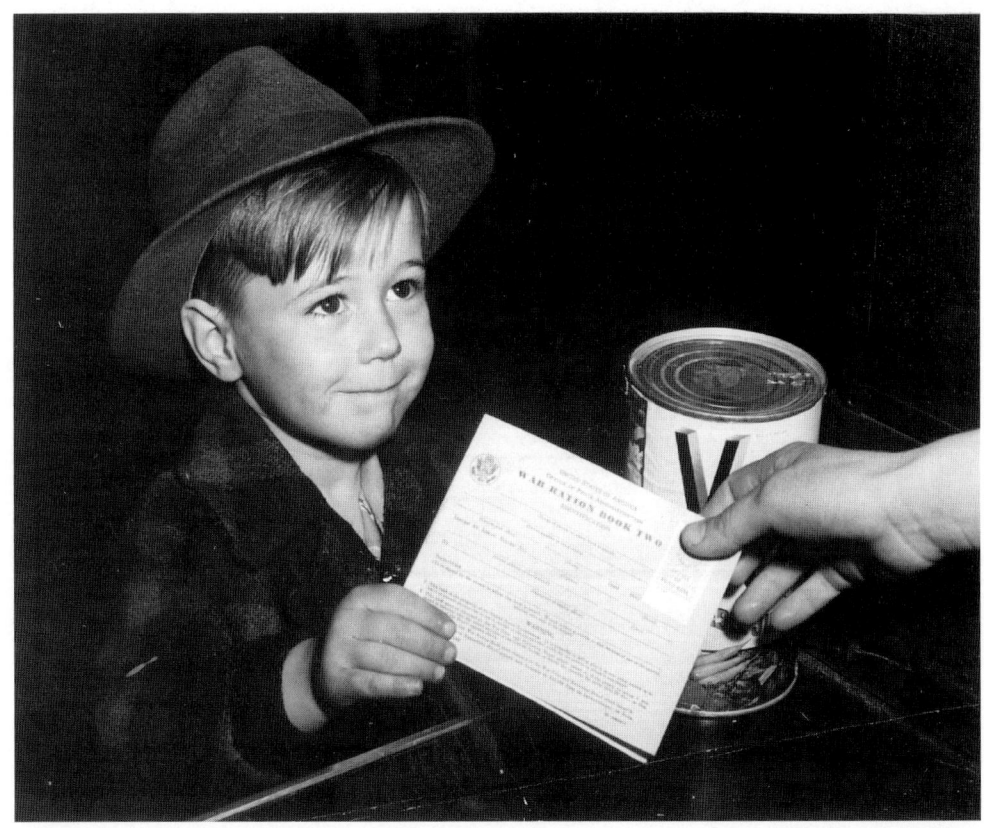

Starting in 1941 these ration books became part of the home front for the duration. (*Public domain image, via Wikimedia Commons*)

A young boy gets his first experience using a ration card. (*Public domain image, via Wikimedia Commons*)

Scrap drives were fun, especially when kids got the day off from school. (*Public domain image, via Wikimedia Commons*)

Gas and tire rationing poster c.1942–3. (*Office for Emergency Management. War Production Board. Public domain image, via Wikimedia Commons*)

Blackout curtains were required as Home Front Americans were ordered to cover all windows and doors to block out all light each night by 11:00 p.m. (*Public domain image; The Library of Congress, Farm Security Administration/Office of War Information*)

Queueing for meat rations in LA. Lines for rationed goods were not uncommon and meat was especially sought after. (*Public domain image, via Wikimedia Commons*)

A group of women workers at Ingalls Shipbuilding yard, Pascagoula, Mississippi, in 1943. (*Public domain image, via Wikimedia Commons*)

'Buy Bonds' bond drive was featured on posters, encouraging Americans to financially contribute to the war effort. (*Public domain image, via Wikimedia Commons*)

Your Victory Garden: encouraging Americans on the Home Front to grow their own fruit and vegetables. (*Public domain image; WPA Federal Art Project*)

Women ordnance workers had a strong sense of identity including uniforms. (*Public domain image; The Library of Congress*)

Woman at work on a Wright R2600 aircraft engine in North American Aviation's plant. (*Public domain image; The Library of Congress, Prints and Photographs Division, Washington DC, 20540. Photograph by Alfred T. Palmer*)

The Mochida Family; A Japanese family headed for an internment camp. (*Public domain image; From the US National Archive. Record Group 210, series G. Photograph by Dorothea Lange*)

Howard Miller's Rosie. This Rosie was originally drawn as a patriotic promotion at Westinghouse Electric. (*National Archives Catalogue*)

Nothing defines home front women more than their loneliness. (*Image by Lawrence Wilbur, 1944. Printed by the Government Printing Office for the War*)

Victory garden poster. Millions of Americans jumped into gardening, including children. (*Public domain image; Library of Congress via Wikimedia Commons*)

The Lockheed assembly plant in Burbank, CA, producing P-38 pursuit planes. (*Library of Congress, Prints & Photographs Division, FSA/OWI Collection, LC-USE6- D-006674 LOT 1985. Photograph by David Bransby*)

A war time store window in Danbury, Connecticut. (*Photograph courtesy of Danbury Museum and Historic Society*)

Bring him home sooner... Join the WAVES (Women Accepted for Volunteer Military Services). (*Public domain image, via Wikimedia Commons*)

Chapter Six

The Impact on Children on the Home Front

The story of wartime children starts, of course, with wartime marriages. The marriage rate for women over the age of 15 rose from 73 percent in 1939 to 93 percent in 1942.[1] Couples were taking happiness where and when they could. Some women, knowing their new husbands would not be coming home from the war, were choosing to be widows rather than old maids. The result was a jump in birth rates from 77.6 per thousand to 94.3 per thousand.[2]

As always, parents held the greatest influence on these children. Children felt the absence of a father profoundly. (The absence of an older brother could be just as painful.) Separation from a parent was seen as so detrimental to a child that the US did not follow Britain's program of evacuating children from danger zones.

Whether a child lived in a city or in rural America, the war was to become central to his growth and values for his lifetime. Here is one story.

Tina B. (b. 1938):

I thought that spies were around every corner, listening and reporting back to Germany or Japan. In downtown Mobile there were posters on lamp posts that said "loose lips sink ships." I didn't want to have loose lips and worried about what that was. The pictures of Japanese soldiers they showed were terrifying to me. The worst was in the movies where we saw the endless lines of German soldiers marching. My friends and I wondered how we could ever beat such an army. My uncle Roy was in the Army and he said we would beat them for sure, so I held on to that.

It's funny that when I talk to people my age today, they mostly say, "Oh, yes, I forgot about that. I was afraid back then." I hope I forget someday.[3]

The majority of children spent the war years in the same home they were born in, but many others were subjected to migration either because of their mother following their father base to base as he served, or from chasing after defense work and its high paycheck. The impact of migration, particularly on children, was judged to be so great that Congress created The Select Committee Investigating National Defense Migration.

No matter where the children spent the home front years, they endured anxiety. Children absorbed the fears and tensions of their surrounding adults. Adding to their fears were the graphic and vivid depictions of war in the newsreels shown at the Saturday matinee. With a father gone and a mother working, a child faced drastic changes. No aspect of life was left unchanged.

Still Fearful
I can confess it now to people who read this who are sort of from the same era. I was terrified.
by Sarah M. (b. 1932):

All day long I heard grown ups and older kids in the street talking about the Germans and the Japs and how they were winning. In the newsreels at the movies I saw how powerful the Germans looked with all the tanks and thousands of marching men. My Uncle Alan told me how mean the Japs were to our Marines.

Two girls in my school lost their brothers and one of them stayed home for a long time. My father worked at the Brooklyn Navy Yard and told me he and the other men were building ships that would go fight them and that we would win, but I was still afraid.

I spent all those years so scared. I had bad dreams about German soldiers breaking into our house. After the war my mother said she thought I was just a quiet kid.

I'm well over 80 now and I still have moments of fear come over me. You just don't forget that.[4]

It was easy for a child to get lost in the shuffle. "Latch key kids" and "dresser drawer babies" became shorthand for neglect. Children were left to watch movies all day. Some were left locked in parking lots at war plants. Some were locked in (or out) of their home. These were by no means the majority, but they were enough to catch notice.

In the beginning most children were cared for by the traditional networking of family and friends, but this proved inadequate. The upshot was the development of a new social entity that would change lives long after the war: day care. Childcare was seen as a mother's responsibility and there was social resistance to government involvement in caring for children.

The well to do could place their children in private nurseries. Other than private nurseries, day care as we know it today did not exist. To provide a subsidized system of care the government called on provisions of the Lanham Act, an act which gave the Federal Works Agency the authority to fund the construction of houses, schools, and other infrastructure for laborers in the growing defense industry. More than 4000 Lanham-funded centers served approximately 600,000 children. Some of the defense plants, the Kaiser Works chief among them, provided childcare for their workers on their own. Separately, Eleanor Roosevelt had urged President Roosevelt to approve US government childcare facilities under the Community Facilities Act of 1942. Seven centers, servicing 105,000 children, were built.[5]

As groundbreaking and helpful as subsidized day care was, it was not fully subscribed. Mothers were not yet comfortable trusting their children to strangers and some of the physical conditions were poor. The programs ended after the war and subsidized day care was not seen again until recent years.

Across the country officials took steps to protect children. There were advocates for creating a master registry. In some locations children were registered and fingerprinted. Children in the San Francisco area had to wear ID tags stamped with numbers corresponding to those on lists held by Civil Defense in case they became evacuees. In Washington DC children were given copper dog tags. In New York City they were fingerprinted.[6]

A very successful program took shape in early 1942. Called Extended School Services (ESS), it simply had school teachers stay on and care for the children until the working mother could get there. FDR managed a grant of $400,000 to kick off the program and it spread very quickly with no added funds to more than 600 locations. So popular was ESS that when the school year ended, locales, parents, schools, and others found ways to keep ESS going through the summer.[7]

Another Washington originated program was "Schools at War," which was used as a platform to engage children in scrap drives, bond drives, and other patriotic activities.

At this time on the home front a change came sweeping over the field of child development. The standard all through the 1930s had been personified by John B. Watson who advocated "habit training" of children in all things, starting at an early age. A parent was not to pick up a crying child if it was bedtime. Feeding took place at a specific time. But Watson's philosophy came under fire from followers of Dr Benjamin Spock who advocated a child-centered and more flexible, natural rhythm of child rearing. In time it would be almost impossible to visit the home with a child without seeing a worn copy of Dr Spock's famous book.

Children who accompanied their mothers to a defense factory town found a different culture where people behaved differently and talked differently, making it difficult to fit in. They could encounter poor living conditions. They might be subject to group living or living in temporary housing or in trailers. Wherever it was, the child knew it was temporary. Friendships and relationships of all kinds, whether with other children or adults, were tempered by the child's awareness of impermanence. When a child did commit to a relationship they could be hurt by its severance when they moved next.

Education

The war exposed colossal deficiencies in American education: massive functional illiteracy, a terrible shortage of people with basic competence in math, foreign languages, and science. And woeful levels of vocational skills. Coming out of the Depression, only one in four had finished high school. Most had not finished grade school.[8] Education in the US, never uniform across the country in terms of quality or even quantity, now came under new, severe pressures.

The first pressure arose from the call for workers, first to replace draftees and second to replace those entering the high paying defense jobs springing up across the country. With teachers' salaries perennially low – teachers' annual salaries in parts of the South averaged less than $500 – the depletion of teachers was rapid and severe. The shortage of teachers forced larger or discontinued classes in some places while in others it broke down the long-standing objection to teachers being married. Conditions led to school systems hiring unqualified teachers, some with barely a high school education themselves.

Pressure came from the need for home front children, now more than ever, to help on farms and other family businesses, which led to longer vacation periods and shorter class days, though in some areas Saturday classes were laid on to lessen the lost educational time.

Pressure also came from the military demanding more functional recruits. leading schools to add more math, vocational, and technical studies. Low salaries had led to low competence of teachers. The Los Angeles School system went as far as ordering physical exams of the county's 10,000 high school seniors with free dental and medical care for those who could not afford it. The seniors were also threatened with a physical fitness requirement to graduate.[9]

While all of this was occurring, a philosophical battle was taking place over teaching methods. The long prevailing pedagogy involved quantification and standards with points, units, and tests, always tests. But a set of progressive ideas had been quietly growing and burst forth during 1941. This progressive methodology put the engagement of students and their personal development at the top of its list of must haves.

A huge experiment completed in 1941 purported to show the progressive method superior to the rigid rules of the past and schools became amenable to changing to the new method. However, as deficiencies were revealed by the draft and as reports of unruliness in progressive schools emerged, the progressive trend went into hibernation on the home front for the duration and more directed rules and 'hard' subjects were in. Though no one seemed to lack patriotism, patriotic fervor entered the curriculum, and teaching of the benefits of democracy became popular. (No doubt with dollops of propaganda such as the *Democracy Reader*, included.)

Higher education also came under pressure. No federal agency existed for its guidance, benefit and help. In addition to the financial pressures from Depression-depleted endowments, enrollments declined prompting some colleges and universities to lower their standards. Once enrolled, students could come under draft rules as they approached draft age prompting some institutions to develop three or even two-year programs. Often these programs now contained such studies as ballistics and other courses useful for military purposes. Colleges also embarked on a hunt for communists. At the extreme were acts of book banning and censorship. Some campuses endured friction between more liberal faculty, which favored intervention, and conservative students who opposed it.

The conditions around the new defense plants were far worse than elsewhere with shortages of everything including classroom space. Students flooded into, often small town, school systems woefully unprepared to handle them. The long-standing demands for local control of education gave way to demands for federal funds to rescue their systems. More than $100,000,000 was appropriated to aid "impacted areas," most of which were in rural and poorer parts of the country. Given the turmoil of the times, the appropriation passed quietly and provided a kind of social aid that such grants still provide.

The government directly inserted itself into education to bolster the country's supply of technically and scientifically trained people. It offered and funded, tuition free, more than 200 programs in those disciplines as the 1941 academic year opened.[10] It also created a registry of those on the home front who held technical degrees or enjoyed scientific experience which resulted in the creation of a vital inventory of a critical resource. These actions demonstrated a measure of thoughtfulness often believed to be lacking in government.

The military, faced with astounding levels of illiteracy in its draftees, began education programs of its own. Using teachers from its own ranks and a "Soldiers' Reader" which conveyed lessons in a more simplified manner, it brought more than 100,000 men up to a fourth-grade level of education.[11]

The school day for almost all now started with the pledge of allegiance and the singing of patriotic songs. In addition to the Star-Spangled Banner, children now might sing God Bless America, Anchors Away, Caissons Go Rolling Along, and the new Air Force song, Off We Go into the Wild Blue Yonder. Students put on patriotic plays. Some teachers asked their class to show hands if they had a family member in the service and then would lead prayers for the servicemen. Children wrote letters to their family members and even to strangers. Teachers sometimes read the (poignant) letters children received in return.

Playground games changed from cops and robbers and Cowboys and Indians to war games with pointed hands for pistols and running, arms spread, making roaring sounds to play at being an airplane, and crying, "bombs away." Girls' dolls wore the uniforms of the WACS or WAVES or nurses. The following depicts how two youngsters enjoyed those times.

Greeting the Troop Train
We all knew when it was a troop train because of the color of the cars.
Frank G. (born. 1934):

The Southern Railway's cars were a bright "livery green" and the troop trains were plain gray or brown. The trains all stopped just outside of Charleston, we guessed as a safety check, and that gave everyone a chance to go down and greet the troops, mostly recruits, heading to Fort Benning, Georgia.

We brought them food, of course, mostly sweets, and we also brought them toilet items like soap and razors. What I remember most about all that was how everyone from all around came down together. It was like all those soldiers were our own family, including the black soldiers.

For that time we were all together. It was too bad it took a war.[12]

How Can I remember So much?
Lynne C. (b. 1940):

I was born in Newark and then moved to Union where the memories of the war click in. How can I remember so much?
The dark green light blocking shades.
Daddy's head lights half blocked.
The running board and rumble seat.
The excitement in the streets on VE and VJ Day.
Mixing the 'butter' at my neighbor's house. (Don't know what we used.)
Saving the 'tinfoil' from gum wrappers.

Party lines at Unionville 2 5057 J.
Mom giving me twenty five cents to walk to the store (Heavens, she'd be in jail today) for a few slices of bologna.
Johnny ride a pony – hide and seek – kick the can – sleigh riding on the street in winter – freedom to roam all over the neighborhood.
My first portable radio – looked like a big lunch box.
Climbing and falling out of many trees...guess I was a real tomboy.
Oh, and I do remember going to the old, old, Newark airport to mail packages to my Uncle Joe who was a cook (chef) in the Navy in the Pacific. (I still have his hat from 1939.) I remember all the things he brought home...a piece of a Japanese Zero, a hand grenade, a bloody Japanese flag.

Another customary activity for children was the movies, mentioned in Chapter Two, where they would see two features, a serial, and a newsreel. It was the newsreel that brought the war to home front children in clear visual images, the war in scenes from air, land, and sea battles uncensored by their parents.

Comic books burst on the scene in a big way. Superman, Batman, and many other characters were bought up to the tune of 20,000,000 copies a month.[13] While most of these characters were male, one female character drew a huge audience: Wonder Woman, who arrived in the comic world in 1941. Attired in red, white, and blue and complete with bullet dodging bracelets and a gold lasso, she battled Axis male villains with the best of them.

In September 1942, the Department of Education created the Victory Corps to involve high school students and prepare them to aid in the war effort at home and in the service. To participate the student must take part in a physical fitness program, enroll in a war-effort class, and volunteer for at least one extracurricular wartime activity. The physical fitness program was deemed important because many of the military inductees were in such poor physical shape.[14]

While Japanese children were removed from most school settings, German and Italian American children remained and could endure taunts and ostracism.

Of course, children's experiences varied by age. Older boys shouldered men's work where needed. Girls became the cook and household cleaner. At 18 girls could join the USO dances but in some communities that was considered daring. The term "Victory Girls" came to mean teen girls who were promiscuous (or appeared so). School enrollment dropped drastically. Part of the reason was that defense factories, short on labor, ignored the age of some teen boys and hired them for factory work. Teenage vandalism became a problem due to urban crowding and general lack of parental supervision due to work schedules.

I Went to the USO – Almost
Some people thought you were a bad girl if you went to the USO
By Mary L. (b. 1930):

I was too young to go into the USO canteen, but I did hang around to see what it was all about. At our USO in Portland it was mostly sailors. The girls who did go said that they were nice. Some were afraid of going overseas and wanted a girl to write to them. My friends, Marie and Claire, would get their names and a bunch of us would write to them. Sometimes we would get letters back from sailors we hadn't even met.

When the war was over, they all went home and the letters slowly stopped coming.[15]

Home front children participated wholeheartedly in scrap drives of every kind, metal, paper, or fat. The Boy and Girl Scouts were often the organizers. Children toiled in Victory Gardens and carried the experience into adulthood. They sold garden seeds and victory stamps and saved for defense bonds and even ran bond drives of their own. They built model airplanes and acted as airplane spotters. They acted as auxiliary fire and police. In short, they rose to the occasion, and they bonded together. (The bond of "war kids" carries over to today.)

They were also, in some cases, more supportive of rationing than their parents. They were disillusioned by the personal dishonesty of adults including close relatives.

Making Rationing Work: "Making Do" Meant Working Together
Lyla (b. 1936):

Prices had been going up fast because of the shortages and then along came rationing. A lot of my memories about those times have to do with all the hitches and squabbles in our big family about rationing and hoarding and swapping rationing stickers. They changed over to tokens and points, and we had to learn about when things expired. Some stores would let you trade one kind of stamp for another. One store in our town was like a bank with lots of tokens, points, stickers, and ration books. Some people said it was illegal. Ads in the newspapers said, "Don't pay above the ceiling price!" I worried when I overheard that one of my aunts had bought meat on the black market because my teacher said you could go to jail.

What I remember are the times when our neighbors and my mother and her sisters would all get together in our kitchen and talk in loud voices about rationing. They argued some about who owed what from last time and who would get extra next time. The stamps, tokens, and checks did not all come on the same day or expire at the same time, and that made things complicated. But they always worked things out, and they always said they could "make do." Which everybody said...[16]

Children on the home front suffered the normal diseases of mumps and measles but were most likely to die from accidents. Accidents were the leading cause of death for children between the ages of 5 and 14.[17]

But home front parents worried much more about polio. Terrified would not be too strong a word to use about how parents felt. There seemed to be no rhyme or reason about how, where, and who polio hit. Even the president of the United States had polio. Accidents were understandable and parents could take positive steps to limit them. Not so with polio. Causes were thrown around for years before its true cause was found. Having tonsils out, swimming in a public pool, going to the movies, chewing a certain gum, flies and other insects were all considered at some point. (Some towns sprayed DDT liberally around garbage cans.) Eventually polio became recognized as a virus.

Polio is an intestinal infection spread by contact with fecal waste. The virus enters the body through the mouth, travels down the digestive tract and is excreted in the stool. Usually the infection is slight, with minor symptoms. In a small number of cases – about one in 100 – the virus invades the central nervous system, destroying the motor neurons that stimulate the muscle fibers to contract. At its worst, polio causes irreversible paralysis, most often in the legs. Most deaths occur when the breathing muscles are immobilized, a condition known as bulbar polio, in which the brain stem is badly damaged.[18]

Parents tried any number of treatments, including those of Sister Kenney who advocated hot blankets, hydrotherapy, and assisted motion in place of splints and frames. Parents were urged to keep children away from public pools, banish flies, and avoid letting children get chilled and overtired. These conditions permeated summer life for most of the war years. A powerful charity arose to combat the disease called The March of Dimes. With President Roosevelt as its spokesman and other celebrities promoting its efforts, the March of Dimes worked hard, especially during the 1944 epidemic. President Roosevelt said the dimes given "were like victory bonds which would be the ammunition to fight the disease." Eventually the Salk vaccine and then the Sabin oral pill would stave off the epidemic, but not until into the 1950s.

The Villain in Our Childhood
C. D. Peterson (b. 1937):

A villain lurked in all our childhoods back then. We talked about the villain, but always in quiet tones. We worried because we didn't know when he might strike or who might be stricken next. We heard he could strike when you took a drink at the water fountain in the Hollis Theater or went swimming in Learned's Pond. Parents couldn't protect you. Nothing could protect you from polio.

One Saturday morning before we went to the movies, a bunch of us went to see a boy who was in an iron lung because he had polio. He lived on a nice tree-lined street near Butterworth Field, where we played baseball. We lined up in silence and walked single file through the house to a quiet, front living room. All I could see was his head lying on a pillow, sticking out from the round cylinder of a machine that made hissing sounds.

He had dark hair, and I didn't know his name, but I said "hello" and he said "hello" back. He was smiling. His mother followed us out and called to us as we walked away, "It was very nice of you boys to come by. It's not contagious, you know. Come back again."

I had never had so much as a cold and couldn't imagine what that boy must have been feeling. I became sad every time I thought about him lying there, trapped in that steel tube, not able to be outside playing baseball.

To address the pitiful cases of pregnant service wives struggling to get by on $50 a month, a groundbreaking effort at maternal and child health was implemented in 1943. Called the Emergency Maternity and Infant Care (EMIC) Act, it provided federal funds for military wives prenatal and childbirth expenses, along with pediatric care for the infant's first year of life. It was the biggest health experiment in history, functioning in all forty-eight states and Alaska and Hawaii. Women had freedom of choice among providers assuming the doctors and hospitals were approved by EMIC, which set standards of care and facility hygiene. Over its lifetime the program authorized more than 1 million maternity cases.

EMIC was resisted by political conservatives and leadership in the American Medical Association, (AMA) who called it socialized medicine. However, the largest survey of physicians overwhelmingly approved of EMIC.[19] There can be no doubt that the children of the million women cared for were able to grow up in better health to become a functioning part of the post-war generation. Nonetheless, EMIC was cancelled in 1946.

Occasionally the war intruded on the home front. A soldier home on leave would flash around a souvenir, perhaps a German Lugar pistol or, if he was a sailor from the Pacific, a Japanese flag with blood red markings. The worst would be gruesome photos.

Not surprisingly, these war time children revered FDR and felt sadness at his passing. He was the leader and the only leader they had known. It seemed to them that every important announcement came from him. He was the person who put every important change in motion. His picture was everywhere, and his deep reassuring voice came to them at home on the radio and in the movie theaters in the newsreels.

One remembrance…
Nick N. (b.1939):

I remember discussing President Roosevelt's death with my elementary school classmates. We were not sure that this might cause our country to lose the war.

Home front children carried on with a great deal of pride. They bonded among themselves and knew they were real contributors to something bigger – the war effort.

Some children, such as those hauled around to military camps and were often intrusive in the lives of their parents who were under emotional strain, never did really bond with their fathers before they shipped out. Those that did, like their mothers, endured high anxiety over separation from their fathers, especially at the last separation before he was shipped overseas. Children often interpreted the goodbye as final and feared they would never see their father again. The scene could be heartbreaking with the child screaming at the vision of the father leaving forever, potentially to be killed overseas. Parents were advised to say goodbye at home, not at the train or bus station.

VJ-Day was a glorious celebration of parades and fireworks for home front children. The end of their fears welled up in tears of joy. Then, as fathers slowly began to return home, the joyous anticipation of their return met with reality: these men were not the same men who had left. In many cases the readjustment was easy but in others the impact of the war had changed the father profoundly. Even when the father returned relatively unharmed, the roles in the family had been changed. The home front child and his family faced a period of, sometimes, difficult readjustment. Just the sound of a male voice in the household could alarm a child. The war had changed everything.

One adult home front child described his memory of the war below.

R. LaRue (b.1937):

The smooth voice of Lowell Thomas comes over the airways. He tells us the news of the day. Most of what he has to say is about the war. The war is not news to me. Like the endless routine of the dairy, it has always been there. It is a part of our lives. We don't feel it; it is far away. But we hear about it constantly. It is like the sound of the ocean when we camp on Laguna Beach. It rumbles in the background without end.

Chapter Seven
The Aliens Among Us

America's modern involvement with the issue of aliens (people living in the US who are not citizens) traces back to the 1940 Alien Registration Act, known as the Smith Act. The act required that each alien living within the US go to their local post office and register their alien status with the government. The registration process included a questionnaire form and a requirement that fingerprints be taken. Each non-citizen would be issued an 'A' number.

This act also made it illegal for anyone in the United States to advocate, abet, or teach the desirability of overthrowing the government.

At the end of 1940 there were approximately 650,000 Italian aliens, 300,000 German aliens and 50,000 Japanese aliens resident in the country. With President Roosevelt's declaration of war on December 8, and his Presidential Proclamations 2525, 2526, and 2527, all German, Italian, and Japanese aliens over the age of 14 were now deemed "enemy aliens" who were required to register and carry certificates of identification.[1]

The president also signed Executive Order 9066, which permitted the Army to exclude not just enemy aliens but "any and all persons" from designated critical areas on the West Coast. Eventually, that same Executive Order led to the "relocation" of all persons of Japanese ancestry, including those who were citizens.

During the 1940s, Americans enjoyed dozens of spy movies, several by famous directors such as Alfred Hitchcock and Fritz Lang. Radio dramas played on the same theme as did propaganda campaigns, the most well-known being "Loose Lips Sink Ships." The idea of a fifth column at work on the home front was never far from mind.

Though not well known, the United States, based on hemispheric security, offered to intern allegedly dangerous enemy aliens living in Latin American countries and even recommended which enemy aliens should be interned. Several Latin American countries accepted the offer and eventually deported more than 6000 individuals of Japanese, German, and Italian ancestry, along with some of their families, to the US for internment.

31,275 enemy aliens were imprisoned in Justice Department camps under the provisions of the Alien Enemies Act during World War II: 10,905 Germans, 16,845 Japanese, and 3278 Italians. In early 1942 thousands more – Germans, Italians and particularly Japanese – were excluded from military zones and interred. 7000 Germans and Italians living on the West Coast were moved inland.[2]

A special interment occurred for 800 Native American Alaskans. In an effort to remove them from a war zone in the Aleutians, the government resettled them in camps 2000 miles away near Juneau. Conditions were by all accounts poor. Their internment ended with the war.

Freedoms were sacrificed in the name of national security. Professions were interrupted or lost, property and businesses were forfeited, and families were torn apart.

The famous among them included Italian opera star, Ezio Pinza, who was detained for months as was Giuseppe DiMaggio, father of baseball's DiMaggio brothers. The elder DiMaggio, a fisherman in California, had failed to register. He became subject to travel restrictions and a curfew. Barred from his family's restaurant, he was even prohibited from boarding his boat and fishing.

By late 1942 however, the government had dropped serious discussion of the mass relocation or detention of unnaturalized Germans or Italians. The move would have been impractical, and officials decided that these enemy aliens did not pose a significant security threat.

The US Attorney General removed Italians from the enemy alien list on Columbus Day, just before the 1942 elections. Critics pointed to Roosevelt's need for the very large Italian American vote for the Democrats.[3]

A Little-Known Case

In August 1944 a ship carrying 983 Jewish refugees who had managed to escape from Germany and get to the allied lines in Italy docked in New York. Because they were here outside immigration quotas, they were taken to a refugee camp in upstate New York. The camp was not unlike an Army stockade.[4]

A Sad Case

The issue of the Japanese in America was quite different. Americans knew and grew up with Italian and German Americans as both citizens and aliens. On the home front people talked about "good Germans" and "good Italians." They looked like any American and were hard to single out, though incidents did occur. The sentiment toward Japanese was never positive but after Pearl Harbor feelings became passionate with hatred.

Most of the 120,000 people of Japanese descent on the mainland lived along the Pacific Coast. The large majority, perhaps 75,000, were full citizens, born and raised in the United States. After the Pearl Harbor attack, however, Americans on the home front became suspicious and fearful of all Japanese. No doubt racial motives played a role in their feelings, particularly on the West Coast where anti-Asian feelings resided ever since Chinese workers arrived to work on the railroads.

American sentiment, fears of sabotage, and news of Japanese victories in the Pacific as well as strong pressure from military leaders led Washington to adopt a drastic policy toward these residents, alien and citizen alike. Virtually all Japanese Americans were forced to leave their homes and property and live in camps for most of the war, although it violated many essential constitutional rights of Japanese Americans. Yet despite this treatment, 33,000 Japanese Americans decided to join the armed services distinguishing themselves as combat interpreters in the Pacific theater and in combat in Europe.

Some of the Japanese were small business owners and many owned their own homes. As they learned that they would be uprooted from their property and belongings, many searched and found non-Japanese neighbors and friends who offered to look after their property for the durations.[5]

The camps were spartan at best, located in arid open areas and surrounded by barbed wire. They were made up of rows of wooden barracks with tar paper roofs which had families crammed into single rooms with steel cots and straw mattresses. Showers and toilet facilities were communal. The lack of privacy broke down family and traditional social norms. Families were referred to by numbers. The Japanese were filled with resentment for their treatment, especially those who were citizens.

1862 Japanese died while in the internment camps. Some died simply from disobeying orders and were killed by guards. The conditions of the internment camps were less than sanitary and caused sickness to be a concern across all ten camps. Extreme weather was also to blame as these camps were not well made. Often the lack of medical care available to prisoners played a role in untreated disease, mental health issues, and stress.[6]

In time the internees were able to construct a more livable environment and a functioning society. They published a newsletter and set up schools. They planted trees and gardens and raised livestock. All internees were to work at paying jobs, some making war supplies. Clothes left from the CCC were distributed. Stoves were installed. Stores were set up with the profits returned to residents.

Americans on the home front did not receive much coverage of the camps. They were treated to news stories portraying the camps as centers with schools and baseball fields. In farming areas the Japanese were permitted to leave the camps and work on farms which were desperate for workers. Internees were credited with saving the sugar beet crop of 1942.[7] Many had been farm workers before their detention. The following is a story that tells of an encounter during that time.

In My Innocence
by R. LaRue (b.1937):

My dad often lets me tag along as he makes his rounds of McMullen Dairy. We live on the dairy in the San Gabriel valley of Southern California. A cacophony of voices fills my memory of these adventures.

"Elgin, Elgin, come have a wee taste," Mr. McMullen's Scottish brogue rings out from his front porch. We climb the stairs and I watch with the curiosity of a four-year-old as the two men share a glass of wine while discussing the status of the dairy and events of the day. I know my dad's name is Eldon and wonder why Mr. McMullen always calls him Elgin.

The house sits back among the trees of McMullen's walnut orchard. I listen curiously to men talking in Spanish as they tend the trees.

We take our leave and walk on out to the cow pasture. Dad opens the gate and we follow the cattle down the lane to the holding pen outside the dairy barn.

The milkers take over and shout the cries of western herdsmen as they sort and move the milk strings into their respective stanchions.

Pete, the dairy operator, comes out of his house. He scoops me up, swings me around, and teases me in his Dutch accented English. He sets me down and he and my dad discuss the condition of the herd. When the cows are locked in their stanchions, Dad straps on his milking stool, sets his bucket under the first cow of his string, and the never-ending task of a dairy farm begins anew. Pete walks me back to our house and hands me over to my mom.

Mom is listening to the Hit Parade on the radio. She sends me out to play while she tends to her household chores. I approach the backyard fence and listen to the singsong voices of the orient coming from the truck farm next door. The people speaking are bent over tending their rows of plants. A pretty little girl about my age leaves the group and crosses the field toward me. She sits down across the fence from me and we play in the dirt.

My parents have tried to explain that these people are Japanese and somehow different. I don't understand. I can see that she is darker than Pete's redheaded granddaughter, Sharon. Her eyes are different. But she is just as fun to play with. We play with few words, but words are not needed. Still, the fence separates us. She does not come to my house and I don't go to hers.

The afternoon wears on. A woman comes and leads the girl away. She smiles and says something that I don't understand. I watch as they walk toward their house. The girl turns and her hand comes up in a small wave. I wave back.

Dad comes home from the afternoon milking. Mom sets out dinner and we eat. After dinner, Dad and I go to the living room while Mom cleans up the kitchen and nurses my baby brother. Dad turns on the radio.

The smooth voice of Lowell Thomas comes over the airways. He tells us the news of the day. Most of what he has to say is about the war. The war is not news to me. Like the endless routine of the dairy, it has always been there. It is a part of our lives. We don't feel it; it is far away. But we hear about it constantly. It is like the sound of the ocean when we camp on Laguna Beach. It rumbles in the background without end.

It is an afternoon like any other. Pete hands me off to Mother. I go out the backdoor to the yard. It is strangely quiet. I can hear the strains of Glen Miller's "Don't Sit Under the Apple Tree" playing from inside the house. But no singsong voices come from the field next door. It is deserted. The plants still stand, green and growing. But no one is taking care of them. The people are gone. I sit by the fence for a while, alone. The death-like silence wraps around me.

I go back in the house and ask my mom where the people have gone. "The Army took them away," she tells me. She tries to explain, but her words are not enough. Not enough to quell the fear welling up inside me. The first chink in my armor of innocence has been opened.

Over the course of the war, and very quietly, the government had been relocating many of the residents to other parts of the country. When the war ended some of the remaining residents were reluctant to leave the camps for fear that the animosity toward them was still strong in California. Governor Earl Warren, later a Supreme Court Chief Justice, made extraordinary efforts to encourage local communities to accept them, many of whom were US citizens.

Much less known was the plight of Korean aliens, many of whom were citizens. Korea had been annexed by Japan and so made Koreans technically Japanese subjects and the US government classified them as Japanese. Yet Koreans had been and were still fighting against Japan through the Korean Nationalist Association.

POWs – A Special Case
More than 400,000 Axis prisoners were shipped to the United States and detained in camps in rural areas across the country. Some 1000 camps and hospitals were built, mainly in the South and Southwest but also in the Great Plains and Midwest. Forty-seven of forty-eight states hosted camps.

Government guidelines mandated placing the compounds away from urban, industrial areas for security purposes, in regions with mild climate to minimize construction costs, and at sites where POWs could alleviate anticipated farm labor shortages.

Other than barbed wire and watchtowers, the camps resembled standard United States or German military training sites with prisoners segregated by service branch and rank. The Geneva Convention of 1929 required the United States to provide living quarters comparable to those of its own military, which meant 40 square feet for enlisted men and 120 square feet for officers. If prisoners had to sleep in tents while their quarters were constructed, so did their guards. The three admirals and forty generals in custody were sent to Camp Clinton and Camp Shelby in Mississippi, where each had his own bungalow with a garden.[8]

POWs subsisted on the same rations as American soldiers. Enlisted men were permitted to buy beer in camp canteens, while officers enjoyed wine. Many POWs wrote home that they ate better in captivity than in the German army with some reporting that they had actually gained weight while in the US. The perks didn't end there. Prisoners could appoint representatives to take part in some decision-making with their jailers or to file complaints with the camp commander. POWs were also provided recreational facilities, religious services and hobby and sports equipment, as well as theaters for plays and movies. Musical instruments, books and magazines were also supplied, as was printing equipment for the production of camp newspapers. Detainees could send and receive letters and packages, subject to approval of military censors.[9]

Tens of thousands of enemy prisoners were put to work in canneries and mills, on farms to harvest wheat or pick asparagus, and just about any other place they were needed and could work with minimum security. In Nebraska, near one camp, passers-by could watch POWs playing soccer while fellow prisoners cheered them on.[10]

German and Italian POWs were given liberty passes to visit nearby towns. Many interacted with the locals; some even became romantically attached to American girls. Ironically, in Southern states, German POWs could eat in segregated diners not open to Black Americans. Italian POWs also had great freedom with passes to dances in town (usually arranged by Italian American groups or Catholic Churches) and even weekends at the home of a sponsor.[11]

The interactions between these prisoners and Americans mostly proved to be friendly and even cordial in some cases. POWs dined with families on occasion and some confessed that they were glad to be prisoners and not getting shot at. Very few attempted to escape and almost all were returned. In Framingham, Massachusetts, Italian POWs from a nearby camp were used to help build a large veteran's hospital. The Italians were excellent masons and were building the chapel. The neighborhood near the site was heavily Italian-American and the not-tightly-supervised POWs would wander away from their work to go into town. They always returned. The following is a report of an encounter.

A POW Remembered
by John B. (b.1935):

I was maybe 10 and playing out front on the sidewalk when this man wearing gray striped clothes with POW stenciled across the front came along. I was told to be afraid of them because they were soldiers who killed people in the war. He looked very sad and I wasn't afraid. I spoke a little Italian and asked him if he ran away from his work. He said he was just taking a walk and was going right back. He said I looked like his little brother in Italy. Then Mrs LaPenta came out and told him to go back to his work and he left. I had to tell the story over and over in the neighborhood. What I'll always remember is how sad he looked.

Of course, as all POWs are required to try, some escaped. A well-known case occurred in Arizona at the Papago Park confinement center. Twenty-five German prisoners led by Captain Jurgen Wattenberg, former commander of the submarine *U-162*, had miraculously managed to tunnel 180 feet under the fences out to a canal and freedom. Bad weather and bad luck doomed most of them to their quick capture, except for Captain Wattenberg. He made his mistake when questioned by a police officer who asked to see his selective service card. The captain said he had left it at home in Glendale.

When further quizzed about which Glendale, he fell afoul of his lack of geography and responded, "Oh, back East." He was quickly reincarcerated. The follow up to the story is unusual. In 1985, Captain Wattenberg and eight of his fellow former prisoners met up for a celebration with several of their former guards.[12]

As soon as the war ended, the US government arranged to repatriate all POWs held on American soil and elsewhere. Many requested permission to stay and even applied for citizenship. Some had been born in the US and already had citizenship but had been conscripted on trips back to Italy or Germany prior to America's entry to the war. A few had managed to escape and survive in the larger American home front. One owned and operated a bookstore for some time before his recapture. On July 23, 1946, one prisoner, an electrician from Heidelberg, was rumored to be the last POW being repatriated. The event was deemed so newsworthy that press photographers had him walk up the ship's gangway several times, some trips in continuous motion for the movie cameras and several trips in stop action for the still photos.[13]

Chapter Eight
Spies and Saboteurs

German Spies and Saboteurs

Well before Pearl Harbor, Germany maintained a spy ring in place in the US. If it hadn't been for the actions of a naturalized German American, the spies could have wreaked untold damage to the US war efforts. His name was William Sebold. On a trip back to Germany in 1939 he was approached by the Nazi spy master, Major Nickolaus Ritter, of the German Secret Service and told he should become a spy for Germany when he returned to the United States. He was informed that if he did not do so his family in Germany might suffer.

So angered, he contacted the American Embassy and began a role as a double agent. Upon his return to the US in 1940 he made contact with the members of the spy ring, led by Frederick "Fritz" Joubert Duquesne. He convinced them that he should be the communication channel between them and German headquarters. The FBI monitored all Sebold's contacts. Once the FBI had enough information to pinpoint the members of the ring and enough evidence for an airtight case, the thirty-three spies were arrested. The *New York Daily News* on June 30, 1941, headlined "Nazi Spy Ring Broken." Nineteen quickly pled guilty. The remaining fourteen spies were brought to trial in Brooklyn and found guilty on September 3, 1941.[1]

The *New York Times* reported on September 4th:

> The trial of fourteen members of an alleged German spy ring was begun yesterday in the United States District Court in Brooklyn before Judge Mortimer W. Byers and a jury of nine men and three women. To the surprise of all, the jury, with two alternates, was completed in three hours and twenty-five minutes.

They were all found guilty by the jury on December 13, 1941, just seven days after Pearl Harbor. No mention was made in the *New York Times*.

Two Midnight Spy Landings

In the middle of the night of June 13, 1942, four men landed on a beach near Amagansett, Long Island, New York, from a German submarine. They wore German uniforms and brought ashore explosives, primers, and incendiaries to sabotage American defense-related production. On June 17, 1942, a similar group landed on Ponte Vedra Beach, near Jacksonville, Florida, equipped for a similar career in industrial disruption, with targets that included Hell Gate bridge in New York, Penn Station in Newark, and three Alcoa Aluminum factories. They also had plans to contaminate New York City's Croton water system.[2]

The raids were prompted by Hitler's anger and frustration over the US supplying European countries with arms, munitions, and other aid. It was said that Hitler himself gave the orders to sabotage US war production and intimidate the American population. Unfortunately for him, the "spies" were not highly trained saboteurs, but merely petty criminals who spoke passable English.

Both groups landed wearing German uniforms to ensure treatment as prisoners of war rather than as spies if they were caught in the act of landing. The Florida group made their way to Jacksonville, then by train to Cincinnati, with two going on to Chicago and the other pair to New York City.

The Long Island group was less fortunate; scarcely had they buried their equipment and uniforms, in fact, one still wore bathing trunks, when a Coast Guardsman patrolling the shore approached. He was unarmed and very suspicion of them, more so when they offered him a bribe to forget they had met. He ostensibly accepted the bribe to lull their fears and promptly reported the incident to his headquarters. However, by the time the search patrol located the spot the saboteurs had reached a railroad station and had taken a train to New York City.

George Dasch, one of the spies, was a naturalized US citizen who came to hate the Nazi regime. He may also have come to believe that their mission was folly. In any event, he eventually talked to one of his compatriots, Ernest Berger, about defecting to the United States. Their plan was to surrender immediately to the FBI. Dasch called the FBI office in New York but the FBI agent did not believe his story, so Dasch and Berger went to Washington D.C. and tried to confess again and again were not believed.

However, the FBI did raid his hotel room and found more than $82,000, enough evidence to arrest and question him.

Dasch was interrogated for eight days. He disclosed the locations of the other men in the sabotage operation including Burger. He revealed that the goals of the sabotage program had been to disrupt war industries and launch a wave of terror by planting explosives in railway stations, department stores, and public places. Armed with the information Dasch provided, the FBI arrested Burger. The three remaining members of the Long Island group were picked up in New York City on June 20. Of the Florida group, two were arrested in New York City on June 23, and two more were arrested in Chicago on June 27.

By June 27, 1942, all eight saboteurs had been arrested without having accomplished one act of destruction. Tried before a military commission, they were found guilty. One was sentenced to life imprisonment, another to thirty years, and six received the death penalty, which was carried out within a few days. The FBI kept secret the circumstances of their arrest prior to the trial of the eight men, including the fact that they did not actually consummate their plans of sabotage.

So shaken was the German intelligence service that no similar sabotage attempt was to ever be taken again. The German naval high command did not wish a valuable submarine to be risked for a sabotage mission.[3]

But by late 1944 Germany was desperate and landed two spies on the rocky coast of Maine. With briefcases full of cash and diamonds the two made their way to New York where they engaged in high living. One of the spies looked up an old friend and actually told him that he was a spy. The old "friend" called the FBI and the two were arrested before accomplishing any part of their mission.[4]

Japanese Spies

For the obvious reason of their appearance, the Japanese did not engage in as much spy activity. There were spies in Hawaii prior to December 7 and they undoubtedly aided in the success of the attack.

Itaru Tachibana, a Japanese spy posing as a student, headed a short-lived spy ring in Los Angeles. Initially the FBI was hesitant to pursue prosecution due to diplomatic issues, but eventually they did and arrested Tachibana at the Olympic Hotel, where he was living. The FBI counted 107 pages of evidence that it had collected from his hotel room.[5]

The State Department, wishing to preserve Japan-United States relations, ultimately asked the United States attorney not to pursue prosecution so long as Tachibana left the country. He boarded the *Nitta Maru* on June 21 in San Francisco and set sail for Japan.

USC PhD student, Pedro Loureiro, wrote that Tachibana's arrest by agents of the FBI "became the most publicized and sensational Japanese espionage case in the United States during 1941."[6]

The Japanese did engage in spy work using ships off the West Coast.

Home Grown Spies and Saboteurs
Home front America was on alert. Well aware that hundreds of thousands of German and Italian Americans lived in the country, fear of espionage and sabotage was rampant.

The port of Boston was closed from dark till dawn. Thousands of Army troops were stationed around key points in New York City. People were banned from the walkway bridges over the East River. Lockers in the subway stations were sealed. "Loose Lips Sink Ships," posters were everywhere. In Chicago, the concern was that the water supply could be poisoned. Residents – and the mayor – demanded that bridges be guarded. A special grand jury was sworn in to deal with cases of espionage and sabotage.

One arms maker offered for sale a military-type rifle complete with sling, bayonet and scabbard – "Immediate Delivery (Tear gas pistols also available)," designed for factory owners to ward off saboteurs.

Taking pictures of anything vaguely related to the war or defense became a tricky proposition. One town banned taking photos anywhere but on one's own property. Weather forecasts became far less detailed to not give away useful information.

I Was a Suspected Saboteur
Donald M. (b. 1937):

It happened when I was about six years old. Our family had enough gas rations to get us to Canada and back, so we all jumped into our

1934 Chrysler Imperial and headed for the border to visit relatives. I had a box of 16 squeaky toys I was bringing as a gift. When we got to the border, the Canadian Mounted Policeman made us stand beside the car while he took every single one of those toys out, squeezed each one of them and put them back. I was plenty frightened.

Although many allegations of sabotage were investigated by the FBI during World War II, not one instance was found of enemy-inspired sabotage. Every suspected act traced to its source was the result of vandalism, pique, resentment, a desire for relief from boredom, the curiosity of children "to see what would happen," or other personal motive.[7]

Chapter Nine

Day to Day Life on the Home Front

Just weeks after Pearl Harbor, Christmas shopping was in full swing. People had agonized feelings about the season. Fear and worry over the war pressed on them but they felt this might be the last real Christmas they would have for some years. Money was plentiful and it was spent freely. Sales of almost everything reached record highs. Retail sales in January 1942 were higher than in any January in history.[1] Much in demand were war toys. Some retailers decided to destroy any goods they had which were made in Japan, (even going so far as to burn a Santa Claus) but the government suggested that did no harm to anyone but US shoppers.

As to be expected, rumors were flying. One rumor had Japanese farmers in California putting poison in the crops they harvested. Others were said to have tainted the seafood they brought to market. No evidence was found for either. Many rumors revolved around anticipated sabotage during the Christmas holidays. None occurred.

In a strange occurrence, the near hysteria of late 1941 settled into an odd mix of overconfidence and complacency. Americans seemed to feel that the war would be a "mop up" affair. The result was a population and, unfortunately, a workforce that was not motivated to put forth full energy. Some blamed the government, especially military censorship, which hid unpleasant war news. Official charts showing the US (projected) capacity likely added to the feeling of certainty of victory. Commentators and politicians openly raged against this lack of fervor. Thankfully, the country awoke as events by mid-1942 unfolded: Bataan falls, the carrier Saratoga is sunk, Japan advances in Burma, MacArthur evacuates the Philippines, Rommel advances in North Africa. The awakening evolved to the determination of purpose we most often associate with home front America.

America, for all its extraordinary exertion at war production, its shortages of foods, gasoline and more, plus the unprecedented disruption of millions of migrating lives, carried on fairly well. Americans enjoyed a kind of unity and collective spirit only enjoyed by people under common threat.

That unity was aided by a powerful and national communications complex of newspapers, magazines, radio, and movies. All Americans anywhere in the country had access to the same news, information and entertainment and much of that for five years was about the war.

What the home front saw and heard, however, was not always the reality of the war. Censorship, voluntary and enforced, prevented coverage of the most gruesome aspects of the war for both security and decency. No doubt communications also carried levels of propaganda for support of the war and assurances of our eventual success. Reports about the war shaded the truth, having the US winning battles in the Philippines. "The newspapers are winning the war for us," said Charles Lindbergh. He and Senators in Washington were warning of a long hard time.

Newspapers were hampered by the shortage of paper but still managed to grow their circulation by 20 percent between 1940 and 1945.[2] The big general interest magazines such as *Life*, *The Saturday Evening Post*, *Colliers*, *Look*, and *Time* expanded their staff and increased their photo-journalism capability to better cover the war. These magazines reached millions of Americans every week as did dozens of Women's magazines. All of these, (and their advertisers) in their own way, kept a focus on the country at war. The Office of War Information (OWI) worked closely with the magazine publishers suggesting stories and providing access to military leaders and facilities to generate positive coverage.

Because more than 80 percent of American families tuned in to radios[3], OWI felt a need to create a special Radio Bureau. The Bureau not only encouraged programing which supported the war effort, it actually wrote and produced spot programs to run in between regular programming. The result was that Americans from coast to coast were reminded daily of their common bond and the need to work toward victory. Early in 1941, FDR appointed Elmer Davis to head up OWI. From this position, Davis helped to whip the home front into a fury over the aggressions of the Nazi's in Europe.

President Roosevelt made great use of the radio for his addresses to the nation's home front. His approval rating was an astounding 84 percent, though his detractors cried about his aim of totalitarian collectivism.[4] Audience measures were not sophisticated, but it is estimated that his audience reached as high as 80 million listeners. He used a common vocabulary, and his delivery was calm and direct. His broadcasts were conversational in tone and became known as "fireside chats." FDR used radio to present his programs and ideas directly to the public, creating an intimate relationship between the president and the American people. The chats became a source of hope and security during the war.

> Early each evening across America households went quiet.
> Children were shushed.
> It was time for the news.

Americans came to recognize the voices of Lowell Thomas, Gabriel Heatter, Edward R Murrow, H. V. Kaltenborn, and Elmer Davis. Among the most famous of these newscasts was Edward R Murrow broadcasting live from London, complete with the sounds of war in the background. These highly professional radio journalists presented Americans on the home front with accurate accounts of the war and of American news in general. The reach of these broadcasts was so broad that it had the effect of giving the entire home front a daily and common update of the progress of the war. That collective experience provided Americans a common basis for conversation and comradeship; that we are all in this together. Radio was an incredibly powerful force for unity.

A special kind of radio programming targeted women: the daytime drama or soap opera, so named because at one time most of the sponsors were soap companies. The programming ran much of the day and as many as sixty came and went during the war years. Among the most popular were *Stella Dallas, Backstage Wife, Bright Horizon, The Brighter Day, Front Page Farrell, The Guiding Light, John's Other Wife, One Man's Family, Portia Faces Life,* and *Young Doctor Malone.* The stories were clearly for women on the home front. Some of the difficulties of the war, such as rationing, were woven in, but most of the programs dealt with women gaining their identity in difficult situations.

Another special type of programing attracted home front children. These were the short, mostly after school adventure programs: *Jack Armstrong – All American Boy*; *Tom Mix*; *Sky King*; *Don Winslow of the Navy*; *Hop Harrigan*; *Gangbusters*; *Tennessee Jed*; *Dick Tracy*; *Terry and the Pirates*; *The Lone Ranger*; *The Green Hornet*; and *Superman*. These programs wove tales of the hero battling Nazi thugs and Japanese villains as well as spies and saboteurs on the home front.

In addition, some of these programs directly involved their young listeners. Those programs offered secret decoder rings (usually for buying a certain cereal) which could decode messages from the show's hero. The messages invariably told the young listener how to be a good American and how he or she could help win the war. Dick Tracy asked children to take a pledge to buy savings stamps and collect scrap. Jack Armstrong encouraged children to write to servicemen. Others touted Victory Gardens. The messages underlying the programs themselves universally focused on patriotism and positive moral behavior.

Evening programming on the radio brought top stars into people's homes. Celebrities like Red Skelton, Bob Hope, Jack Benny, Glen Miller, Fred Allen, Kay Kyser (and his Kollege of Musical Knowledge), Amos and Andy, Edgar Bergen and Charlie McCarthy, Henry Aldrich, and Al Jolsen, who was once cut off the radio for letting the word "hell" slip out on the air as he was warming up his studio audience.

While those were comedy and variety shows, thrillers and dramas held big audiences. The most famous of which were *The Shadow*, *Inner Sanctum* (which opened with a squeaking door), *Suspense*, *Lux Theater*, *Gang Busters*, *The FBI in Peace and War*, *Lights Out*, *The Whistler*, *Boston Blackie*, and *Sam Spade*.

A big development in radio, the music variety show, brought music to the entire nation. A top program of its type was *Your Hit Parade*. Every Saturday evening, the program offered the most popular and bestselling songs of the week. The format involved a presentation of the top 15 songs. A countdown with fanfares led to the top three finalists, with the number one song for the finale.

Popular songs included peppy numbers such as *Don't Sit Under the Apple Tree*, *Boogie Woogie Bugle Boy*, *Praise the Lord and Pass the Ammunition*, and

Coming in on a Wing and a Prayer. The big bands like Glen Miller with swing tunes *In the Mood* and *Pennsylvania 6–5000* were big hits. More memorable, perhaps, were the sentimental titles such as *I'll Be Seeing You, White Christmas, You'll Never Know, Don't Get Around Much Anymore, I'll be Home for Christmas, Long Ago and Far Away,* and *The Last Time I Saw Paris.* Slotted in there was one by Frankie, *The House I Live In.* Hailing the war's end were songs like *When the Lights Go on Again,* and one by Harry James and Kitty Kallen, *It's been a Long, Long Time.*

Another top musical program was the *Camel Caravan* named for its sponsor, Camel cigarettes. The nationally broadcast musical variety show featured the big stars of music such as Benny Goodman, Artie Shaw, and Bob Crosby. It later became the *Camel Comedy Caravan* with performers such as Abbott and Costello, Jimmy Durante, Garry Moore, Jack Carson, and Mel Blanc.

The Camel Caravan and radio brought the home front another music phenomenon. Spawned in places like Nashville and Memphis and now carried all over the country by southern servicemen and migrating war workers, "hillbilly' or country and western music found a home on radio. The music had gained popularity on local radio even before the war, but now it was beamed nationally via a variety format known as "barn dance" typified by the top-rated *Grand Ole Opry* out of station WSM in Nashville.

The touring revue of the *Camel Caravan* featured Opry stars and was created as a morale booster. After the Japanese attack on Pearl Harbor, the troupe kicked into high gear, playing 175 shows in 1942 at 68 military facilities in 32 states. Radio station WSM contributed transcriptions of its radio broadcasts to the Armed Forces Radio Services and the Opry's blend of country music and down-home comedy was played around the world. Yankee servicemen raised on Bing Crosby were exposed to country performers like Roy Acuff, Hank Snow and Pee Wee King.[5]

Top Country-Western (Hillbilly) Hits
Bouquet of Roses – Eddy Arnold
Lovesick Blues – Hank Williams
Walking the Floor Over You – Ernest Tubb
Candy Kisses – George Morgan

Smoke on the Water – Red Foley
New San Antonio Rose – Bob Wills and His Texas Playboys
Pistol Packin' Mama – Bing Crosby and the Andrew Sisters
'Slippin' Around – Margaret Whiting and Jimmy Wakely
Smoke! Smoke! Smoke! (That Cigarette) – Tex Williams
Blue Moon of Kentucky – Bill Monroe

In general, radio programs treated the war as background material, not the central subject. A program might include some special mention or recognition at the close of their broadcast.

Special Communications

Two special forms of communication arose. One involved the placing of photographs of service men and women in lighted store windows. The lights were left on all night. During shopping hours friends and family members stopped to view their loved ones Another form was the "Honor Roll." It was printed in the local newspaper and was also posted on some form of bulletin board placed in a prominent place in town. The Honor Roll listed men and women who had entered the service and reserved a special section, usually in gold, for those who gave their lives. The knowledge that the newspapers and the board provided often led to acts of kindness, sympathy, and help. Here is a simple story of kindness:

J. Kinkade (b.1935):

I grew up in a small town near Dallas. My cousins and I played marbles games back then. We had lots of kinds of marbles; glass, stone, "aggies" of agate, and there was the rare 'steely' that my cousin, Maryann, used for her shooter.

Our games were simple: draw a circle, put in a marble from every player and then take turns trying to knock the other players' marbles out of the circle. She won lots of games with that steely and prized it above anything she owned.

When my father was killed in France, Maryann came to our house for the wake. We were both about 10 years old. As a kid, she didn't know the right things to say, but she gave me her steely. I knew what it meant to her and understood what she was doing.

I won some games with the steely, but never used it against Maryann. Today the steely is in my jewelry box where I see it and think of Maryann's war time kindness often.

Movies

At times it seemed as though everyone on the home front was at the movies. Attendance skyrocketed with an estimated 80 million people per week buying tickets.[6] People had few ways to spend the big money they were making, and gas rationing further reduced their options. Movies were not only convenient and cheap, but they helped relieve the tensions and anxieties of the war.

Hollywood had made a few pre-war movies about the war – Disney's cartoon *In Der Fuhrer's Face* (complete with rude sounds), *A Yank in the RAF*, and *International Squadron* among them – but the flood of films began after Pearl Harbor.

Movie makers turned out thousands of feature films as well as short documentaries, newsreels, and serialized dramas. Some turned out to be classics such as *Citizen Kane, Rebecca, The Lady Eve, Sergeant York*, and *How Green Was My Valley*. The sample of the war-oriented films includes *Casablanca, Bataan, Bombardier, Five Graves to Cairo, Guadalcanal Diary, Thirty Seconds Over Tokyo, Since You Went Away*, and *The Fighting Sullivans*. These films united people on the home front in support of their war efforts and sacrifices. The films also carried a propaganda undertone emphasizing the profound evilness of the Axis and the righteousness of our cause.

The Saturday matinee serials attracted a very loyal audience of youngsters. The top titles included *Superman, Batman, The Green Hornet, Flash Gordon*, and *Nyoka the Jingle Girl*. Young people just had to see if their hero, who was trapped and doomed at the end of last week's episode, would manage to escape. (Even though they knew he/she would.) These serials were the perfect medium to infuse patriotic messages.

The newsreels held a place of special importance which can only be likened to the role television plays today. They were the equivalent of today's evening news, covering current events and showing what the war actually looked and sounded like. The fact that the same graphic reports were seen by millions of home front Americans provided another way for common experience and bonding.

With attendance at all-time highs, Hollywood was able to survive its big problem: the loss of its top stars and directors. Clark Gable, James Stewart, Henry Fonda, Alan Ladd, Robert Taylor, and many other stars left for the military, as did such top directors as John Ford, Frank Capra, William Wyler, George Stevens, and John Huston.

In a case of doing well by doing good, the studios often released hundreds of prints of a new film to first go to Army and Naval stations at home and around the world. Sometimes servicemen wrote home telling about a new movie they had just seen. *Variety*, in April 1943, indicated that this unique form of word-of-mouth promotion generated "considerable pre-selling value," and the advance release setup with the army and navy was "developing into an important merchandising channel."

As might be expected, such a rush to the movies brought a desire to know about the stars in those movies. Movie and gossip magazines such as *Pictoplay, Movie Life, Filmland, Photoplay,* and *Modern Screen* to name just a few, met that need with color photos and breathless prose!

Breathless prose was in order for Errol Flynn and his adventures with young girls, and for Charlie Chaplin and his fascination with, and marriages to, very young women which was revealed in lively courtroom dramas. Another breathtaking tale dealt with Gary Cooper and his entanglement with actress Lupe Velez, "The Mexican Spitfire." Cooper, reportedly quite a Lothario, had decided to break off his relationship with Miss Velez. He went to the train station to leave for New York when Miss Velez appeared on the platform, whipped out a gun and started shooting. She missed and Cooper went on to New York and then to Italy to rendezvous with Countess Dorothy di Frasso.

Celebrity marriages were aplenty during these times: Cary Grant and Barbara Hutton, Humphrey Bogart and Lauren Bacall, and Gloria Vanderbilt and Leopold Stokowski. (Only Bogart/Bacall worked out.)

In addition to commercial features, several Hollywood directors produced documentaries for government and military agencies. Among the best-known of these films, which were designed to explain the war to both servicemen and civilians, are Frank Capra's seven-part series *Why We Fight* (1942–44), John Ford's *The Battle of Midway* (1942), William Wyler's *The Memphis Belle* (1944), and John Huston's *The Battle of San Pietro* (1944). The last three were shot on location and were made especially effective by their immediacy.[7]

Hollywood underwent huge changes during the war. In addition to deciding on what films to produce, they had to adjust to the rules for blackouts by starting their shooting earlier and ending earlier. Some shooting locales such as bridges and tunnels were off limits. Scenes could not show airports, harbors or rail centers. Rationed wood and steel meant they had to reuse old sets. It was widely known that they even had to reuse nails.

Gangsters wielded toy guns, but only on backlots as location shooting was prohibitive. Some films in production had to be edited to reflect the reality of the war. The military comedies of early 1941 gave way to more serious fare.

And the Winner is......

1941

Best Picture: "How Green Was My Valley"
Actor: GARY COOPER in "Sergeant York"
Actress: JOAN FONTAINE in "Suspicion"
Supporting Actor: DONALD CRISP in "How Green Was My Valley"
Supporting Actress: MARY ASTOR in "The Great Lie"
Director: JOHN FORD for "How Green Was My Valley"

1942

Best Picture: "Mrs. Miniver"
Actor: JAMES CAGNEY in "Yankee Doodle Dandy"
Actress: GREER GARSON in "Mrs. Miniver"
Supporting Actor: VAN HEFLIN in "Johnny Eager"
Supporting Actress: TERESA WRIGHT in "Mrs. Miniver"
Director: WILLIAM WYLER for "Mrs. Miniver"

1943

Best Picture: "Casablanca"
Actor: PAUL LUKAS in "Watch on the Rhine"
Actress: JENNIFER JONES in "The Song of Bernadette"
Supporting Actor: CHARLES COBURN in "The More the Merrier"
Supporting Actress: KATINA PAXINOU in "For Whom the Bell Tolls"
Director: MICHAEL CURTIZ for "Casablanca"

1944

Best Picture: "Going my Way"
Actor: BING CROSBY in "Going My Way"
Actress: INGRID BERGMAN in "Gaslight"
Supporting Actor: BARRY FITZGERALD in "Going My Way"
Supporting Actress: ETHEL BARRYMORE in "None But the Lonely Heart"
Director: LEO MCCAREY for "Going My Way"

1945

Best Picture: "The Lost Weekend"
Actor: RAY MILLAND in "The Lost Weekend"
Actress: JOAN CRAWFORD in "Mildred Pierce"
Supporting Actor: JAMES DUNN in "A Tree Grows in Brooklyn"
Supporting Actress: ANNE REVERE in "National Velvet"
Director: BILLY WILDER for "The Lost Weekend"

Life was hectic. The longing to live life to the fullest during wartime was a new phenomenon on the American home front. Combine that "live for today" temperament with the fact that Americans had more money to spend than they had in years and far fewer places to spend it and you have a recipe for a consumer explosion. Just about anything that was for sale got sold, often depleting the available stock. The hectic life led to a dramatic increase in automobile accidents. 1941 saw an all-time high in auto deaths.

The era also saw a tremendous wartime boom in nightclubs and restaurants, in live music and dancing, spectator sports, and in various other forms of entertainment. While entertaining the troops had its place, entertaining the workers who stoked the war machine was crucial as well.

Dancing was an easy way to relax, socialize, and be entertained. Most nightclubs offered dancing to big swing bands. USO centers and some restaurants also offered dancing often from jukeboxes. Even some factories set aside space for employees to dance during breaks. The war years are most often known as the time of jitterbugging. While that may be true, the Latin influence mentioned earlier brought the rhumba and the samba, with songs like Brazil and Amor.

For Americans who lived near New York City, or who had gas rations to get there, Broadway during the war years offered some of the biggest hits of all time: *A Bell for Adano*; *Carousel*; *Dark of the Moon*; *Harvey*; *I Remember Mama*; *Life with Father*; *Oklahoma!*; *On the Town*; *Song of Norway*; and *The Glass Menagerie*. The problem was finding a seat even at the top ticket price for *Carousel* – $6.00!

The war years were also the years of the big bands, girl bands, the Andrew Sisters and a true phenomenon – Frank Sinatra. This skinny crooner from New Jersey captivated the female audience, especially the young girls who typically wore the fashion of the day and were nicknamed "bobby soxers." It's doubtful that any American on the home front could avoid Frank Sinatra either on the radio, in the fan magazines or in the newspapers where he often showed up in a fracas at some night spot.

Sports
Sports suffered more than other forms of entertainment and distraction. In the United States the major spectator sports were boxing, horse-racing, major-league baseball, and professional and college football. Professional basketball was still in its infancy.

Boxing was very popular and Joe Louis, who became the heavy-weight champion, was a big part of the reason. A poor Black man from Alabama who swore he would never throw a fight because, "I want to fight honest so that the next colored boy can get the same break I got. If I 'cut the fool' I'll let my people down." His fights drew radio audiences second only to

FDR's addresses. He served honorably in the Army. Other top boxers also served and so boxing titles were frozen during the war which opened up the sport for others, including more Black boxers.

Horse racing survived until it was banned in 1945 when the Office of War Mobilization in Washington viewed it as a waste of valuable resources. The Board felt that men that could be serving in the war instead were working in track operations. In addition, gas and tire rubber was being consumed heavily in transporting bettors and horses to tracks.

College football and its bowl games had always occupied American's attention all through the Fall and up to New Year. Like professional teams, college teams lost players to the armed services. (There was no deferment for college.) The anomaly here was that two college teams were composed of players already in the services: Navy from its Naval Academy and Army from West Point. They dominated the college field with Army posting one of the best teams in college history.

Military training bases also fielded college-level teams, but the rosters changed frequently, and they lacked the tradition of college sports.

The Rose Bowl was normally played in Pasadena, California, and continued to be played there throughout the war except for January 1942, shortly after Pearl Harbor, when it was moved to Durham, North Carolina.

Two other bowl games were played far from the home front. The Spaghetti Bowl was played between teams from the Fifth Army and the Twelfth Air Force in Florence, Italy, on New Year's Day 1945. The game was won by the Army 20–0.

The other such bowl game had fewer festivities. The Mosquito Bowl was played on Christmas Eve 1944 between two regiments of Marines on Guadalcanal. The Marines were training for the invasion of Okinawa where they would face the bloodiest fighting in the Pacific. The game ended in a scoreless tie.

Pro football, like everything else, was hit by the draft taking away key players. Nonetheless, with a reduced eight team roster, the National Football League, (NFL) had banner attendance during the war years.

Baseball was by far the most watched. The question arose at the start of the war about whether baseball should be banned for the duration. Here is what President Roosevelt thought about it:

Baseball provides a recreation which does not last over two hours or two hours and a half, and which can be got for very little cost. If 300 teams use 5,000 or 6,000 players, these players are a definite recreational asset to at least 20,000,000 of their fellow citizens – and that in my judgement is thoroughly worthwhile.

Among the 500 or so major leaguers who entered the services were some of the biggest names in the sport: Ted Williams, Bob Feller, Stan Musial, Joe DiMaggio, Warren Spahn, Yogi Berra, Pee Wee Reese, Phil Rizzutto, and Hank Greenberg.

The players left were unfit for drafting because of either age or disability so the level of play was not top notch. Even using these players some teams could not fill a full roster and merged their team with another as did Pittsburgh and Philadelphia. One fill-in player who drew a lot of fan attention was Pete Gray of the St. Louis Browns. He wasn't a great hitter, though he could bunt, but he was a fine outfielder made all the more special because he had only one arm. He certainly helped attendance and he stood as an inspiration to returning disabled servicemen about overcoming disability.

In baseball as in defense plants, women stepped up to take the place of men. In 1943, Philip K. Wrigley, the owner of the Chicago Cubs, formed the All-American Girls' Professional Baseball League. The league consisted of fifteen Midwestern teams and lasted until 1954.

The women's game underwent some changes. The size of the ball was altered to that of a regulation softball and the pitcher's mound was moved to 40' from home plate. The size of the field shrank, as well, with the distance between bases shortened to 65 feet as opposed to the standard 90 feet.

Like many of the industries that women took over as men went to war, when the war was over and the men started to return home to their jobs, women were pushed out, many to their previous role as housewives. But, of all the sports, only baseball advanced women's athletics.

War-time baseball cannot be discussed without mentioning the special performances of two legendary players during the 1941 season. Joe DiMaggio of the New York Yankees hit in 56 consecutive games, a record that still stands. Ted Williams of the Boston Red Sox batted for an average of 406, also a record that still stands. (Both records are likely to stand for the foreseeable future due to changes in the game of baseball.)

Sports entered the American home front in another way. The draft revealed a nation of physically unfit Americans; the nation was flabby. The response, led by the Office of Civil Defense, was a nationwide exercise program called Hale America, and corralled local CD officials to join up. The program was promoted across the country with a full media push, including personal appearances by professional sports stars. Contests, matches, meets, and tournaments of all kinds were held. Schools and colleges added physical exercise to their curricula. Scouts introduced a fitness merit badge.

The physical fitness thrust expanded to include nutrition which was also seen to be a big factor in draftee rejection.

Spectacles and Big Events

In another paradox, in this pre-war time of contradictions, Americans on the home front were presented with two huge spectacles.

San Francisco's Golden Gate International Exposition celebrated the recent completion of two landmark bridges – the San Francisco–Oakland Bay Bridge, and the Golden Gate Bridge.

The entertainment zone featured mechanical rides and numerous shows by such performers as Count Basie, Bing Crosby, Eddie Duchin, Benny Goodman, and the Folies Bergere from Paris. Esther Williams swam in Billy Rose's Aquacade. Sally Rand, the fan dancer, performed in her Nude Ranch. Military bands and roaming Mexican folk musicians played amid camels and rickshaws giving tourists rides.

Despite predictions of a robust tourist season, the fair was a financial disaster, losing more than $4,000,000 in 1939. A court order forestalled bankruptcy and permitted a second season. The fair closed in the red in September 1940, despite 17 million visitors.[8]

The 1939–40 New York World's Fair was held at Flushing Meadows, Corona Park in Queens, New York. It was an expensive extravaganza. Many countries around the world participated, and more than 44 million people attended its exhibits in two seasons. Its theme was based on the future, with an opening slogan of "Dawn of a New Day," and it offered a look at "the world of tomorrow."

The fair was open for two seasons, from April to October each year The first year piled up financial losses and the fair changed its emphasis from educating about the future – television was demonstrated at one point broadcasting a speech by FDR – to emphasizing traditional America and providing more amusement and entertainment opportunities. The fair attracted more than 45 million visitors and generated roughly $48 million in revenue. But, since the Fair Corporation had invested 67 million dollars (in addition to nearly a hundred million dollars from other sources), it was a financial failure, and the corporation declared bankruptcy.[9]

Big Events

It seems that some officials in America were looking beyond the rationing of gas and rubber. In 1940 fortunate Americans could drive on the Arroyo Seco Parkway, the first "freeway." It connected downtown Los Angeles with Pasadena, California.

In the East, in 1940, those with gas and tires could drive on the first section of the Pennsylvania Turnpike, the country's first long-distance controlled-access highway that opened between Irwin and Carlisle.

As they drove, they might have seen the billboard advertising campaign for a shaving cream in a series of five small rhyming billboards about 100 yards apart:

> Don't stick your elbow,
> Out so far.
> It may go home,
> In another car.
> *Burma Shave*

> Don't lose your head,
> To gain a minute.
> You need your head,
> Your brains are in it.
> *Burma Shave*

Drove to long,
Driver snoozing.
What happened next,
Is not amusing.
Burma Shave

Around the curve.
Lickety-Split.
Beautiful car,
Wasn't it.
Burma Shave

At intersections,
Look both ways.
Harps sound nice,
But they're hard to play.
Burma Shave

Passing school zone,
Take it slow.
Let out little,
Shavers grow.
Burma Shave

A fire at the Rhythm Night Club in Natchez, Mississippi killed 209 people on April 23 1940. Bandleader, Walter Barnes, and nine members of his band were among the victims. The band was credited with attempting to calm the crowd and Barnes was praised as a hero for leading the song "Marie" by Irving Berlin as the fire raged.[10]

Another nightclub tragedy gripped the attention of all Americans on the home front. On Thanksgiving weekend in 1942, in the Coconut Grove nightclub in Boston, crepe decorations caught flame and in 15 minutes, 463 people died, many crushed in the scrum to get through revolving doors.

A circus fire claimed 167 lives in Hartford Connecticut on July 6, 1944, when the big top tent of the Ringling Brothers circus was set on fire by an arsonist. The tent had been coated with paraffin thinned with gasoline to make it waterproof.

In July 1945, less than a month before Japan's surrender, a B25 flying in fog, crashed into the Empire State building between the seventy-eighth and seventy-ninth floors killing ten office employees and the crew of three. Photos of the wreckage filled newspapers, magazines, and movie newsreels.

The cost of World War II far exceeded federal tax revenues. To address the deficit the Revenue Act of 1942 created the Victory Tax, the broadest and most progressive tax in American history. To ease taxpayers' burden of paying a lump sum, and to create a regular flow of revenue into the Treasury, the government required employers to withhold money from employees' paychecks. By the end of the war in 1945, about 90 percent of American workers submitted income tax forms.

The stock market had its own reaction to these events. After gut wrenching lows in the Depression, it began a slow rise in 1933 up to 1937 where it hit a high before entering a severe but short-lived recession. Americans would not see those highs again until after the war. The market then started a slide, hitting a low in March 1938 when Hitler annexed Austria. The next sharp low came in April 1940 when Hitler entered Paris. The market then drifted downward, ignoring Pearl Harbor, until it hit bottom in the Spring of 1942. Then, as the war began to turn in the favor of the Allies, the market began an up-trend, strongly bolstered by D-Day success, which continued to the end of the war and beyond.

Leisure
There were just so many football games, baseball games, movies and shows to see or nightclubs to visit and dance in. Even with a resurgence of roller skating, Americans spent much of their time at home. They read. They listened to the radio and phonograph records, now available for less than a dollar in five and ten cent stores. They played cards and board games like Monopoly, Scrabble, Life, checkers, chess, backgammon, Chinese checkers, and dominoes. The sales of these amusements skyrocketed.

A fad was resurrected: the Ouija board. It was played by resting your fingers lightly on a palm sized triangular piece and letting the piece "guide" you to letters painted on the edge of the Ouija board. Ask the piece a question and the piece would guide you and spell out an answer.

Home front children played with Tinker Toys, Erector Sets, Lincoln Logs, electric or wind-up trains, Army figures, and model airplane kits. Outdoors, children played at war games, had pedal cars, Radio Flyer wagons, and – if parents approved – Daisy Red Ryder air rifles.

The sale of books broke records each year of the war while Book-of-the-Month Club membership doubled. The newly introduced paperback book used less paper and was cheaper and further bolstered sales. The books of the war years reflected the times with a shift from fiction to non-fiction. Nonetheless, some great fiction was published: *A Bell for Adano*, *The Heart is a Lonely Hunter*, *A Tree Grows in Brooklyn*; and *The Little Prince* as examples. But it was non-fiction that dominated the market.

John Steinbeck's *The Moon is Down*, a story of German occupiers in Norway, boiled up controversy and criticism about the author's perceived sympathetic treatment of the occupiers.

One religious themed book, *The Robe*, and one racy novel, *Forever Amber*, were both best sellers.

The humorous reporting of a 'regular guy' who joins the Army, *See Here, Private Hargrove*, was an enormous bestseller. As the war wore on more serious war themed books emerged such as *Guadalcanal Diary* and *They Were Expendable*. Other firsthand accounts that sold well were Ernie Pyle's *Here is Your War*, and Bill Mauldin's *Up Front*, which contained several of his now famous cartoons.

Curiously, at the height of the war in 1943, a book not about the war, but about what would come after became the fastest home front seller of all, selling 1,000,000 copies in less than 60 days: *One World* by Wendell Wilkie. He had been a candidate for president in 1940, and this was his account of his trip around the world which molded his hopes for post war collaboration among nations. The Armed Services Edition program produced popular paperback books that were wider than they were high for fitting into pockets. Over the course of the war around 100,000,000 copies were distributed free to service men and women.[11]

Politics

And of course, there were discussions of politics to fill the hours. President Roosevelt enjoyed enormous popularity during the war years. His political enemies despised him and hurled the epithet "that man" around when discussing him. FDR enjoyed Democratic majorities in both the House and the Senate, but Southern, more conservative, Democrats could – and did – often join in voting with Republican opposition requiring extraordinary political dexterity on FDR's part to move his programs forward.

Throughout the 1930s the Democratic Party dominated politics in the South. Party leaders upheld White supremacy and segregationist Jim Crow laws denying Black citizens their rights. The party led the Confederacy through the Civil War and subsequently controlled what was dubbed "the solid South." FDR counted on the South's support to win the 1932 election. He took no steps to distance himself from their policies of White supremacy. Eleanor endeared herself to Black communities, however, by supporting Marion Anderson, a Black opera star, and her controversial recital at the Lincoln Memorial.

In building support for the war in Europe, FDR formed a bipartisan alliance with moderate Republicans, including Henry Stimson, whom he appointed Secretary of War in 1940. FDR and Stimson declined to desegregate the armed services, rejecting pleas from the NAACP.

However, in June 1941, A. Philip Randolph, President of the Black Sleeping Car Porters union, urged the administration to end the segregation of workers in the vast defense industry. He threatened a huge march on Washington DC. Four days before the march, FDR agreed to do so. What followed was a watershed moment in civil rights history. For the first time, the machinery of the federal government was put to work on ending racial discrimination in employment. FDR signed an executive order creating the Committee on Fair Employment Practices (FEPC) charged with investigating complaints of discrimination in defense plants and taking "appropriate steps to redress grievances which it finds to be valid."

Soon, the FEPC began issuing orders to federal contractors requiring them to hire Black workers. Black workers and their champions were thrilled, but Southern Democrats railed against the FEPC, warning that its attacks on segregation would cause violence and lead southerners to abandon the Democratic Party.

As the 1944 presidential election drew closer, the Democrats sorted out their choice for a running mate for the president. They settled on Missouri senator, Harry S. Truman. Truman was making a name for himself leading the special committee investigating waste and fraud in defense contracting. Dubbed "the mousey-looking little man from Missouri" by *Time* magazine, he was also faithful to the party line and a strong campaigner.

The Republicans, on the other hand, were engaged in internal conflict over who should be the nominee. Wendell Willkie had alienated the conservative wing with his "one world" outlook. The traditional Midwestern block had Ohio Governor, John Bricker, and Senator Robert Taft, to put forward. Bricker's very aggressive style against the internationalists set him up as the vice-presidential choice.

In New York, Thomas Dewey was winning accolades as New York District Attorney and then as Governor. He campaigned well and was poised to gain the presidential nomination when a profound event slowed everything down. Southern Democratic states had always held that maintaining segregated primaries was legal because political parties were private organizations and free to set their own rules. Challenged in Texas, the Supreme Court (by an 8 to 1 vote) ruled that such primaries were unconstitutional. The Democratic party, already devolving into a racial divide, continued its spiral.

Dewy did win the nomination and with Bricker at his side went forth to battle FDR and his new running mate, Harry S. Truman.

In a harbinger of modern times, the 1944 election season featured an election initiative in Massachusetts that would allow doctors to disseminate birth control information. It went down to defeat under the predominantly Democratic Catholic majority.

During campaign season country music super star, Roy Acuff, was a sometimes candidate for President and Governor. Pushed by his supporters, he finally told them that while he was a good guitar picker, he didn't think he had it to be Governor.

One event during the presidential campaign captured a moment of absurdity. Someone had begun a rumor that the President's dog, Fala, had been left behind in Alaska and a US Navy destroyer was sent, at great expense, to fetch the dog back to Washington. His opponents and their press seized on the issue, though false, and the president addressed it in a radio talk that gave weary Americans on the home front a good reason to laugh.

> "These Republican leaders have not been content with attacks on me, or my wife, or on my sons. No, not content with that, now they include my little dog, Fala. Well, of course, I don't resent attacks, and my family doesn't resent attacks, but Fala does resent them."

Columnist, Ray Clapper, described the war time 77th Congress as "composed of a collection of two-cent politicians who could serve well enough in in simpler days. But the ignorance and provincialism of Congress render it incapable of meeting the needs of modern government… What you hear in Congress is 99 percent tripe, ignorance, and demagoguery and not to be relied upon." Clapper continued to be dismayed at Congress' selfish and destructive conduct when Congress voted itself a very generous pension. A whopping 84 percent of Americans opposed the pension![12]

However, the record of the 77th is one of extraordinary work. It convened in 700 out of 730 possible days and dealt with some of the most critical issues in US history. It's ironic that with the Allied victories in November of 1942, if the election was held just one month later, in December, the 77th would have been viewed as a great success.[13]

None the less, the American home front was making it through.

The new conservative-minded coalition in Congress managed to dismantle several large liberal initiatives born in the Depression, including three that enjoyed a degree of public popularity: The Works Progress Administration, (WPA), the Civilian Conservation Corps, (CCC) and National Youth Administration (NYA). Meanwhile the liberal wing of the Democratic party was working to pass a bill ensuring that servicemen stationed abroad would be able to vote – all 10 million servicemen, Black and White – using a special ballot. Southern Democrats were, of course, opposed. They felt voting laws were the province of states' rights. There were threats by the southerners that they would leave the democratic party.

The bitter debate had FDR suffering deteriorating health, fighting WWII abroad while re-fighting the Civil War at home. After months of wrangling, a compromise was reached, and states could determine for themselves whether to approve the use of those soldier ballots. With the full support of labor, FDR easily won the election of 1944, and there is no evidence the soldier vote had any impact.

Southern Democrats remained unmoved. The leadership of the Democratic Party, however, had made its decision: they would not countenance White supremacy and injustice for Black citizens.

People refer to the events by which the two parties traded places as the "Roosevelt Inversion," because it began when the Democratic president embraced civil rights, causing civil rights supporters to shift into the Democratic Party and segregationists to shift into the Republican Party, ironically, the party of Lincoln. Americans on the home front in 1944 were worrying more about their loved ones overseas and the importance of the struggle wasn't fully realized. Begun in the crucible of war, the story is long forgotten, and misunderstood, but the outcome is starkly visible when looking at America's political map today.

Propaganda
From the Latin word *propagare*, meaning "to spread" or "to propagate."

Propaganda is the dissemination of information – facts, images, arguments, rumors, half-truths, or outright lies – to influence public opinion.

> "The principal battleground of the war is not the South Pacific. It is not the Middle East. It is not England, or Norway, or the Russian Steppes. It is American opinion."
> – Archibald MacLeish, Director of the Office of Facts and Figures

In June of 1942, FDR created the Office of Wartime Information (OWI) to counter the confusion resulting from the huge flow of information about the war, and to mobilize support for the country's war effort. Almost at once there were concerns in Congress that the OWI might come to resemble the Nazi propaganda machine. FDR appointed Elmer Davis, a respected newsman, to head the effort. The Government launched an aggressive propaganda campaign with clearly articulated objectives to galvanize public support, and it recruited some of the nation's foremost intellectuals, artists, and filmmakers to wage the war on that front. Persuading the American home front became a wartime industry, almost as important as the manufacturing of bullets and planes.

Two divisions were created: overseas and domestic. The overseas division earned praise from Congress, but Congress expressed concern that the domestic division might become too political or overtly manipulative in the model of Nazi propaganda.

The domestic division had bureaus for motion pictures, magazines, and radio. The Radio Bureau itself produced several series and reviewed the scripts for others. The magazine bureau published *The Magazine War Guide* which listed suggested topics for articles. It offered guidelines such as setting fiction in war plant locations. It suggested showing minorities, women and men working together, stressing the interdependence of the war effort. It published ration-aware recipes, and other hints.

The Bureau of Motion Pictures (BMP) worked very closely with the movie studios. BMP reviewed scripts and suggested edits which would show the better aspects of American life. Elmer Davis, the head of the OWI, said that "The easiest way to inject a propaganda idea into most people's minds is to let it go through the medium of an entertainment picture when they do not realize they're being propagandized."[14]

A much-praised movie series developed by Frank Capra, "Why We Fight," was intended not for the public but for men in the services who might not be certain of the reasons for the war. WWI had left a bad residue with many, including the military.

During its existence OWI and Davis were in persistent conflict with the military. OWI wanted to be more truthful with the American home front while the military wanted secrecy and censorship. (Of course, OWI did censor what it considered sensitive information.) OWI also butted heads with advertising agencies and advertisers who OWI felt were not depicting realistic images and were also encouraging needless consumption. Advertisers feared they could lose the tax deductibility of advertising expenses and so were more or less cooperative.

The government had many objectives for its propaganda. Its major stated aim was to rally support for FDR's four freedoms: freedom of speech, freedom of worship, freedom from want, and freedom from fear, further justifying the country's entry into the war and the sacrifices Americans were obliged to make.

Other aims included:

- convincing women to join the work force,
- urging the public to honor rationing rules,
- rallying people to buy bonds,
- supporting scrap drives and other conservation measures,
- encouraging the races to work together,
- pressing Americans to be vigilant for home front spies and sabotage,
- calling for the achievement of (or exceeding) production goals,
- inspiring military recruiting,
- buoying home front spirits,
- depicting the enemy as fearsome and evil

(Some were concerned that this last aim could foster racial hatred. Some older Americans to this day will not buy a Japanese car.)

While adults were certainly the prime target of OWI's propaganda efforts, children were the target of specialized messages. A "Schools at War" program urged children to join in planting Victory Gardens and conducting scrap drives. Children were told to ask their principal about joining. Dr. Seuss introduced children to *Private Snafu*. Disney produced an award-winning Donald Duck cartoon *Der Fuehrer's Face*, complete with rude noises. Disney also produced *Education for Death: The Making of a Nazi*, an animated propaganda short film showing how a young German boy is indoctrinated and corrupted into conforming with the Nazi social mindset.

The *Wartime Handbook for Young Americans*, an OWI publication for children, contained similar urgings and pictured children in adult roles, as did many of the posters aimed at children.

Posters were just one way propaganda was deployed. OWI employed movies, advertising, radio, mail, speeches, songs, and flyers, but nothing compared to posters for reach and coverage. *Rosie the Riveter* stands as the most iconic example of a poster even though there were two versions of her. *Loose Lips Sink Ships*, *Uncle Sam Wants You*, *Remember Pearl Harbor*, and *When You Ride Alone You Ride with Hitler* are among the more memorable poster slogans.

Even with grudging recognition of its success, Congress remained unhappy with OWI's more than frequent depiction of FDR in the role of the great man and war time leader. Consequently, it cut the program's budget in 1943 and ended the program completely and abruptly one month after Japan surrendered.

Communism
Americans on the home front were subject to whiplash when it came to communism and the USSR. The US was cool to the dictatorship of Josef Stalin and its aggressions, particularly with Finland. Despite pressures from both conservatives and liberals to sever relations with the USSR, FDR chose to implement trading restrictions while publicly condemning the Soviet Union as a "dictatorship as absolute as any other dictatorship in the world." But the USSR appeared firmly in the camp of those opposing Hitler, and Roosevelt never lost sight of the fact that Nazi Germany, not the Soviet Union, posed the greatest threat to world peace. To defeat that threat, Roosevelt confided that he "would hold hands with the devil" if necessary.[15]

The USSR did indeed appear to be the devil when, in August of 1939, it signed a ten-year non-aggression pact with Germany. But FDR persisted. Beginning in July of 1940, a series of negotiations took place in Washington between Under-Secretary of State, Sumner Welles, and Soviet Ambassador, Constantine Oumansky. Welles refused to accede to Soviet demands that the United States recognize the changed borders of the Soviet Union after the Soviet seizure of territory in Finland, Poland, and Romania and the reincorporation of the Baltic Republics in August 1940, but the US Government did lift the embargo in January 1941.

Furthermore, in March of 1941, Welles warned Oumansky of a future Nazi attack against the Soviet Union. Finally, during the Congressional debate concerning the passage of the Lend-Lease bill in early 1941, Roosevelt blocked attempts to exclude the Soviet Union from receiving US assistance.

Earlier, a temporary linkage occurred earlier between Black and communist factions. In the 1930s, Black union members were making their first attempts at organizing themselves to obtain some economic justice. The Southern Tenant Farmers Union (STFU) was an alliance of Black and White tenant farmers organized to resist evictions, foreclosures, and wage cuts. STFU had 75,000 members, one third of whom were Black farmers. The Communist Party of the USA (CPUSA) aided the STFU in its efforts and won more support for its legal aid in cases of injustice against Black farmers. The front-page case which held the attention of Americans on the home front involved the 1931 "Scottsboro Boys." Nine young Black men were accused of raping two White girls while riding in a box car. Eight of the men were sentenced to death. After three Supreme Court appeals the death penalties were overturned. What appeared to be a possible partnership came to an end when the Soviet Union signed its pact with Germany in 1939.[16]

Anti-communist purges, many centered around unions, were flourishing. The American home front was on board with the anti-communist fervor. A major reinforcing event was a strike at North American Aviation, a large defense contractor in California, in early 1941. One of the union executives was an admitted communist and that fired up enough anger that FDR ordered the Army to break the strike, which they did with fixed bayonets and a display of machine guns. Even the pro-union left applauded.

But just a few weeks later Hitler committed what many consider the greatest military blunder of all time: he invaded the USSR opening up a second front. Abruptly the USSR was an ally! FDR had (wisely) preserved Lend-Lease for the Soviet Union and soon food and arms were on their way. Overnight our policies changed. *Life* magazine treated readers on the American home front with a complete and laudatory issue on the Soviet Union. It stressed the positive nature of the Russian people and praised their armed forces – all without mentioning communism.

Communists on the home front made their own flip-flop. They went from vocal isolationists to full-throated support of the war against the Nazis. Earl Browder, Chairman of the Communist Political Association (the Communist Party of the USA having been disbanded), who had once denounced FDR on the floor at Madison Square Garden, now praised him as a great leader.

It was widely assumed that with the US and the communist Soviet Union now linked against Hitler, that strikes would cease. The opposite occurred. The incidence of strikes in defense plants rose by 50 percent and now they could not be blamed on a communist conspiracy. In fact, no one was more adamantly opposed to strikes at this point than the Communist newspaper the *Daily Worker*![17]

The 1944 election, in which the Republicans put forth New York's Thomas Dewey, became an occasion to revive the old fears of communist subversion. The campaign was rife with accusations that FDR was, if not a communist, soft on communism. (The "soft on communism" charge became a staple of political campaigns for the next half century.)

Religion

Americans on the home front turned to religion for comfort and understanding. This is an article from long-gone *Click Magazine*, December 1942, page 20:

> **America Goes Back to Church**
> War Weary Mankind finds Comfort in the Faith of Our Fathers.
> "Two years ago most churches were considered fortunate if 45 people attended the morning service. Today, devout worshipers fill the pews morning and night – in Sunday school, formal church services, and in old fashioned camp meetings, men and women are, in the words of Paul, Taking the shield of faith, the helmet of salvation, and the sword of the spirit."[18]

The same magazine reported a renewed interest in religion in the armed services.

Most American Christians supported the war. But some objected to military service on religious grounds. They registered as conscientious objectors with their local draft boards. Some served in the military as noncombatant medics or chaplains.[19]

Not all religious activity was positive. A number of fundamentalist lay preachers could be heard on Sundays on the radio preaching racial hatred. One-time presidential candidate, Father Coughlin, preached his antisemitic and anti-negro tracts until his show was pulled by the Catholic church in 1942.

Many members of the clergy felt that they had been duped by propaganda in WWI and walked a fine line supporting US efforts in WWII. Most were anti-interventionists until Pearl Harbor, but then rallied their support. American clergy was confident that the Allied cause was right, and that the enemy was wrong. God would therefore vindicate them.

Their support, however, had some reservation and ambivalence. Religious organizations wanted to maintain the principles of humanitarianism and justice. For example, they expressed their objection to segregation in the military and supported the Double V campaign. They also objected to the internment of the Japanese. (They established ministries in the internment camps.) They ministered to the spiritual needs of the nation and supported the war effort even though they sometimes offered criticism. It was a cautious patriotism. Religious groups also sponsored some 10,000 military chaplains and initiated various ministries in and around military bases.

A Young Life Gets Direction
I Was Inspired on a Sunday Morning
Dave P. (b. 1934):

In 1944 I was 10 years old. One Sunday morning I was at home in Leaksville, North Carolina – now called by the nicer name Eden – waiting for my sister and brother to walk to Sunday school. The skies were clear but for a few puffy white clouds. From out of nowhere roared a Lockheed Lightening P-38 at chimney top level! It must have sent a million volts up my spine. The war was on and I said to myself, "I'm going to do that someday." Well, I did, but that's another story.

Some events were simple and from the heart, like the following story.

Home Front Memories From the Heartland
Patty H. (b. 1928):

Those times are very clear to me as a teenager in Mason City, Iowa. My father had two big maps in the basement: one for the European theater and one for the Pacific. Almost every night he would mark on the maps to keep track of the action.

Every other Saturday my mother would bake bread and my uncle would bring a live chicken from his farm. I didn't enjoy getting the chicken ready for the table, but it sure tasted good. We couldn't get much beef – it was rationed. Potatoes were plentiful but I tired of potato soup. We did get an occasional fish if someone got lucky! I often had to stand in line to buy rationed food. I especially remember standing in line for mayonnaise, of all things.

All the women sewed not just because they wanted to, but because there wasn't much for sale. I didn't have a store-bought dress until I was 16. I knitted warm caps for several years during the war. I was never sure where they went. As a high school girl, I wanted nice shoes – leather shoes – which were very hard to come by. I don't know if how I got those leather shoes was allowed. Here's the story. We didn't have a car, but we had a gas ration. Our neighbor had a car and wanted our gas ration which we traded for his shoe ration. (I don't think I'll get arrested at this late date.)

Those leather shoes were really important to me on Friday nights, the night the Minneapolis and St. Louis railroad train came through town. The train came down from Minneapolis carrying men (boys) going down to St. Louis to enlist. When the train stopped around 8p.m. in Mason City the townspeople would set up tables on the platform and load the tables up with homemade cookies and donuts along with coffee and soft drinks, compliments of our local Piggly Wiggly. The boys would get off the train and enjoy the snacks. My mother sometimes worried about me down there, but there were always lots of adults around.

Some of those adults were there to see off their own Mason City sons who were boarding the train to go down to enlist. I remember two of them who did not return. Both were airmen; one went on to fly P51's and the other B-17's.

Of course, the war did end and on August 8, Mason City, (which we natives believe was the inspiration for Meredith Wilson's "River City" in the Music Man) held a rousing spontaneous celebration with marching bands, blowing horns and fireworks!

Not too much later, I enrolled at Principia College and met this wonderful man named Charlie Hathaway who, as a veteran, was there on the G. I. Bill. We were married for 64 years.

Of course, central to day to day life life was the war. Even though the country was not under direct attack, it was never certain until early 1944 that the war would be won. Almost every American had family or friends facing the brutality of combat. Day-to-day life with its shortages and inconveniences did have moments of normalcy and even live-for-the-day happiness, but the American home front, in repose, was serious and restrained.

Chapter Ten
After the War

The post-war period properly begins with three deaths in April 1944: President Franklin D. Roosevelt on April 12,[1] Benito Mussolini on April 28, and Adolph Hitler on April 30. The D-Day assault on Europe by the Allies on June 6, 1944, led to Germany's surrender and VE-Day on May 8, 1945.

> The western world has been freed of the evil forces which for five years and longer have imprisoned the bodies and broken the lives of millions upon millions of freeborn men. They have violated their churches, destroyed their homes, corrupted their children and murdered their loved ones. Our armies of liberation have restored freedom to those suffering peoples, whose spirit and will the oppressor could never enslave."
> – President Harry S. Truman, V-E Day Proclamation

On the home front, the victory was dampened by the recent death of President Roosevelt. His successor, Harry S. Truman, dedicated the day to Roosevelt and ordered that flags be kept at half-staff. The American home front was in deep mourning. FDR had been at the center of everyone's life for thirteen years in a time of great peril. He, through his grand presence, had provided leadership, protection, reassurance, and confidence.

Because few people in the general public knew of the president's failing health, the nation was shocked. Reporters and close associates were well aware of his deteriorating condition and honored such personal confidence.

His body was transferred from his Georgia retreat, where he had been posing for an artist, to Washington DC by train. Mourners lined the train route no matter the hour. They stood atop overpasses and threw flowers. Black citizens counted heavily in the mourners. At every stop fresh flowers were carried aboard. After a state service in Washington, FDR was transferred to his family estate at Hyde Park, New York and buried with full military honors.

For generations, people who were alive on April 15, 1945, could tell you exactly where they were when they learned of FDR's passing.

The war was not won yet in the Pacific, where US and Allied forces fought the Japanese in Okinawa, the Philippines and other Far East locations. President Truman urged Americans to temper their elation until all hostilities ended.

Despite this, many Americans rejoiced. New York was the site of the largest VE-Day celebration. Crowds gathered in Times Square, and thousands marched down Fifth Avenue with confetti raining down on them.

Some US cities observed VE-Day in a subdued fashion, adhering to Truman's advice. From coast to coast, Americans flocked to houses of worship to pray. In Chicago, churches arranged special services, reported the *Chicago Daily Tribune*. Government and labor leaders asked workers to stay on their jobs, and liquor stores were closed for twenty-four hours. New Orleans "had no frenzied celebration," and a similar calm prevailed in Dallas, Boston and Denver, according to *Newsweek*. The mood in Atlanta was "somber, reflective," while in Los Angeles, the mayor proclaimed: "This is not a holiday."[2]

As joyous was the victory, revulsion spread as the world learned more about the hideous atrocities in the concentration camps, sobering the joy. The revelations added to the belief that the war was just.

In August the world, including Americans on the home front, were shocked to learn about the employment of a new and frightening weapon, as the US dropped two atomic bombs on Japan. The weapons produced Japan's surrender and introduced the world to the nuclear age.

The surrender brought a three-day spree of home front VJ-day celebrations. The mainstay of the celebrations were parades, spontaneous and organized, big and small. Pots were banged, flags waved, firecrackers lit, horns blared all amid screams and cries of joy. Many of the parades' most enthusiastic, and sometimes tipsy, members were servicemen recently returned home and exultant that their nightmare was over.

Often the ordeal of war was replaced by the ordeal of fitting back in both to work and the family. Some veterans slipped smoothly into college or a technical school. Others found their jobs gone and had to latch on to a job, which became less difficult as 1945 wore on.

The difficult place to fit back into was the family. There would be the sad cases of men returning to children who were not theirs or wives who no longer wanted to be married. In some cases, the returning father had never really known his children when he shipped out. The small child could have difficulty adjusting to this new, large, loud entity now in his life. Often mothers may have created false expectations in their children about what to expect, describing all the great things that Dad would be doing with them not aware that the Dad who left was not the Dad who was coming home.

One problem arose from the human tendency to fashion a good version of reality. A man who was away for the duration with only letters to remind him of home, could come to remember his wife as the embodiment of beauty and love. Likewise, the wife might remember only the very best of her husband. The expectations these fantasies created could make the man's homecoming even more difficult.

Women were quicker to realize that the man standing at the door in his uniform was not the same man who left. Most were prepared to do what it would take to help him readjust to peacetime life in a family. The returning men, however, were often not prepared for the changes that their women had undergone in their absence. A common denominator for the returning men was surprise. They found their women independent-minded and full of a confidence they had not had before the war. Women now knew how to make household repairs, change a tire, balance a checkbook and more. The men who felt diminished by the loss of their old roles had a harder time. Some, sadly, could not make the adjustment. Many men felt that they had lost time out of their lives, that they needed to "get caught up" as they expressed it. Embracing materialism, buying things that they had longed for was one way of coping, but the lost time could not be reclaimed.

When a serviceman returned disabled, the problems were far more difficult, particularly if the veteran was classified as NP, a shorthand for neurotic-psychotic (also nicknamed shell-shock) which did not mean mentally disabled but did mean that professional counselling was advised.

Unfortunately, while veterans with physical disabilities could find ample rehabilitation, NP veterans had difficulty finding help.

Any high expectations that life would quickly and happily pick up where it left off before the war were severely tested. At a peak spike in 1946, nearly 40 percent of wartime marriages ended in divorce.[3] "Marry in haste – repent at leisure," certainly rang true. The proof was that in just a year or two the frequency of divorce quickly slid back to its long-term rate.

Stirred by the great relocation of both servicemen and civilians adjusting to changing economic conditions, Americans got to know their country and each other. Educational institutions had been shaken to their core and came out better for it, narrowing the huge regional disparities in quality. The war boom gave second chances – even first chances – to many Americans who had been held down by poverty and social injustice.

The relocation and mobility did displace some Americans creating rootlessness for them. It altered, and somewhat homogenized, regional provincialism. It was now a different America.

The Boom Begins

August 1945. The war was truly over. The American home front was now freed to be simply home. What happened in a very short space of time reshaped the country. As with so many things connected with the war, reconversion and absorbing the millions of returning servicemen was bumpy. For much of 1945 returning servicemen scrambled to find jobs as defense plants wound down and their conversion to civilian goods was slow, but by the end of the year "help wanted" ads filled the papers. For those who did have trouble finding work, the government provided what was called the 52–20 Club which provided $20 a week for 52 weeks giving the veteran the security of a guaranteed income for a year to aid in readjustment.

My 52–20
By Joseph A (b. 1935):

When most of us who were there at the time think about the end of the war we think about the parades and celebrations, but the readjustments were difficult – for both the servicemen and their families. We had four boys in our town who had what we called shell shock. They stayed to themselves mostly, but it was awful to see them on the street.

But lots of other boys who came home found it hard to get back into civilian life. My uncle James had trouble adapting. He tried some work but just needed more time to settle in. One day he told me he was joining the "52–20 Club." It was a program that gave men like him $20 a week for 52 weeks, or until they got a job, to help them. He joked about it, but he was a little embarrassed I could tell. He got a job in a short time.

We don't often talk about these kinds of things that happened after the war. There were lots of problems.

These returning servicemen were a big driver for change. They needed housing and they needed the appliances and furniture to fill the houses. And they wanted cars. The billions of dollars Americans had piled up because of rationing were now available to be spent and spend it they did, aided by the new installment plans. The economy began a four-decade march upward. The war had sized everything bigger: business, labor, government, education, farming, transportation, construction.

Arguably the greatest agent of change, one that changed every aspect of American life forever, was a bill signed on June 22, 1944 – the Servicemen's Readjustment Act, commonly known as the G.I. Bill of Rights. Congress had been told that returning veterans wanted educational opportunities which traditionally had been available only to wealthy Americans and the G.I. Bill provided just that.

But the G.I. Bill went much further. It not only provided money for college and vocational education, it provided government backed loans. The so-called VA loans permitted veterans to buy a home with no money down. The result was a building boom never seen before. Instead of building a house or two, people like William Levitt were building whole communities all at once. Levittowns and similar developments seemingly popped up overnight.

Often unnoticed was a special way the G. I. Bill aided the Black community. Many Black people opted to pursue vocational education, setting themselves up for work in the trades to become electricians, plumbers, and carpenters. It was not uncommon for them to then set themselves up in their own business and hire other Black workers as employees. Black entrepreneurship was another G.I. Bill breakthrough.

Thus the G.I. Bill democratized two pillars of American life: education and housing. In doing so it is not too strong a statement to say that the G.I. Bill created the American middle class. With its stored-up wealth, America jumped into its new affluence. After a brief pause, fears of a postwar depression flew out the window as aircraft plants quickly returned to making cars and other factories learned how to make the new labor-saving devices like washing machines and vacuum cleaners which freed women up to address their changed aspirations.

Affluence created a brief, often wistfully discussed era: the era of the stay-at-home mom. Women came off their defense jobs and the family was able to live on the father's income. The myth has mom baking pies and doing housework, greeting the kids as they came home from school every day. That did happen, but the era was short lived. Women's changed aspirations and the rising cost of living drew women back into the work force to help support the family.

In fact, changed aspirations may be considered the most long-lasting consequence of the war. Depression-era men now aspired to economic security. Black people who glimpsed parity now aspired to equality; women who experienced independence now aspired to full emancipation.

The US had never been bombed or invaded and, in fact, it was stronger after the war, not weaker. The war reaffirmed people's faith in the promise of the country. WWII was, in fact, the greatest social experiment in the country's history. While the services did not alter segregation, they did promote social democracy among members drawn from every level of society and every religious and ethnic group. Collective living threw college graduates together with illiterates, Christians with Jews, Catholics with Protestants, Yankees with Southerners, and farm boys with street kids. The services provided reading classes for illiterates, hygiene courses for those needing them, and a well-balanced diet for all.[4]

The groundbreaking, though limited, efforts at establishing equality for Black people and women certainly impelled the way for advances thirty and forty years later. Segregation did reappear and millions of women defense workers did become unemployed and, as always, disillusionment was the product of raised expectations. But both the Black community and women now had the tools and experience to move forward.

It's been said that our wildly heterogeneous nation was more completely united in purpose and spirit than at any time in our history. Those were simple times. Good had triumphed over evil. Things were going to get better. It was a rich emotional experience that gave everyone a vital sense of community. America has lived on that accumulation of cultural capital for nearly eighty years. To some, that account now seems almost exhausted.[5]

Four Essays – Reflections on the Home Front

1. A Child's Life During the War   188
2. The Short Happy Era of the Stay-at-Home Mom   192
3. At the Saturday Matinee   194
4. Children of the 1930s – "The Last Ones"   196

By C. D. Peterson

A Child's Life During the War

"If the Japanese win any more battles, they could win all the way to California," I heard my grandmother say. She was sitting at the scarred desk that served as the hub of our small dairy farm speaking on our only telephone. I was sure I shouldn't be listening, so I slipped out to be with the men in the dairy.

Yesterday I overheard some of the men talking about how all the Japanese out west were being rounded up and sent out to the desert. Today they were talking about which of their friends were going off. We were a Navy family – my father and two uncles were gone to fight. Two of our men were headed for the army. That would leave just my grandparents, my mother, one hired man and me to handle the farm. We did share help and work with our neighbor farms.

When the Depression eased a bit, we had bought a more modern tractor and a portable gasoline engine but with gasoline sometimes hard to get, work was tough. My grandfather broke out two draft horses we had hung onto, pretty much out of affection, and so Tom and Jerry became part of the war effort. My mother's pleasure horse was fit enough to pull a small wagon that we had fun outfitting to deliver milk. We had farm rations for truck gasoline, so it wasn't needed too often but the newspapers loved capturing my pretty young mother delivering milk from a horse drawn wagon. On the farm she was teased about her celebrity.

Besides having to relearn how to use horses, we had to learn how to save grease in cans, how to peel tinfoil, save metal parts and pull down shades at night. Managing ration books became part of life. For a time, my grandmother served on the ration board and told us that some people were trying to cheat and others were hoarding. She also spoke about "draft dodgers" who pretended to be sick. I was surprised that people were doing bad things.

No surprise that I won the Victory Garden contests. We didn't have a lot of cash for me to buy the black war bond stamps sold every week at school, but I wasn't embarrassed. I felt like my garden and my farm work were helping the war effort. The very few letters my father sent us always had a place where he told me to help take care of the farm. He reminded me about my first job when I was 4 or 5 years old, standing with a stick in my hand at the top of the farmyard drive that led down to the state highway. My job was to keep the cows that were coming up for milking from wandering out. My father teased me into making fierce faces and sounds at the cows to scare them off. I don't remember one coming near me.

During the build-up and early years we didn't talk much about the war at school but later, with news flashes on the radio and war movies at the theater, we younger ones quizzed each other in constant curiosity about what we were all making of it.

Older kids – boys – took up playing at war on the playground and especially on the rowdy walks home from the Saturday matinees. Mostly they used their hands as guns or else spread their arms wide and made airplane sounds as they ran shouting "Bombs away!" There were afternoon radio shows like Jack Armstrong or Dick Tracy where they chased spies, and you could get a secret decoder ring but that was my chore time and I didn't listen often. My cousins who lived in town had lurid war tales they picked up hanging around shops and garages. One boy said he saw a German submarine when he was out on Cape Cod. Under merciless playground grilling he admitted that he hadn't actually been the one who saw it, but he knew the boy who did.

In school we wrote letters to servicemen, sometimes to relatives and sometimes to strangers. Our teachers, when they learned that someone's father had gone off, would ask the rest of us to say a prayer. I remember a boy and a girl in my second grade losing their fathers. No one knew what to do or say. If a kid was absent for a few days we might wonder about it, but no one would ask. For a couple months during the war we had a boy live with us. He was very quiet and didn't know anything about farming. His mother had moved away to be near his father but he was sent overseas and she came back and got the boy.

The girl on our neighbor farm was in my class and she told me that German planes were going to come in the night. She said she knew they were coming because her uncle was an air raid warden and he knew for sure. She, like I, held responsibility for pulling down the blackout shades during the drills.

Every day we pooled our eavesdropping, snooping and overheard talk of war from each of our homes. Roosevelt's radio talks were occasions for excitement and serious deliberation by adults. We watched adults closely for signs of fear. We figured out they intended to keep bad news from us. They didn't want us to be afraid and I think they did a pretty good job. (I never heard Edward R. Murrow's chilling reports from London until I was a grown man.)

Nevertheless, fear came anyway. It came from watching newsreels of Hitler and especially the massed thousands of goose-stepping soldiers. Even we could read headlines about the war in the Pacific and see the pictures of Europe in *Life* magazine. The air raid drills and blackout curtains were daily reminders. My in-town cousins told me about German spies. But, except for the girl on the neighboring farm, we kids never spoke out loud about our fear, not even the fear for our fathers and brothers in the war. Perhaps giving voice to our fears would have given them a toehold on our reality.

Reality, too, came anyway. Boys were coming home wounded. Parents hung gold stars in windows to silently attest the loss of a son. Every time I went out delivering milk I would watch for any new ones.

We had big excitement in my town when the Army decided to build a hospital for the boys coming home. What made it so exciting was that we heard POWs were being used to build it and if you went by you could see them! It turned out they were Italian prisoners being used to build the stone chapel for the hospital. I went by delivering milk one day and told my school mates that the prisoners didn't look scary, just sad.

Sometimes in class we would have young student teachers come down from the Normal School. In the third grade one student teacher came and had me sit in a special chair rigged with a broom handle, wires and pedals and explained how to fly a plane. (Years later on my first training flight at Pensacola I remembered everything she taught.)

The end of the war was as intense as its beginning. News of D-Day was everywhere and on everyone's lips. VE-Day, a year later, was stirring even though by then we all expected it. Then came VJ-Day and, along with the rest of the country, our town exploded with joy. The war was truly over!

I was 8 years old when my mother drove us down from the farm to see a spur-of-the-moment VJ-Day parade. Not far out of town we began to form in a loose caravan with other packed cars and trucks. Gas rationing just ended the day the war ended and Bill Crawford, who owned the ESSO station, said he would pump whatever gas anybody needed for the parade.

We wound all around the crowded downtown blowing our horn and joining in with the shouting. I had never heard such noise. A bunch of boys and girls jumped in the back of the truck and, all laughing, we became part of the mayhem for a while. We found a place to pull over and joined the crowd waiting for the soldiers and sailors to come marching by.

We found a viewing spot at the curb and soon were witness to a ramble of cops and firemen, air raid wardens and clubmen and smiling shirt-sleeved political glad handers. Anybody who could play an instrument and walk had been conscripted for the parade band. As the band passed us with music in the air, the boys came in to view. There were no more than a few dozen who had made it home by that time and half of those were banged up one way or another limping, staring at things the crowd would never see.

On a Saturday shortly after the war I joined a pack of boys downtown who were moving from one veteran's house to another to look at their treasures. I recall seeing a real German Luger, Japanese flags and some grainy gruesome pictures among other things.

One sad impact of the war involved an older cousin. He volunteered early and returned only after the war. He had been hospitalized with a head injury for years in an Army hospital. While he was away his family moved just a few streets over. When he returned, he could not accept that his old house was no longer his. He would stand in front of his old house and cry for hours on end, demanding the new owners give back his house. Family efforts to get him to stop, to convince him of the new situation did not work. Kids were hustled away when he came out because he could be frightening. Then one day he was gone. No one would say where he went. The sight of his tortured face and the sound of his anguished cries remain vivid to me.

Looking back over the war years I recall something about my childhood friends and schoolmates that I have never seen in children since that time. I can only describe it as a deep watchful quietness. I saw it and felt it all around me, even during play. To us, bonded by the war, the world seemed ominous but we recognized that we had no agency over anything. We watched; dependent, impotent, and obliged to be silent. We waited for things to get better, and they did.

We are the last ones who remember.

The Short, Happy Era of the Stay-at-Home Mom

Those were the days. Dad went off to work while Mom stayed home and took care of the house. She helped out at the PTA. She baked cookies for the kids. She was always there when they came home from school. That's the way it used to be. That's how it should be. That's the way it always was.

No, it wasn't. That idealized image did exist, but only for a short time, maybe little over a decade. Like so many things, this phenomenon requires going back to the WWII era. In the early 1940s the 25 percent of women working outside the home mostly followed traditional roles as teachers, nurses, and office assistants though some worked in sewing and other factories. By 1944, at the height of the war, about one third of women worked outside the home, the increase caused by their working in war production factories. With mothers at work and fathers in the service, some children were called "eight-hour orphans."

The other two thirds may have been at home, but they were not just baking cookies. Women at home in the 1940s worked hard in addition to helping in the war effort. They washed and dried laundry by hand. They managed the family's food by shopping frequently, gardening, canning, and supervising the schedule for ice. Floors, walls, and windows required hand sweeping, scrubbing and wiping. Rationing meant detailed planning and making everything last. "Making do" was the catch phrase.

The war ended and things changed. Rationing was over. A factory that was making tanks now introduced refrigerators and that meant no more ice, no need to shop every day or can garden-raised vegetables. In fact, newly introduced frozen vegetables even saved cooking time as did the new Betty Crocker ready-to-use cake mixes. Vacuum cleaners and automated washing machines further lightened the workload and gave women time. The post-war boom brought good jobs and wages; wages enough that only Dad had to go to work.

Thus, the era of the stay-at-home mom was born, somewhere around 1946 to 1950. It may have been just as many remember it, cookies and all, Mom at the door when the kids came home. But it wasn't forever. In fact, as eras go, it was short. In 1950, the number of women working outside the home returned to the pre-war 25 percent. But women, now with time available to them, were questioning their roles, and expectations. By the 1960s, the universal ideal of the stay-at-home mom was already beginning to wane. During the 1970s, single income households faced higher living costs and more moms went out to work so, by 1980, 50 percent of women were working outside the home, double the 1950s figure. The number now hovers around 60 percent.

Nostalgia isn't a bad thing, but in this case our longing to return to those times triggers not only sweet yearning, but needless guilt. "If we just had better values today. Our children would be better off. Crime would go down." In fact, the era was not a lost Eden that we somehow poisoned. The stay-at-home mom ideal was a modern, mostly middle-class phenomenon and a short-lived one at that. For many a latchkey kid it never existed except as a myth.

At the Saturday Matinee

He was big and I was fast. It wasn't talked about, it was just understood the way kids understand things among themselves. My cousin Dick, at age 13, stood as big as some of our teachers and I could run like the wind. These facts took on significance on Saturdays as we prepared for the matinee at the Hollis Theater.

Our Saturday matinees were probably like Saturday matinees everywhere in the 1940s. We saw two features, usually one western and a war picture. Five cartoons ranked OK but seven was better. The serials, though, were pretty poor. We could always spot where they changed something that allowed the hero, who was doomed last Saturday, to cheat death this Saturday. The oldest of my four cousins did like *Nyoka the Jungle Girl*, however.

The whole thing began with some previews and a newsreel which involved our participation. When the familiar concluding credits to the newsreel rolled on screen we kids always shouted along with each word – "The eyes and ears of the world. The end. Paramount News!" proclaiming the start of the show.

Tribal-like social order dominated our Saturday matinee. Rigid protocols determined who could cut line in front of whom, and under what circumstances. A noisy breach of the rules usually caused the convening of a hasty court of bystanders to adjudicate. By and large kids wanted to cluster with kids from their neighborhood so that, once inside, they could rush by the lobby posters announcing "Free Dishes Every Thursday" to claim their usual seats.

Any real rowdiness in line was risky because the hooligan might suffer a cuffed ear from an aunt or neighbor passing by, any of whom were empowered to enforce discipline.

A few kids from well to do neighborhoods actually got dropped off. The cacophony of us kids standing in line was brought down to a hush when a car pulled up. With no anger or envy, we figured that those kids probably had movie money given to them.

I don't remember why, but for me, my cousins, and most of my friends, movie money was our own responsibility. We weren't really poor, and it didn't cost that much but for some reason we had to generate our own movie money. Some boys had paper routes, shined shoes or stocked shelves, but for many of us returning bottles was our source of cash. Small bottles were worth two cents and large ones a nickel. Because most people had milk delivered to them, those bottles couldn't be returned to a store. That left us soda and beer bottles.

One boy, a bully I didn't like, used to steal bottles from the back of his own father's package store and try to get one of us to return them and split the take. Only a few boys would do it.

The magic number for me was twenty-six cents; twelve cents for the ticket, ten cents for the popcorn, and four cents for the candy – if I bought it at Bond's Drug Store, not in the movie. It might take a little longer if I found a steel penny because I was collecting them, assured they would be worth a lot of money one day. While I had a job, it was on our dairy farm and it came with lots of compensation, but not the cash kind. So, on Saturday I would ride my bike to town to meet up with my cousins and we would decide how much we needed. Often, we could find enough just by scouring for bottles around the streets or asking a nice neighbor for hers.

But not always. That's when my cousin Dick and I worked our special and dangerous plan. We had a railroad yard in town and while the era of "riding the rails" was pretty much over, we still had our hobo jungle where (unfortunate) men lived and where they drank Pickwick Ale. An empty of Pickwick Ale was worth a nickel to Dick and me but it was also worth a nickel to its owner. As I mentioned, he was big and I was fast. The plan worked like this. We would walk along the edge of the tracks bordering the hobo jungle looking down to spot a bottle. My job was to slip down on the cinders, grab the bottle and run while his job was to fight off anybody who came after us. Only once did we have an encounter. My cousin Dick told it that while I was reaching for a bottle a hobo rushed out of the brush and he ran down and chased the man away. The truth was that there was a man in the brush, but he was relieving himself and he was too old to chase anybody. Even so, our adventures entitled us to a certain swagger waiting in line at the Hollis Theater.

My wife and I went to a movie recently. We shared a box of popcorn and a bottle of water. It cost $34.

Children of the 1930's – "The Last Ones"

Born in the 1930s, we exist as a very special age cohort. We are the "last ones." We are the last, climbing out of the Depression, who can remember the winds of war and the war itself with fathers and uncles going off to fight. We are the last to remember ration books for everything from sugar to shoes to stoves. We saved tin foil and poured fat into tin cans. We closed ranks and worked together. We saw cars up on blocks because tires weren't available. My mother delivered milk in a horse drawn cart.

We are the last to hear Roosevelt's radio assurances and to see gold stars in the front windows of our grieving neighbors. We can also remember the drama of D-Day and the parades in August 1945 for VJ-Day.

We saw the "boys" home from the war build their cape style houses, pouring the cellar, tar papering it over and living there until they could afford the time and money to build it out.

We are the last who spent childhood without television; instead imagining what we heard on the radio. As we all like to brag, with no TV we spent our childhood "playing outside until the streetlights came on." We did play outside and we did play on our own. There was no little league.

With war-busy parents and no television in our early years we picked up little real understanding of what the world was like. Our Saturday afternoons at the movies gave us newsreels of the war and the holocaust sandwiched between westerns and cartoons. Newspapers and magazines were written for adults. We are the last who had to find out for ourselves.

As we grew up, the country was exploding with growth. My small New England town saw General Motors come and bring hundreds of jobs and a boom in real estate. A futuristic mall, the first of its kind, transformed our state highway and powered commercial growth. A local truck farmer was so short of labor that he brought in summer workers from Puerto Rico; another demarcation of before and after.

The G.I. Bill gave returning veterans the means to get an education and spurred colleges to grow. VA loans lit off a housing boom. Pent up demand, coupled with new installment payment plans, put factories to work. New highways would bring jobs and mobility: shipbuilding to the South, aircraft manufacturing to the Midwest and West. The veterans joined community civic clubs and became active in politics. In the late 1940s and early 1950s the country seemed to lie in the embrace of brisk but quiet order. The war had solidified the working class and now the post-war boom gave birth to a new middle class.

Our parents, understandably, became absorbed with their own new lives. They were free from the confines of the Depression and the war. They threw themselves into exploring opportunities they had never imagined. We weren't neglected but we weren't the all-consuming family focus of today. They were glad we played by ourselves "until the streetlights came on." They were busy discovering their post-war world.

We could see over the horizon to adulthood that there were opportunities everywhere. The ghost of shortage was banished. Most of us had no life plan, but with the unexpected virtue of ignorance and an economic rising tide we simply stepped into the world and went to find out. We entered a world of overflowing plenty and opportunity; a world where we were welcomed. Based on our naïve belief that there was more where this came from, we shaped life as we went.

We enjoyed a luxury; we felt secure in our future. Of course, just as today, not all Americans shared in this experience. Depression poverty stayed deep rooted. Polio was still a crippler and segregation was rampant.

The Korean War was a dark presage in the early 1950s and by mid-decade school children were ducking under desks and families were building bomb shelters. China became Red China. Eisenhower sent the first "advisors" to Vietnam. Castro set up camp in Cuba and Khrushchev came to the Kremlin.

We are the last to experience an interlude when there were no threats to the existence of our homeland. We came of age in the late 1940s and early 1950s. The war was over. The cold war, terrorism, climate change, technological upheaval and perpetual economic insecurity had yet to haunt life with insistent unease.

Only we can remember both a time of apocalyptic war and a time when our world was secure and full of bright promise and plenty. We experienced both.

We came of age at the best possible time, a time when the world was getting better.
We are the "last ones."
– C. D. Peterson

Contributors

Joining the New Hampshire State Guard – Roy Hoopes.
Migration to California – Duncan Eisley.
For Grandad, WWII (and Fate) put an End to the Depression – Emil Stefanik.
First story about an arsenal – Anonymous.
Second story about an arsenal – Julia Anton Wiggins.
Parachutes for Their sons – Claire Stafford.
Blackouts in Miami – "Nick" Nickerson.
CAP patrols – Captain Bob Mosely.
Hiding during the drills – Sherill Janowski Cunning.
Seattle's first blackout – Samuel Hynes.
Front Row Seat for the War – Michael Cranston.
Blackout drills – Robert "Lash" LaRue.
"Pig Clubs" – Dovey Sommers.
Chicago Victory Gardens – Jim Kelly.
Scrap Day – No School! – Janet Olmstead.
Just get it Done – George Ames.
Reminiscence of a Black American – Samuel Hyman.
Who's Sorry Now? – Albert Scioffi.
Left Alone as Soon as the War Started – Claire McConnell.
Waiting for the Mailman – Richard Sharon.
I Thought that Spies were Everywhere – Tina Bouchard.
Still Fearful – Sarah M.
Greeting the Troop Train – Frank Galvin.
How Can I Remember So Much? – Lynne Coppoletta.
I Went to the USO – Almost – Mary Long.
Making Rationing Work – Lyla Burns.
The Villain in Our Childhood – C. D. Peterson.
Roosevelt's Passing – "Nick" Nickerson.
Home Front Child's Memory – Robert "Lash" LaRue.
In My Innocence – Robert "Lash" LaRue.
A POW Remembered – John Boiardi.
I was a Suspected Saboteur – Don Metz.
An Act of Kindness – Janet Kinkade.
A Young Life Gets Direction – Dave Pace.
Home Front Memories From the Heartland – Patty Hathaway.
My 52–20 – Joseph Adquist.

Notes

Chapter One
1. America was not an Eden for everyone on December 6. Black communities lived segregated lives of poverty. Antisemitism was alive. Large pockets of the country suffered low literacy and poor healthcare.
2. Wilk, Gavin (2021), "Hasty Departures: The Evacuation of American Citizens from Europe at the Outbreak of World War II" in *Journal of Transnational American Studies* 12 (1): pp.108–128.
3. The National WWII Museum, New Orleans (www.nationalww2museum.org).
4. Yellin, Emily, *Our Mothers' War*, Free Press (New York), 2004 pp.333–341.
5. Seeley G., *Mudd Manuscript Library*, Princeton University.
6. With thanks to University of Chicago Library (https://www.lib.uchicago.edu/).
7. CSU Northridge University Library, Northridge CA (https://library.csun.edu/).
8. Perrett, Geoffrey, *Days of Sadness Years of Triumph*, (New York), 1973, pp.164–165.
9. Kline, Maury, *A Call to Arms*, Bloomsbury Press (New York), 2013, p.111.
10. Perrett, Geoffrey, *op.cit.*, p.191.
11. *Fortune*, July 1941, p.116.
12. Perrett, Geoffrey, *op.cit.*, pp.27, 38.
13. The National WWII Museum, New Orleans (www.nationalww2museum.org).
14. Naval History and Heritage Command (www.history.navy.mil).
15. National Archives and Records: *A People at War* (https://www.archives.gov/exhibits/a_people_at_war/a_people_at_war.html).
16. UC Santa Barbara: *American Presidency Project* (presidency.ucsb.edu).
17. Brinkley, David, *Washington Goes to War*, Alfred A. Knopf (New York), 1988, p.88.

Chapter Two
1. *Time*, December 15, 1941.
2. Perrett, Geoffrey, *Days of Sadness, Years of Triumph: The American People 1939–1945*, Coward, McCann, & Geoghegan, (New York), 1973, p.205.
3. Klingaman, William K., *The Darkest Year, The American Home Front 1941–1942*, St. Martin's Press (New York), 2019, p.51.
4. The National WWII Museum, New Orleans (www.nationalww2museum.org).
5. Wessels Living History Farm, York, Nebraska (https://livinghistoryfarm.org/).
6. Ibid.
7. Ibid.
8. *The Women's Land Army Works for Victory*, USDA pamphlet, April 1945.
9. Cosworth, Paul D. *Let the Good Times Roll*, Paragon House (New York), 1989, p.6.
10. Lingeman, Richard R., *Don't You Know There's a War On?* Paperback Library (New York), 1970, p.171.

11. www.amemoirfromthehomefront.com.
12. Weatherford, Doris, *American Women and WWII*, Castle Books (Edison, NJ), 1970, p.119.
13. Tuttle, Jr, William M., *Daddy's Gone to War*, Oxford University Press (New York), 1993, p.59.
14. Jeffries, John W., *Wartime America, The World War II Home Front*, Ivan R. Dee (Chicago), 1996, p.135.
15. Tolan Committee, *Hearings*, part 22, pp.8534–8563.
16. https://www.federalreservehistory.org/essays/feds-role-during-wwii.
17. Perrett, Geoffrey, *Days of Sadness, Years of Triumph: The American People 1939–1945*, Coward, McCann, & Geoghegan (New York), 1973, p.67.
18. In 1941 the US Army was still buying horses.
19. www.warbirdsandairshows.com.
20. The Henry Ford Museum, Michigan (https://www.thehenryford.org/).
21. Willow Run was glorified in the press though it left a legacy of empty housing and overbuilt infrastructure.
22. Naval History and Heritage Command (https://www.history.navy.mil/).
23. Los Angeles Conservancy (https://www.laconservancy.org/wartime-shipbuilding-at-terminal-island/).
24. The Jacksonville Historical Society, Jacksonville, Florida (www.jaxhistory.org).
25. US Bureau of Labor Statistics Bulletin: 839.
26. www.amemoirfromthehomefront.com.
27. Maine Maritime Museum, Bath, Maine (https://www.mainemaritimemuseum.org/).
28. Lingeman, Richard R., *op.cit.*, p.165.
29. Jeffries, John W., *Wartime America*, The American Way Series.
30. *The Jeep: An American Icon*, The National Museum of the United States Army, July 16, 2012.
31. *Motor Trend Magazine*, September 24, 2020.
32. The National WWII Museum, New Orleans (www.nationalww2museum.org).
33. Yellin, Emily, *Our Mothers' War*, Free Press (New York), 2004, p.62.
34. With thanks to ACS.org (American Chemical Society).
35. *Missing in Action: Unions in WW II*, Arthur Herman (https://www.writersreps.com/feature.aspx?FeatureID=214).
36. *"Billion Dollar Watchdog*, Time Magazine, March 8, 1943.

Chapter Three
1. Geoffrey Perrett, *Days of Sadness, Years of Triumph*, (New York), 1973, pp.232–234.
2. As told by permission of N. Nickerson.
3. World War II: The American Experience (www.visitww2.org).
4. Perrett, Geoffrey, *op.cit.*, pp.232–234.
5. Wikipedia: *Aircraft Warning Service*.
6. Lingeman, Richard R., *op.cit.*, p.49.
7. Keefer, Louis, *From Maine to Mexico: With America's Private Pilots in the Fight Against Nazi U-Boats*, C O T U Pub; 1st edition January 1, 1997.
8. World War II: The American Experience (www.visitww2.org).
9. https://sos.oregon.gov/archives/exhibits/ww2/Pages/protect-raids.aspx.

10. Harris, Mark Jonathan; Mitchell, Franklin; & Schacter, Steven, *The Homefront*, Putnam Sons (New York), 1984, p.69.
11. www.Rosietheriveter.net.
12. The National WWII Museum, New Orleans (www.nationalww2museum.org).
13. Klingaman, William K., *The Darkest Year, The American Home Front 1941–1942*, St. Martin's Press (New York), 2019, p.75.
14. https://www.adn.com/alaska-life/2021/02/01/blackouts-and-air-raid-preparedness-were-taken-seriously-in-nearly-all-american-cities-during-wwii-not-anchorage.
15. Lingeman, Richard R., *op.cit.*, p.26.
16. www.smithsonianmagazine.com (January 19, 2018).
17. www.smithsoniamagazine.com (*op.cit.*).
18. www.Rosietheriviter.net.
19. Lingeman, Richard R, *op.cit.*, p.324.

Chapter Four
1. www.amemoirfromthehomefront.com.
2. Lingeman, Richard R., *Don't You Know There's a War On?* (New York), 1970 p.66.
3. National Women's History Museum (www.womenshistory.org).
4. www.amemoirfromthehomefront.com.
5. Klingaman, William K., *The Darkest Year, The American Home Front 1941–1942*, St. Martin's Press (New York). 2019, p.260.
6. Kennett, Lee, *For the duration: the United States goes to war, Pearl Harbor-1942*, (New York: Scribner), 1985, pp.118, 124.
7. Perrett, Geoffrey, *Days of Sadness, Years of Triumph*, (New York), 1973, p.382.
8. *The Washington Post* Health and Science article dated Sept 25, 2012, entitled "Milkweed fruits: Pods of plenty."
9. Klingaman, William K., *The Darkest Year The American Home Front 1941–1942*, St. Martin's Press (New York), 2019, p.115.
10. Perrett, Geoffrey, *Days of Sadness, Years of Triumph*, (New York), 1973, p.188.
11. Klingaman, William K. *op.cit.*, p.209.
12. Lingeman, Richard R. *op.cit.*, p.307.
13. Miller, Keith, *How Important Was Oil in WW II?* historynewsnetwork.org.
14. "Bulletin," Consumer Division, Oregon State Defense Council, Aug. 7, 1942. Folder 12, Box 28, Defense Council Records, OSA.
15. https://en.wikipedia.org/wiki/Lucky_Strike.

Chapter Five
1. Wynn, Neil A., *The African American Experience During World War II*, Rowman & Littlefield, (Lanham,) 2002, p.73.
2. Brown, Lloyd L., "Brown v. Salina, Kansas" in The *New York Times*, February 26, 1973, p.31.
3. Goodwin, Doris Kearns, *No Ordinary Time, The Home Front in World War II*, Simon & Schuster (New York), 1995, p.165.
4. National Park Service (https://www.nps.gov/subjects/worldwarii/african-americans.htm).
5. Takaki, Ronald, *Double Victory, A Multi-Cultural History of America in World War II*, Little Brown (Boston), 2000, p.20.

6. Yelli, Emily, *Our Mothers' War*, Free Press (New York), 2004, pp.221–222.
7. Perrett, Jeffrey, *Days of Sadness, Years of Triumph*, Coward, McCann, & Geoghegan (New York), 1973, p.323.
8. *Newsweek*, September 6, 1943, p.74.
9. Brock, Julia et. al., *Beyond Rosie, A Documentary History of Women and World War II*, University of Arkansas Press (Fayetteville), 2015, p.8.
10. Goodwin, Doris Kearns, *op.cit.*, pp.417–418.
11. The Khan Academy (https://www.khanacademy.org/humanities/us-history/rise-to-world-power/us-wwii/a/american-women-and-world-war-ii).
12. Weatherford, Doris, *American Women and World War II*, Castle Books (Edison, NJ), 2008, p.120.
13. Weatherford, Doris, *op.cit*, p.164.
14. Jeffries, John W., *Wartime America, The World War II Home Front*, Ivan R. Dee (Chicago), 1996, p.101.
15. *African American Women in World War II*: The Gilder Lehrman Institute of American History (www.gilderlehrman.org; subscription required to access).
16. Weatherford, Doris, *op.cit.*, p.16.
17. *Women in the Military – WWII: Overview*: Minnesota Historical Society (https://libguides.mnhs.org/wwii_women).
18. Weatherford, Doris, *op.cit.*, p.101.
19. *A Question of Equity: The WASP in WWII* (https://texashistory.unt.edu/ark:/67531/metapth908307/).
20. https://www.history.com/news/black-rosie-the-riveters-wwii-homefront-great-migration.
21. Yellin, Emily, *Our Mothers' War*, Free Press (New York), 2004, p.15.
22. *How "Allotment Annies" Scammed Men – And the US Army* (https://bust.com/allotment-annies-fyeahhist/).
23. Litoff, Judy Barrett and Smith, David C., *Since You Went Away*, University Press of Kansas, 1991.
24. *V-Mail:* The Smithsonian National Postal Museum, Washington (https://postalmuseum.si.edu/exhibition/victory-mail).
25. Tuttle, William, M., *Daddy's Gone to War*, Oxford University Press (Oxford), 1993, p.36.

Chapter Six
1. US Census Bureau, *Historical Statistics of the United States, Bicentennial Edition*, (1975), Part 1, pp.49, 64.
2. Ibid.
3. www.amemoirfromthehomefront.com.
4. Ibid.
5. https://www.wwiimemorialfriends.org/blog/the-lanham-act-and-universal-childcare-during-world-war-ii.
6. Tuttle, William M. Jr, *Daddy's Gone to War*, (New York), 1993, p.8.
7. Tuttle, William M. Jr., *op.cit.*, p.85.
8. Perrette, Geoffrey, *Days of Sadness, Years of Triumph*, Coward, McCann & Geoghegan (New York), 1973, p.375.
9. Klingaman, William K., *The Darkest Year, The American Home Front 1941–1942*, St. Martin's Press (New York), 2019, p.158.

10. Klingaman, William K., *op.cit.*, p.115.
11. Klein, Maury, *A Call to Arms*, Bloomsbury Press (New York), 2013, p.631.
12. www.amemoirfromthehomefront.com.
13. Tuttle, William M. Jr., *op.cit.*, p.158.
14. De Quesada, Alejandro, *The US Home Front 1941–45*, Osprey Publishing (New York), 2008, p.56.
15. www.amemoirfromthehomefront.com.
16. Ibid.
17. Tuttle, William M., *op.cit.*, p.198.
18. https://medicine.yale.edu/news/yale-medicine-magazine/article/breaking-the-back-of-polio/.
19. *American Journal of Obstetrics and Gynecology*, Volume 66, Issue 3, September 1953, pp. 569–579.

Chapter Seven

1. German American Internee Coalition (www.gaic.info).
2. Perrett, Geoffrey, *Days of Sadness Years of Triumph*, (New York), 1973, p.218.
3. German American Internee Coalition (www.gaic.info).
4. Casdorph, Paul D., *Let the Good Times Roll*, Paragon House (New York), 1989, p.157.
5. Regrettably not all the caretakers were honorable, and some made off with the owners' property.
6. https://www.britannica.com/story/what-was-life-like-in-japanese-american-internment-camps/.
7. Lingeman Richard R., *Don't You Know there's a War On?* (New York), 1973, p.417.
8. *Nazi POWs in America. History Channel*, 2004-04-18.
9. https://militaryhistorynow.com/2018/04/10/pows-in-the-usa-10-amazing-facts-about-americas-ww2-prisoner-of-war-camps/.
10. Casdorph, Paul D., *Let the Good Times Roll*, Paragon House (New York), 1989, p.74.
11. https://militaryhistorynow.com/2018/04/10/pows-in-the-usa-10-amazing-facts-about-americas-ww2-prisoner-of-war-camps/.com.
12. Cohen, Stan, *V for Victory America's Home Front During World War II*, Pictorial Histories Publishing (Missoula, Montana), 1991, p.244.
13. Casdorph, Paul D., *Let the Good Times Roll*, Paragon House (New York), 1989, p.74.

Chapter Eight

1. https://www.fbi.gov/history/famous-cases/duquesne-spy-ring.
2. Ibid.
3. Ibid.
4. https://meandermaine.com/tale/nazi-spies-in-downeast-maine/.
5. Loureiro, Pedro (1989). "The imperial Japanese Navy and espionage: The Itaru Tachibana case" in *International Journal of Intelligence and CounterIntelligence*.
6. Loureiro, Pedro *op.cit.*, p.22.
7. https://vault.fbi.gov/world-war-ii.

Chapter Nine

1. US Department of Commerce, *Data and Reports* (https://www.commerce.gov/data-and-reports).

2. https://www.pewresearch.org/journalism/collection/fact-sheets-state-of-the-news-media.
3. Wikipedia: *Golden Age of Radio*.
4. Klingaman, William, K., *The Darkest Year, The American Home Front 1941–1942*, St. Martin's Press (New York), 2019, p.149.
5. *How World War II Helped the Grand Ole Opry Go National* (https://www.military.com/).
6. Casdorph, Paul D., *Let the Good Times Roll*, Paragon House (New York), 1989, p.34.
7. https://www.britannica.com/art/history-of-the-motion-picture/The-war-years-and-post-World-War-II-trends.
8. *Trail's End for '39ers* (https://sfmuseum.org/hist5/treasis.html).
9. Wikipedia: *1939 New York World's Fair*.
10. Rugel, Michael, *Natchez Burning: Anniversary of The Rhythm Club Fire*, in April 23, 2011 Mississippi Blues (https://www.americanbluesscene.com/2011/04/natchez-burning-anniversary-of-the-rhythm-club-fire/).
11. Lingeman, Richard, *op.cit.*, p.339.
12. Klingaman, William K., *op.cit.*, p.211.
13. Perrett, Geoffrey, *Days of Sadness, Years of Joy*, Coward, McCann, & Goeghegan (New York), 1973, p.253.
14. "How Hollywood became the unofficial propaganda arm of the US military". *CBC News*, 2020-05-11.
15. https://www.brainyquote.com/quotes/winston_churchill_111298.
16. Wynn, Neil A., *The African American Experience in World War II*, Rowman & Littlefield Publishers, Inc. (Plymouth, UK), 2010, p.19.
17. Perrett, Geoffrey, *Days of Sadness, Years of Triumph*, Coward, McCann, & Geoghegan (New York), p.183.
18. http://www.oldmagazinearticles.com/WW2-church-attendance-American-church-attendance-increased-during-world-war-two-pdf.
19. https://www.nps.gov/subjects/worldwarii/homefront.htm.

Chapter Ten
1. Curiously, the announcements of Roosevelt's death were first heard by children as their afternoon radio serials were interrupted.
2. US Army Airborne and Special Operations Museum, Fayetteville, North Carolina (https://www.asomf.org/).
3. *National Bureau of Economic Research*, Vol. 23 (www.nber.org).
4. Harris, Mark Jonathan, et al., *The Homefront, America During WWII*, G. Putnam's Sons (New York), 1984, p.47.
5. Perrett, Geoffrey, *Days of Sadness, Years of Joy*, Coward, McCann & Geoghegan (New York), 1973, p.443.

Index

100,000 Black Civil Rights March, 98
1939 Neutrality Act, 37 *see also* Neutrality Acts
45th Infantry Division, 8
52-20 Club, 182
87th Mountain Division, 8

A Night at the Garden, 4
A-26 Invader, 38
Academy Awards, 12, 102
Air Force *see* United States Army Air Force
Air Raid Warden, 56, 62, 63, 64, 66, 189, 191
Aircraft Production statistics, 36, 38-39
Aircraft Warning Service, (AWS), 58, 59
Alien Enemies Act, 136
Alien Registration Act, 135
Aliens, 135-136,
Allotment Annies, 117
America First Committee, 2, 3
American Chemical Society (ACS), 50
American Medical Association (AMA), 132
American Women's Voluntary Services (AWVS), 114-115
Anderson, Marion, 167
Arkies, 28 *see also* Oakies
Army Air Corps *see* United States Army Air Corps
Army *see* United States Army
Atlantic Charter, 15
Atlantic Conference, 14
Austria, 6, 165

B-24 bomber, 36, 37
B-25 hits Empire State building, 165
B-29 Superfortress, 38

Baby Boom, 182
Bataan, 149
Battle of Los Angeles, 69
Beaverbrook, Lord, 16
Belgium, 6
Bell Isle Amusement Park riot, 99
Bennett, Philip, 54
Benny, Jack, 22
Berger, Ernest, 145, 146
Berkman, Dr Boris, 83
Big Inch, The, *see* Pipelines
Black Americans, Impact of the War on 98-120
Black market, 77, 85, 88, 90, 92-93, 94, 130
Black Rosies, 113 *see also* Rosie the Riveter
Black women soldiers, 114
Blackout Drills, 64, 65, 71
Blackout Kit, 70
Blackouts, 56, 62, 63-67, 68, 69, 70, 157
Bomber City, 37
Book sales and bestsellers, 166
Bowder, Earl, 174
Bureau of Motion Pictures (BMP), 171
Byers, Judge Mortimer W., 144

Capra, Frank, 171
Ceiling prices, 74
Censorship, 126, 149, 150, 171
Chanel, Coco, 85
Chaney, Maris, 54
Children, 121-134
Christian Front, 2
Churchill, Winston, 12, 14, 16-17
Circus fire (Hartford, CT), 164
Citizen Kane, 13, 155
Civil Air Patrol (CAP), 59, 60, 61, 62

Civil Defense, 19, 67, 70, 71, 114, 123, 162
Civil Rights Movement, 114
Civilian Conservation Corp (CCC), 50, 138, 169
Clapper, Raymond, 6, 34, 169
Clothing and fashion, 84-86
Coca Cola, 94
Coconut Grove fire, 164
Comic books, 128
Commercial television, 14
Committee to Defend America by Aiding the Allies, 4, 6
Communist Party of the USA (CPUSA), 174
Community Facilities Act of 1942, 123
Copacabana, 5
Coughlin, Charles, 2
Country music, 153
Croton Water System, 145
Czechoslovakia, 6

Daily Worker, The 175
Daniels, Jonathan, 55
Dasch, George, 145, 146
Davis, Elmer, 150, 171
Daylight saving time, 49
Days of Sadness – Years of Triumph, 34
DC-3, 36
DDT, 130
Declaration by United Nations, 15
Democracy Reader, The 125
Der Fuhrer's Face, 172
Dilling, Elizabeth, 3
DiMaggio, Guiseppe, 136
DiMaggio, Joe, 14, 136, 161-162
Donald Duck, 172
Double V campaign, 102, 103, 176
Douglas, Melvyn, 54
Draft for Women, 109
Draft, military, 7, 15, 23, 24
Drip wells, 81
DuPont, 44, 85
Duquesne, Frederick Fritz Jouberet, 144

Education, 124-127
Educational training orders, 38

Eleanor Clubs, 100 *see also* Roosevelt, Eleanor
Emergency Maternity and Infant Care Act (EMIC), 132
Executive Orders: (EO9112, EO9336) 31; (EO9066) 135; (EO8802) 99, 114
Extended School Services, (ESS), 123

F6F-Hellcat, 38
Fair Employment Practices Committee (FEPC), 50, 99, 167
Farm Security Administration (FSA), 50
Farming and Farm labor, 24-26
Federal Bureau of Investigation, (FBI), 8, 21, 42, 144, 145, 146, 147, 148
Federal Works Agency, 123
Fifth Column is Here, The, 8
Fight for Freedom (FFF), 4
Firestone Rubber Company 47
Food Co-ops, 78, 79
Ford Motor Company, 36
Ford, Leland, 54
Fort Stevens, OR, 68
Franco, Generalissimo Francisco, 5
Furloughs and Leaves, 117

G.I. Bill *see* Servicemen's Readjustment Act
Gas rationing stickers, 90 *see also* Rationing
German American Bund, 4
German Americans, 135, 136
Germany, 4, 5, 6, 13, 21, 30, 34, 35, 37, 39, 100, 121, 136, 143, 144, 146, 173, 174, 179
Golden Gate International Exposition, 162
Good Housekeeping, 108
Goodrich Rubber Company, 47
Goodyear Rubber Company, 47
Grable, Betty, 22
Grand Coulee Dam, 12
Gray, Adeline, 46
Great Britian, 2, 3, 4, 6, 9, 10, 15, 30, 73, 89, 114, 121
Greatest Generation, 46
Greenland, US acquisition of defense rights, 13

Grew, Ambassador Joseph, 12, 16
Guthrie, Woody, 10, 20

Harassment, 107-108
Harper's, 33
Harriman, Averell, 16
Hathaway, Charlie, 178
Hathaway, Patty, 178
Hercules Powder Company, 44
Higgins Boats, 43
Hitchcock, Alfred, 135
Hitler, Adolph, 4, 82, 93, 106, 145, 165, 173, 174, 175, 179, 190
Hobby, Oveta Culp, 112
Honey, Dr Maureen, 114
Honor Roll, 154
Hoover, J. Edgar, 8
Hope, Bob, 12, 13, 17, 152
Horne, Lena, 102
House Naval Affairs Committee, 29
House Un-American Activities Committee, 8
Housing, 11, 27–28, 29, 33, 37, 53, 115, 124, 183, 184, 196 *see also* National Housing Act
Hull Note, The, 16
Hyman, Samuel, 103
Hynes, Samuel, 68

Individual Income Tax Act of 1844, 22
Inflation, 11, 21, 22, 32, 73, 87
Ingalls, Laura, 2
Isolationists, 2, 6, 30, 174
Italian Americans, 128, 135, 136, 142, 147

Japan, 5, 6, 8, 9, 10, 12, 14, 16, 17, 18, 19, 21, 30, 37, 46, 57, 85, 89, 121, 140, 147, 149, 173, 180
Japanese Americans, 135, 136, 137, 138, 139, 146, 147, 149
Jeep, The, 43
Jefferson, State of, 17
Jewish refugees, 136
Jim Crow Laws, 100, 102, 103, 167

Kaiser Permanente, 107
Kaiser Works, 123

Kaiser, Henry J., 41, 107
Kaltenborne, H. V., 151
Kapok, 83
Korean Aliens, 140
Kraft Macaroni and Cheese, 94
Krupp, 34

L.A. Nippons, 21
LaGuardia, Fiorello, 17, 53, 54, 55
Landing Craft Personnel Large, (LCP/L), 43
Landing Craft Vehicle, (LCV), 43
Lang, Fritz, 135
Lanham Act, 107, 123
Latin America and influence, 5, 25, 135, 159
League of Nations, 4
Lend-Lease, 9, 13, 16, 24, 30, 32, 173, 174
Levitt, William, 183
Levittowns, 183
Liberty ship, 15, 40, 41, 42 *see also* Victory Ship
Lindbergh, Charles, 2, 12, 13, 15, 65, 150
Lindley, Betty, 55
Lindley, Ernest K, 55
Little Big Inch, The, *see* Pipelines
"Little people" at Willow Run, 37
Loneliness, 117
Long Island Spies *see* Spies
Long, Breckinridge, 1
Los Angeles School System, 125
Louis, Joe, 159-160
Loureio, Pedro, 147

MacArthur, General Douglas, 14, 149
MacLeish, Archibald, 170
Magazine War Guide, The 109, 171
Manning, Thomas, 59
Manpower, 23-25
March of Dimes, 131
Marine Corps, 23, 38, 39, 101, 111, 122, 160
Marriage, 7, 115, 117, 121, 156, 182
Marshall, General George, 101
Mass migration, 26, 28, 29, 98, 103, 104, 113, 122

McAllister Volunteers, 7
McDaniel, Hattie, 102
Meat rationing, 95 see also Rationing
Medal of Honor, 101
Mexican Farm Labor Program, 25
Migrants, 28, 29
Miller, Howard, 106
Miranda, Carmen, 5
Molly Pitcher Rifle Brigade, 7
Molotov, Vyacheslav, 15
Moscow Conference, 15
Mosely Zack, 60
Mosely, Bob, 60-62
Mothers' Movement (MOM), 3
Movies, 155-158
Munitions, 9, 30, 44, 45, 46, 51, 94, 105, 106, 145,
Murrow, Edward R., 151
Mussolini, Benito, 5, 179

NAACP, 167
National Housing Act (NHA), 49-50 see also Housing
National Resource Planning Board (NRPB), 50
National Roster of Scientific and Specialized Personnel (NRSSP), 34
National War Labor Board (NWLB), 50
National Youth Administration (NYA), 169
Native American Alaskans, 136
Naval Expansion Act, 7, 11
Navy see United States Navy
Netherlands, 6
Neurotic-psychotic (NP or shell-shock), 181-182
Neutrality Acts, 2, 8, 9, 37
New Deal, 1, 3, 11
New York Daily News, 144
New York Times, 100, 144
New York World's Fair, 162-163
Newlyweds, 115
Newspapers, 25, 57, 65, 77-78, 89, 102, 118, 130, 141, 150, 154, 159, 165, 188, 196
Newsweek, 105, 180

Nomura, Admiral/ Ambassador Kichisaburo, 12, 16
Nursing, 111
Nylon, 46, 47, 85; stockings 18, 85, 86,

Oakies, 28 see also Arkies
Octopus, The, 3
Office of Civilian Defense (OCD) 8, 12, 17, 53, 54, 55, 56, 57, 59, 62
Office of Defense Transportation, 25
Office of Price Administration (OPA), 11, 25, 49, 73, 75, 90, 91, 92, 93, 97
Office of Production Management (OPM), 88
Office of Scientific Research and Development (OSRD), 50
Office of War Information (OWI), 50, 150, 170-173
Office of War Mobilization (OWM), 50, 160
Okinawa, 180
Ordnance Department, 44
Oregon State Defense Council, 63, 92
Oumansky, Ambassador Constantine, 173

P-51 Mustang, 38
P-61 Black Widow, 38
Panama Canal, 5
Parachutes, 46, 47, 85
Peacetime draft, 7
Pearl Harbor, 6, 7, 9, 11, 12, 13, 18, 19-21, 23, 32, 33, 36, 40, 44, 45, 49, 53, 68, 71, 73, 85, 89, 102, 137, 144, 149, 153, 155, 160, 165, 176
Pennsylvania Turnpike 163
Philadelphia Transit Company strike, 99
Phonograph records, 94
Pinza, Ezio, 136
Pioneer Parachute Company, 46-47
Pipelines: War Emergency Pipeline "Big Inch" and Little Big Inch, 44, 89
Pittman, Senator Key, 2
Playground games, 127
Poland, 6, 173
Polio, 130-131, 197
POWs, 102, 140-143, 190

Presidential Proclamations (2525, 2526, 2527), 135
Propaganda, 2, 32, 50, 74, 80, 106, 110, 111, 125, 135, 155, 170-172, 176; posters 21

Radford Ordnance Works, 44
Radio: Bureau 150, 171; children's programming 152, 196; dramas 135; evening programs 152-153; FDR 'Fireside Chat' broadcast 151, 189, 196; Hit Parade 139; news 151; soap operas 151; sport 159
Randolph, A. Phillip, 98, 167
Rationing, 11, 32, 49, 71, 73-97, 105, 108, 110, 114, 117, 129, 130, 141, 151, 157, 171, 172, 177, 183, 192; ration books, 74-76, 80, 130, 188, 196; gas rationing 61, 88-92, 147, 155, 159, 163, 177, 188, 190; oddities 93-94; stamps 74-76, 78, 94 see also Rubber
Reconstruction Finance Commission (RFC), 31
Red Cross, 6, 57, 114, 115
Religion, 175
Relocation, 135, 136, 140, 182 see also War Relocation Authority
Reserve banks, 32
Revenue Act of 1943, 22
Rhythm Night Club fire, 164
Rinker, Marshall, 59
Ritter, Major Nickolas, 144
Rockwell, Norman, 106
Roosevelt, Eleanor, 19, 53, 54, 55, 107, 123, 167 see also Eleanor Clubs
Roosevelt, President Franklin D. (FDR), 3, 4, 5, 6, 7, 8, 9, 10, 11, 12, 13, 14, 15, 16, 17, 22, 30-31, 33, 35, 39, 48, 49, 50, 53, 55, 71, 73, 89, 90, 91, 95, 98, 99, 107, 123, 131, 132, 133, 135, 136, 150, 151, 160, 163, 167, 168, 169, 170, 171, 173, 174, 175, 179, 180, 189, 196
Rosie the Riveter, 105-106, 110, 172, 220 see also Black Rosies
Rubber, 9, 32, 47-48, 65, 92, 94, 96, 160, 163; rubber rationing 73, 81, 86-88, 91; Rubber Committee, 47; Rubber Reserve Company (RRC), 9; *The Baruch Rubber Report* 91 see also United States Rubber Corporation
Rural Electrical Administration, (REA), 50

Saturday Evening Post, The, 5, 106, 150
Schools at War, 124
Scottsboro Boys, 174
Scrap drives, 57, 80-84, 94, 124, 129, 172
Sebold, William, 144
Select Committee Investigating National Defense Migration, 122
Servicemen's Readjustment Act of 1944 (G. I. Bill), 78, 103, 182-184, 196
Shell-shock see Neurotic-psychotic
Shipbuilding production statistics, 39
Shipbuilding, Los Angeles, 40
Shipbuilding, San Fransisco, 40
Small businesses, 42
Smith, Kate, 7, 22
Soldiers' Reader, 126
South America, 5, 87
Southern Tennant Farmers' Union, (STFU), 174
Soviet Union, 4, 16, 173, 174, 175 see also USSR
Spam, 24, 25
Sparks, Wilbur, 52
SPARS, 111-113
Spies 121, 144-148, 152, 172, 190; Florida, 145; Japanese, 146; Long Island, 145-146; Maine, 146Spock, Dr Benjamin, 124
Sports, 159-162
SS Patrick Henry, 15, 41
SS Robert E Peary, 41
SS Robin Moor, sinking of 13
Stalin, Josef, 5, 29-30, 173,
Stimson, Henry, 101, 167
Stock market, 165
Stockings see Nylon
Submarines, 13, 15, 16, 39, 40, 44, 56, 59, 60, 61, 62, 66, 68, 69, 88, 89, 142, 145, 146, 189
Sullivan family, 119-120
Swift Brands, 108-109

Tachibana, Itaru, 146, 147
Thomas, Lowell, 134, 139, 151
Thompson, James G., 102
TNT, 44, 45
Travelers' Aid, 115
Truman Committee, The, 42, 51, 52
Truman, Harry S: as Senator 3, 42, 51, 168; as President 179, 180
Tuskegee Airmen, 102

United Service Organization (USO), 12, 13, 102, 114, 129, 159
United States Army Air Corps 8, 13, 34, 35, 60, 101; formation of, 14
United States Citizens Defense Corps, The 8; Handbook 56
United States Rubber Company, 47, 87
US Aircraft Industry, 35, 36
US Army 6, 43, 62, 99, 101 see also WACS
US Army Air Force 14, 17, 33, 38, 39, 60, 113, 126 see also WASPS
US Navy, 10, 15, 16, 18, 35, 38, 39, 83, 112, 113, 196 see also WAVES
US, War Divisions, 34
USS Cleveland, 41
USS Greer, 15
USS Kearny, 10, 16
USS Niblack, 13
USS Reuben James, 10, 16
USS Saratoga, 149
USS Tutuila, 14
USSR, 5, 39, 173, 174 see also Soviet Union

VA Loan program, 104
Van Hyning, Lyral Clark, 3
VE Day, 179, 180, 190
Vickers, 34
Victory Corps, 128
Victory Gardens, 79-80, 129, 152, 172
Victory Girls, 129
Victory ship, 40 see also Liberty Ship
Victory Speed limit, 92

Victory Tax, 22, 165
VJ Day, 127, 133, 180, 190, 196
V-mail, 118
Volunteering, 25, 79, 114
Voorhies, Jerry, 54

WAC (Women's Army Corps) 84, 111, 112, 127
Walt Disney Studio, 4, 16
War bonds, 8, 13, 21-23, 80, 109,
War Emergency Pipeline see Pipelines
War Manpower Commission, 106
War Production Board, (WPB), 25, 33, 35, 49, 80, 84, 93
War Relocation Authority (WRA), 50 see also Relocation
War Time Agencies, 49
Warren, Governor Earl, 140
Wartime Handbook for Young Americans, 172
WASPS (Women Airforce Service Pilots) 111, 113
Watson, John B., 124
WAVES (Women Accepted for Volunteer Military Service) 84, 111, 112, 127
Wells, Sumner, 173
What to Do in an Air Raid, 57
Wilkie, Wendell, 168
Williams, Ted, 161-162
Willow Run ("Willit Run"), 26, 36, 37
Women Accepted for Volunteer Military Service see WAVES
Women Airforce Service Pilots see WASPS
Women in the Armed Forces, 111-115
Women Ordnance Workers (WOW), 45
Women's Army Corps see WAC
Women's Land Army (WLA), 25
Works Progress Administration (WPA), 49, 169

"Zoot suit" riots, 29

Dear Reader,

We hope you have enjoyed this book, but why not share your views on social media? You can also follow our pages to see more about our other products: facebook.com/penandswordbooks or follow us on Twitter @penswordbooks

You can also view our products at www.pen-and-sword.co.uk (UK and ROW) or www.penandswordbooks.com (North America).

To keep up to date with our latest releases and online catalogues, please sign up to our newsletter at: www.pen-and-sword.co.uk/newsletter

If you would like a printed catalogue with our latest books, then please email: enquiries@pen-and-sword.co.uk or telephone: 01226 734555 (UK and ROW) or email: uspen-and-sword@casematepublishers.com or telephone: (610) 853-9131 (North America).

We respect your privacy and we will only use personal information to send you information about our products.

Thank you!